To Little Ann
On her birthday . June 1946
from Mary & Bill

THE GOLDEN BOOK
OF CATHOLIC POETRY

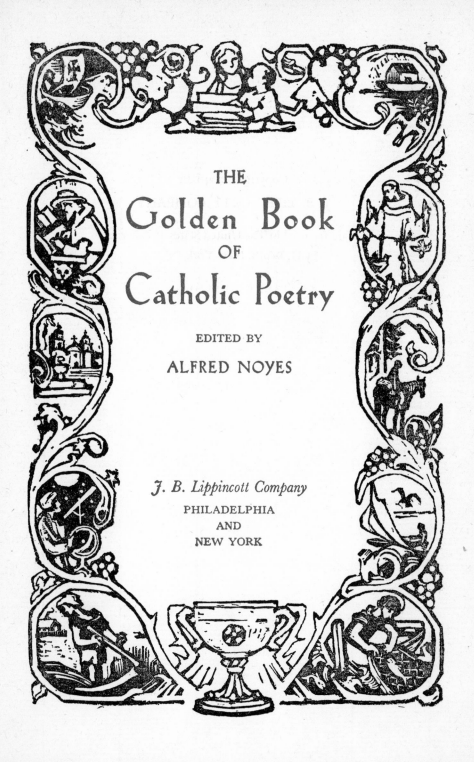

THE
Golden Book
OF
Catholic Poetry

EDITED BY

ALFRED NOYES

J. B. Lippincott Company

PHILADELPHIA
AND
NEW YORK

DEDICATION TO FATHER LEO WARD

Dear Leo,

This book cannot now reach you; but I inscribe it to you in this open letter for several reasons. Your mother, Mrs. Wilfrid Ward, inscribed her novel, *Tudor Sunset,* to me, in an open letter which has been one of the chief treasures of my life. Your own friendship, the talks we had at her fireside, and at my own, in London, are among my happiest memories. For years I carried your ordination card in my own missal; and the words on that ordination card have now been fulfilled by you with the last measure of devotion to your high calling. *Quid retribuam Domino pro omnibus quae retribuit mihi. Calicem salutaris accipiam, et nomen Domini invocabo.* What return shall I make to the Lord for all that He hath given unto me? I will take the chalice of salvation and call upon the name of the Lord.

You were always one of the happiest of human beings, radiating laughter that had no bitter springs, and full of charity for the weaknesses of your fellow-men. There was an additional sharpness, therefore, for all your friends, in the thought that you of all men—you, with your poetry, your fine scholarship, your great intellectual background, across which all that was noblest and best in English life had moved—that you, with your sensitive mind, and kindliness of heart, should have been subjected to the physical humiliations and brutalities of a prison camp in Tokyo. Your death ensued at an age when your gifts were hardly past their youth. But it was said of you, in the prison camp, that through all the humiliations and brutalities, you never for a moment lost the dignity of your priesthood, or allowed the enemy for a moment to imagine that you could ever lose it. That was, perhaps, your best poem; and I therefore venture to place it in the forefront of this anthology.

ALFRED NOYES

Wood Engravings

by

Margaret Ely Webb

ACKNOWLEDGMENTS

For the use of the copyright material in this volume the editor's thanks are due to the following:

AMERICA for *Venite Adoremus* by Margery Cannon; *Prodigal* by Ellen Gilbert; *The Case of Thomas More* by Sister Mary St. Virginia, B.V.M.; *Boy Playing an Organ* by Francis Sweeney (July 31, 1943).

D. APPLETON CENTURY COMPANY for *Signum Cui Contradicetur* by Sister Mary Angelita, from "Starshine and Candlelight."

HILAIRE BELLOC for *Tarantella, The South Country, Stanzas Written on Battersea Bridge, Our Lord and Our Lady, Crusade, Her Faith, Duncton Hill.*

KATHERINE BRÉGY and DAVID MCKAY COMPANY for *The Maid* from "Ladders and Bridges."

SIMON CAMPBELL for *I Am the Mountainy Singer, I Will Go with My Father A'ploughing, The Old Woman,* by Joseph Campbell.

CATHOLIC WORLD for *Peace is the Tranquillity of Order* by Robert Wilberforce (October 1944).

J. M. DENT & SONS, LTD. for *The Donkey* by G. K. Chesterton.

DODD, MEAD & COMPANY and MISS DOROTHY COLLINS, Executrix, for *The House of Christmas, Lepanto, Wine and Water, Convert,* from "The Collected Poems of G. K. Chesterton."

DOUBLEDAY, DORAN & COMPANY for *Prayer of a Soldier in France,* from "Poems, Essays and Letters," by Joyce Kilmer, copyright 1914, 1917, 1918 by Doubleday, Doran & Company.

E. P. DUTTON & COMPANY for *A Christmas Carol,* from "The Wild Knight and Other Poems" by G. K. Chesterton.

HOUGHTON, MIFFLIN COMPANY for *Prayer to the Virgin of Chartres* from "Mont St. Michel and Chartres" by Henry Adams, by permission of and arrangement with the publishers; and for *Ode for a Master Mariner Ashore, The Kings, Song,* by Louise Imogen Guiney.

THE MACMILLAN COMPANY for *The Plougher, An Old Woman of the Roads, A Cradle Song, Fuchsia Hedges in Connacht, The Stations of the Cross,* from "Collected Poems" by Padraic Colum; for *Gates* from "Selected Poems" by Sister M. Madeleva; and for *Of an Orchard* from "Collected Poems" by Katharine Tynan Hinkson.

MCCLELLAND & STEWART, LTD. for *Compline* by Duncan Campbell Scott.

WILFRID MEYNELL for *The Shepherdess, The Young Neophyte, Thoughts in Separation, I Am the Way, Christ in the Universe, To W. M.,* by Alice Meynell; for *Daisy, The Kingdom of God, Ode to the Setting Sun, The Hound of Heaven,* by Francis Thompson; and for *The Folded Flock* by Wilfrid Meynell.

THE REVEREND HUGH J. O'DONNELL and NOTRE DAME UNIVERSITY for *The Spinner, Address to the Crown, Resolution, A Rime of the Rood,* by Charles L. O'Donnell, from "Collected Poems."

FLORA WARREN SEYMOUR for *Ad Matrem in Cælis* by Linda Lyon Van Voorhis.

SPIRIT and CATHOLIC POETRY SOCIETY OF AMERICA for *Repeated Pilgrimage* by John Gilland Brunini (January, 1937); *Esther* by Fray Angelico Chavez; *Do What You Will* by Dorothy Hobson; *Quarrel* by Jean McDougall; *For A Girl in Love* by Florence Hynes Willette; *Requiem, Dwell With Me, Lovely Images,* by Theodore Maynard; *Convent Cemetery: Mount Carmel,* by Sister Mary St. Virginia.

JOHN HALL WHEELOCK and CHARLES SCRIBNER'S SONS for *Exile from God* from "Poems 1911-1936," by John Hall Wheelock, copyright 1936 by Charles Scribner's Sons.

The editor also wishes to give grateful acknowledgment to the following:

ALFRED BARRETT, S.J. for his poems, *Chant of Departure, Unearth, The Rosebush and the Trinity, A Martyr's Mass.*

ALICE CECILIA COOPER for *San Juan Capistrano.*

BELLE COOPER for *The Vintage, A Street Melody.*

JAMES J. DALY for *The Latin Tongue.*

WALTER DE LA MARE and FABER & FABER for *In Memory of G. K. Chesterton.*

HERMANN HAGEDORN for *Solomon* and *Evening Prayer.*

The late CAROLINE HAZARD for *In Shadow.*

HOUGHTON MIFFLIN COMPANY for *Divina Commedia* by Henry Wadsworth Longfellow.

BLANCHE MARY KELLY for *The Housewife's Prayer, The Mirror, The Kingfisher, Brother Juniper.*

PATRICK F. KIRBY for *Sequel to Finality, Rain, Song for These Days, Consecration, Riddles, Compline.*

SISTER MARIS STELLA for *It is the Reed, San Marco Museum— Florence, Oxford Bells, This One Heart-Shaken, The Voice, I Who Had Been Afraid, Now That Can Never be Done, Love is Not Solace, The Pelicans My Father Sees, Afternoon in a Tree, Bay Violets, Grapes.*

MOTHER MARY JOSITA for *To a Poet* by Sister Mary Angelita.

SISTER MARY JUSTITIA for *Whatsoever I Do* by Mary Louise Hector.

MOTHER M. ROSE ELIZABETH for permission to use poems by members of her order: *Exchange* by Sister M. Dorothy Ann; *November Afternoons, Peace by Night, New Things and Old, Design for a Stream-Lined Sunrise, Snow Storm, Wardrobe,* by Sister M. Madeleva; *Poet's Bread, To-day,* by Sister M. Philip; *Joculator Domini,* by Sister M. John Frederick; *Archers of the King,* by Sister Genoveva; *Identity,* by Sister Mary Helen; *Ordination,* by Sister Mary Immaculate.

F. A. STOKES COMPANY for *I See His Blood Upon the Rose* from "Complete Poems" by Joseph Mary Plunkett; *Wishes for My Son,* from "Complete Poems" by Thomas MacDonagh.

A. M. SULLIVAN for *Late Autumn, The Sextant.*

LINDA LYON VAN VOORHIS for *That Which Hath Wings Shall Tell.*

The editor wishes to thank Miss Belle Cooper and Dr. Alice C. Cooper (editor of *Poems of Today*) for invaluable help in the collection and preparation of this material.

PREFACE

he literature of our Western culture is not a series of disconnected explosions, but a living, growing tree, an organic development, with roots deep in the past, and a central trunk, with branches, leaves, and blossoms." The quotation is from an essay I wrote, some years ago, on Chaucer, the first great Catholic poet of our tongue. "It was a gracious act of the Muses," the essay continued, "to set at the head of that long and glorious pageant of our poetry, the many-coloured company of Chaucer's pilgrims, winding down through the lanes of that flowering April to Canterbury, old England's noblest shrine."

But Chaucer, the beginning of the new poetry in England, was himself the offspring of a great poetry that had already reached maturity in Europe. Some of the subtlest thoughts in Dante flowed through Chaucer's "Prologue to the Second Nun's Tale" (included in this volume). Both were Catholic; but the verse of Chaucer is like a young green spray unfolding its first leaves to April shower and sun, while that of Dante is like the dark and massive arm of a central trunk, with centuries of growth recorded in its concentric rings.

This process may be illustrated by one of the most beautiful lines in the *Divine Comedy:*

"In la sua volontade è nostra pace."

Matthew Arnold chose this line as one of his examples of great poetry; but he did not point out that it was derived almost directly from the Latin of St. Augustine:

"In voluntate sua pax nobis est."

Dante endowed it, of course, with a deep undertone of poetry. The exquisite little tremor at the point of elision between the fourth and fifth words of the Italian line does something which can only be compared with the fingering of a violin in the hands of a supreme master. But the process is there—the flow of the life-giving spirit from generation to generation. It need hardly be pointed out that the real origin of both lines is in the one perfect prayer of Christendom.

Among innumerable other instances there is the passage which Shakespeare in *The Tempest* seems to have derived almost directly from Thomas à Kempis:

> "The powers, delaying, not forgetting, have
> Incensed the seas and shores, yea, all the creatures,
> Against your peace."

The remarkable likeness of this to a passage in *The Imitation of Christ* has again escaped notice.

There is a curious connection, too, between Walt Whitman's praise of death and a famous passage in St. Francis. In Whitman's lines

> "Come, lovely and soothing death . . .
> Praised be the fathomless universe
> For life and joy, and for love, sweet love,
> But praise! praise! praise!
> For the sure enwinding arms of cool-enfolding death."

We are carried right back to the praise of Sister Death by the Troubadour of Assisi:

> "Praised be my Lord for our Sister, the death of the body."

Whitman gives us a musical variation, of course, but the theme is unmistakable; and it may be added that, whenever Whitman's long catalogues of things to be praised achieve real beauty, he may add considerably to the length of the list, but he is no more than improvising on the great theme of St. Francis—the praise of the creatures.

Other aspects of the same interdependence are Blessèd Sir Thomas More's variation on the theme of Pico della Mirandola; Matthew Arnold's original tribute to Jacopone da Todi; or the tributes by Tennyson and Longfellow to the author of the *Divine Comedy*. The Petrarchan sonnets of Alice Meynell have not forgotten Arqua or the far hills from which they flow. There is a similar interdependence in the poetry of paganism. Virgil followed Homer; but when Dante took Virgil for his guide, the bond between them assumed a new and deeper

xii

character. In fact, the poetry of Catholicism is a perfect illustration of Gilson's remarks on the culture of the Western World:

"inherited from the Greeks by the Romans, transfused by the Fathers of the Church with the religious teachings of Christianity and progressively enlarged by countless numbers of artists, writers, scientists and philosophers from the beginning of the Middle Ages up to the first third of the nineteenth century."

At a time when that culture is threatened by the new barbarism of a mechanized world, rolling along on the surface of things, unaware of the heights and depths of the human spirit, and even of its history, there is a salutary strength and vitality in those writings which are still rooted in the *philosophia perennis*. During the last half century the material for a Catholic anthology has grown steadily richer, and this growth coincides with the revival of the *philosophia perennis* which has been one of the most striking developments of constructive modern thought.

In this book the principle of selection is as follows: the main body consists of poems by Catholics, roughly from the time of Chaucer to the present day. Translations are included only when they are in themselves fine poetry. There is a section of tributary poems by non-Catholics; but these have been included only when they embody some essentially Catholic idea. In the case of Catholics I have felt freer to choose poems on any subject, since Catholicism naturally touches every side of human life.

An anthology of Catholic poetry in English can hardly give more than an indication of the richness of its sources, or of that unity in variety which makes it a contemporary of all the ages. No anthology in any one language can do justice to its universal character or give an adequate representation of it. Yet throughout Christendom this poetry forms a symphonic whole. *The Song of Roland* and the *Te Deum;* the lyrics of the troubadours and the epics of the Crusades; the spiritual depth of the *Divine Comedy* and the broad humor of Chaucer's *Canterbury Tales;* the love sonnets of Petrarch; the roses of Ronsard; the dark night of St. John of the Cross; the visions of the mystics from St. Francis to Crashaw; the cries of spirits in prison from Villon to Verlaine;

the phantasmagoric river of satirical romance from Ariosto to Chesterton, from *Orlando Furioso* to the songs in *The Flying Inn*—all these have a great community of spirit. There is a comradeship in arms between du Bellay and Belloc; a timeless alliance between Petrarch and Coventry Patmore. It is a coherent whole, developing, but never for an instant contradicting itself. Unlike much of the pagan art of the modern world, it represents, not *chaos* but *cosmos*.

The question of Shakespeare's place in such an anthology is controversial; but in many passages, some famous and others less often quoted, Shakespeare has revealed his religion. A distinguished modern critic, Mr. George W. E. Russell—not himself a Catholic—in his recent autobiography says that Shakespeare was "as Catholic as the sea is salt." He is represented here by a series of passages which reveal something of his own mind.

In other controversial cases I have followed the rule that poets, like Ben Jonson and John Donne, who were formally inducted into the Catholic body, may legitimately be included in a Catholic anthology. There are cases where a man has abandoned his religion, but this surely does not unwrite his Catholic poems. Mr. Shane Leslie excludes from his collection what he calls the "sublime sonnet" on "Night" by the Catholic priest, Joseph Blanco White, on the ground that later in life the author "benighted himself." This is a witty statement; but, as it seems to me, a mistake. If a Catholic architect had built a sublime cathedral and, later on, had abandoned his religion, the most rigid of formalists would hardly pull down the cathedral, or refuse to use it for purposes far more sacred than any that are involved in the arrangement of an anthology. Nor would I exclude Ben Jonson; or—from the tributary section—even Donne, who, after being baptized a Catholic, surrendered to political and economic pressure. In his poetry Donne shows again and again the battering to which his heart and mind were subjected. It seems to me entirely wrong for the editor to assume in such cases the power of literary excommunication. If the poem itself is Catholic, I feel that it may justly be included.

Undoubtedly some of the great Italian painters failed at one time or another in their allegiance to their religion, but there are few churches that would exclude a Holy Family by Leonardo. There are doubts about the complete orthodoxy of Michelangelo, but he painted the Last Judgment for the Sistine Chapel, and I have heard of no proposals for its removal. Other men, like Dryden, have apparently abandoned their religion for a time and returned later. It is not the function of an editor in such cases to excommunicate the author. His concern is simply and solely with the nature of the work actually before him.

In the short section devoted to tributary poems by writers who were not themselves Catholics, there is one poem in particular to which I would call attention, "The Virgin of Chartres," by Henry Adams. I believe it to be among the greatest, perhaps itself the greatest, in American literature. It is one of the most remarkable pieces of self-revelation in modern times: the work of an outwardly skeptical and sophisticated man, disillusioned by a long "education" in the realm of high politics and international affairs, acquainted with all the tendencies of modern materialistic thought; and it suddenly lays bare the profound hunger of a mind robbed of its spiritual heritage. The tremendous realization of all that has been lost in the realms of the spirit during the material progress of a mechanistic age is expressed with passionate conviction, and driven home by the shattering contrast between the "Prayer to the Dynamo" and the lost prayers of Christendom. It is an expression of the modern mind, far in advance of the chaotic pseudo-modernism of our time; and its own vital integrity is manifested by its deep feeling for the continuity of Western culture, and the grave danger it faces in this generation. Written a good many years ago, it actually anticipates the fearful hour when man would tear out the secret springs of the atom.

In this section I have also included poems by Dante Gabriel Rossetti and Christina Rossetti. Racially, and in other respects, they had Catholicism in their blood, though exiled from it by the political views of their father. Some of D. G. Rossetti's Catholic poems are as magnificent in their own way as the religious art of Giotto. Some of his translations from the Italian poets therefore find their place in the main body of the book; and some of his own in the tributary section.

The number of poems allotted to any one writer does not imply any superiority over those with less. For instance, of Digby Mackworth

Dolben, an unusual writer who died at the age of nineteen, I have included more than would be justifiable if numbers alone were the test. But his books are out of print now, and not generally available.

Particularly notable in the great revival of Catholic poetry at the present day is the beautiful work which is being done by some of the women in the religious orders.

Just as in former years it was Catholicism that saved and handed down to us not only the art and letters of Christendom, but the masterpieces of antiquity, so it may not be too much to say that in this confused age Catholicism may once again save the world's inheritance of art and literature. A distinguished American critic, Ralph Adams Cram, himself a master of one of the few vital arts of our time, believed that our Western culture, if it is to survive at all, will be saved in just that way.

ALFRED NOYES

CONTENTS

The Thirteenth to the Eighteenth Century

xviii

The Eighteenth, Nineteenth, and Twentieth Centuries

Tributary Poems by Non-Catholics

Epilogue

THE
THIRTEENTH
TO THE
EIGHTEENTH
CENTURY

A Carol to Our Lady

AUTHOR UNKNOWN
(15th Century)

I sing of a maiden
    That is makeles; [1]
King of all kings
    To her son she ches.[2]

He came all so still
    Where his mother was,
As dew in April
    That falleth on the grass.

He came all so still
    To his mother's bower,
As dew in April
    That falleth on the flower.

He came all so still
    There his mother lay,
As dew in April
    That falleth on the spray.

Mother and maiden
    Was never none but she;
Well may such a lady
    Goddes mother be.

[1] *makeles*—matchless
[2] *ches*—chose

Rosa Mystica

AUTHOR UNKNOWN
(*Medieval*)

There is no rose of such virtue
As is the rose that bare Jesu.
Alleluia.

For in this rose containèd was
Heaven and earth in little space,
Res miranda.

By that rose we may well see
There be one God in persons three,
Pares forma.

The angels sang, the shepherds too:——
Gloria in excelsis Deo.
Gaudeamus.

Leave we all this worldly mirth,
And follow we this joyful birth.
Transeamus.

Adam Lay Ibounden

AUTHOR UNKNOWN
(*Medieval*)

Adam lay ibounden,
bounden in a bond,
four thousand winters
thought he not too long:
and all was for an apple,
an apple that he took,
as clerkës finden
written in their Book.

Ne had the apple taken been,
        the apple taken been,
ne had never our lady
        been Heaven's queen.
Blessèd be the time
        that apple taken was!
therefore we may singen
        Deo gracias.

Alysoun

AUTHOR UNKNOWN

(*c. 1 3 0 0*)

Lenten ys come with love to towne,
With blosmen ant with briddes roune,
That all this blisse bryngeth;
Dayes-eyes in this dales,
Notes suete of nyhtegales,
Uch foul song singeth;
The thresltecoc him threteth oo,
Away is huere wynter wo,
When woderove springeth;
This foules singeth ferly fele,
And whyteth on huere wynter wele
That al the wode ryngeth.

Of Order in Our Lord Christ

ST. FRANCIS OF ASSISI

(*1 1 8 1 – 1 2 2 6*)

Set Love in order, thou that lovest Me,
        Never was virtue out of order found;
And though I fill thy heart desirously,
        By thine own virtue I must keep My ground;

5

When to My love thou dost bring charity,
    Even she must come with order girt and gowned.
      Look how the trees are bound
      To order, bearing fruit;
      And by one thing compute
In all things earthly, order's grace or gain.

All earthly things I had the making of
    Were numbered and were measured then by Me;
And each was ordered to its end by Love,
    Each kept, through order, clean for ministry.
Charity most of all, when known enough,
    Is of her very nature orderly.
      Lo, now! what heat in thee,
      Soul, can have bred this rout?
      Thou put'st all order out,
Even this love's heat must be its curb and rein.

From the Italian, by Dante Gabriel Rossetti

The Song of the Creatures

ST. FRANCIS OF ASSISI

O most high, almighty, good Lord God, to Thee belong praise, glory,
    honor and all blessing!

Praised be my Lord God with all His creatures, and especially our
    brother the sun, who brings us the day and who brings us
    the light; fair is he and shines with very great splendor;
    O Lord, he signifies to us Thee!

Praised be my Lord for our sister the moon, and for the stars, the which
    He has set clear and lovely in heaven.

Praised be my Lord for our brother the wind, and for air and cloud,
    calms and all weather by which Thou upholdest life in all
    creatures.—

Praised be my Lord for all those who pardon one another, for His love's
    sake, and who endure weakness and tribulation; blessèd are
    they who peaceably shall endure. For Thou, O Most Highest,
    shalt give them a crown!

Praised be my Lord for our sister, the death of the body, from which
no man escapeth. Woe to him who dieth in mortal sin!
Blessèd are they who are found walking by Thy most holy
will, for the second death shall have no power to do them
harm.
Praise ye and bless the Lord, and give thanks unto Him and serve Him
with great humility.

From the Italian, by Matthew Arnold

Alysoun

AUTHOR UNKNOWN
(*c.* 1 3 0 0)

Bytuene Mershe ant Averil,
    When spray biginneth to springe
The lutel foul hath hire wyl
    On hyre lud to synge.
    Ich libbe in love—longinge
    For semlokist of all thynge:
    He may be blisse bringe;
Icham in hire baundoun.
    An hendy hap ichabbe y-hent;
    From alle wymmen mi love is lent,
Ant lyht on Alysoun.

On heu hire her is fayr y-noh;
    Hire browe brieve; hire eye blake—
With lossum chere he on me loh!—
    With middel small, ant wel y make,
    Bote he me wolle to hire take,
    Forte buen hire owen make,
    Longe to lyven ichulle forsake,
Ant feye fallen a-doun.
    An hendy hap ichabbe y-hent;
    From alle wymmen mi love is lent,
Ant lyht on Alysoun.

7

Nightes-when y wende ant wake;
    For-thi myn wonges waxes won:
Levedi, al for thine sake
    Longinge is y-lent me on.
    In world nis non so wyter mon
    That al hire bounte telle con:
    Hire swyre is whittore then the swon,
Ant feyrest may in towne.
    An hendy hap ichabbe y-hent;
    From alle wymmen mi love is lent,
Ant lyht on Alysoun.

Of the Gentle Heart

GUIDO GUINICELLI
(1 2 4 0 ? – 1 2 7 4 ?)

Within the gentle heart Love shelters him
    As birds within the green shade of the grove.
Before the gentle heart, in nature's scheme,
    Love was not, nor the gentle heart ere Love.
    For with the sun, at once,
So sprang the light immediately; nor was
    Its birth before the sun's.
And Love hath his effect in gentleness
    Of very self; even as
Within the middle fire the heat's excess.

The fire of Love comes to the gentle heart
    Like as its virtue to a precious stone;
To which no star its influence can impart
    Till it is made a pure thing by the sun:
    For when the sun hath smit
From out its essence that which there was vile,
    The star endoweth it.

And so the heart created by God's breath
      Pure, true, and clean from guile,
A woman, like a star, enamoureth.

In gentle heart Love for like reason is
      For which the lamp's high flame is fanned and bowed;
Clear, piercing bright, it shines for its own bliss;
      Nor would it burn there else, it is so proud.
          For evil natures meet
With Love as it were water met with flame,
      As cold abhorring heat,
Through gentle heart Love doth a track divine,—
      Like knowing like, the same
As diamond runs through iron in the mine.

The sun strikes full upon the mud all day:
      It remains vile, nor the sun's worth is less.
'By race I am gentle,' the proud man doth say:
      He is the mud, the sun is gentleness.
          Let no man predicate
That aught the name of gentleness should have,
      Even in a king's estate,
Except the heart there be a gentle man's.
      The star-beam lights the wave,—
Heaven holds the star and the star's radiance.

God, in the understanding of high Heaven,
      Burns more than in our sight the living sun:
There to behold His Face unveiled is given;
      And Heaven, whose will is homage paid to One
          Fulfils the things which live
In God, from the beginning excellent.
      So should my lady give
That truth which in her eyes is glorified,
      On which her heart is bent,
To me whose service waiteth at her side.

My lady, God shall ask, 'What daredst thou?'
(When my soul stands with all her acts review'd);
'Thou passedst Heaven, into My sight, as now,
To make Me of vain love similitude.
To Me doth praise belong,
And to the Queen of all the realm of grace
Who slayeth fraud and wrong.'
Then may I plead: 'As though from Thee he came,
Love wore an angel's face:
Lord, if I loved her, count it not my shame.'

From the Italian, by Dante Gabriel Rossetti

Sonnets

[From *La Vita Nuova*]

DANTE ALIGHIERI

(1 2 6 5 – 1 3 2 1)

Of Beatrice de' Portinari, on All Saints' Day

Last All Saints' holy-day, even now gone by,
I met a gathering of damozels:
She that came first, as one doth who excels,
Had Love with her, bearing her company:
A flame burned forward through her steadfast eye,
As when in living fire a spirit dwells:
So, gazing with the boldness which prevails
O'er doubt, I knew an angel visibly.
As she passed on, she bowed her mild approof
And salutation to all men of worth,
Lifting the soul to solemn thoughts aloof.
In Heaven itself that lady had her birth,
I think, and is with us for our behoof:
Blessèd are they who meet her on the earth.

Beatrice Has Gone Up into High Heaven

Beatrice is gone up into high Heaven,
    The kingdom where the angels are at peace;
        And lives with them: and to her friends is dead.
Not by the frost of winter was she driven
    Away, like others; not by summer heats;
        But through a perfect gentleness, instead.
        For from the lamp of her meek lowlihead
Such an exceeding glory went up hence
    That it woke wonder in the Eternal Sire,
    Until a sweet desire
Entered Him for that lovely excellence,
    So that He bade her to Himself aspire;
Counting this weary and most evil place
Unworthy of a thing so full of grace.

Wonderfully out of the beautiful form
    Soared her clear spirit, waxing glad the while;
        And is in its first home, there where it is.
Who speaks thereof, and feels not the tears warm
    Upon his face, must have become so vile
        As to be dead to all sweet sympathies.
        Out upon him! an abject wretch like this
May not imagine anything of her,—
    He needs no bitter tears for his relief.
    But sighing comes, and grief,
And the desire to find no comforter,
    (Save only Death, who makes all sorrow brief)
To him who for a while turns in his thought
How she hath been among us, and is not.

With sighs my bosom always laboureth
    In thinking, as I do continually,
        Of her for whom my heart now breaks apace;
And very often when I think of death,
    Such a great inward longing comes to me
        That it will change the colour of my face;

* * * * *

I scare could tell indeed how I am thus.
 All joy is with my bitter life at war;
  Yea, I am fallen so far
That all men seem to say, 'Go out from us,'
 Eyeing my cold white lips, how dead they are.
But she, though I be bowed unto the dust,
Watches me; and will guerdon me, I trust.

He Will Gaze Upon Beatrice

Because mine eyes can never have their fill
Of looking at my lady's lovely face,
 I will so fix my gaze
That I may become blessed, beholding her.
Even as an angel, up at his great height
Standing amid the light,
 Becometh blessed by only seeing God:
So, though I be a simple earthly wight,
Yet none the less I might,
 Beholding her who is my heart's dear load,
 Be blessed, and in the spirit soar abroad.
Such power abideth in that gracious one;
Albeit felt of none
 Save of him who, desiring, honours her.

From the Italian, by Dante Gabriel Rossetti

A Tribute to Dante

GIOVANNI BOCCACCIO
(1 3 1 3 - 1 3 7 5)

To One Who Had Censured His Public Exposition of Dante

If Dante mourns, there wheresoe'er he be,
 That such high fancies of a soul so proud
 Should be laid open to the vulgar crowd,
(As, touching my Discourse, I'm told by thee,)

This were my grievous pain; and certainly
   My proper blame should not be disavowed;
   Though hereof somewhat, I declare aloud
Were due to others, not alone to me.
False hopes, true poverty, and therewithal
   The blinded judgment of a host of friends,
   And their entreaties, made that I did thus.
But of all this there is no gain at all
   Unto the thankless souls with whose base ends
   Nothing agrees that's great or generous.

Inscription for a Portrait of Dante

Dante Alighieri, a dark oracle
   Of wisdom and of art, I am; whose mind
   Has to my country such great gifts assigned
That men account my powers a miracle.
My lofty fancy passed as low as Hell,
   As high as Heaven, secure and unconfined;
   And in my noble book doth every kind
Of earthly lore and heavenly doctrine dwell.
Renownèd Florence was my mother,—nay,
   Stepmother unto me her piteous son,
   Through sin of cursèd slander's tongue and tooth.
Ravenna sheltered me so cast away;
   My body is with her,—my soul with One
   For whom no envy can make dim the truth.

From the Italian, by Dante Gabriel Rossetti

Fiammetta

GIOVANNI BOCCACCIO

To Dante in Paradise, after Fiammetta's Death

Dante, if thou within the sphere of Love,
   As I believe, remain'st contemplating
   Beautiful Beatrice, whom thou didst sing
Erewhile, and so wast drawn to her above;—

Unless from false life true life thee remove
    So far that Love's forgotten, let me bring
    One prayer before thee: for an easy thing
This were, to thee whom I do ask it of.
I know that where all joy doth most abound
    In the Third Heaven, my own Fiammetta sees
    The grief which I have borne since she is dead.
O pray her (if mine image be not drowned
    In Lethe) that her prayers may never cease
    Until I reach her and am comforted.

Of Fiammetta Singing

Love steered my course, while yet the sun rode high,
    On Scylla's waters to a myrtle grove:
    The heaven was still and the sea did not move;
Yet now and then a little breeze went by
Stirring the tops of trees against the sky:
    And then I heard a song as glad as love,
    So sweet that never yet the like thereof
Was heard in any mortal company.
"A nymph, a goddess, or an angel sings
    Unto herself, within this chosen place,
    Of ancient loves"; so said I at that sound.
And there my lady, 'mid the shadowings
    Of myrtle trees, 'mid flowers and grassy space,
    Singing I saw, with others who sat round.

Of His Last Sight of Fiammetta

Round her red garland and her golden hair
    I saw a fire about Fiammetta's head;
    Thence to a little cloud I watched it fade,
Than silver or than gold more brightly fair,
And like a pearl that a gold ring doth bear,
    Even so an angel sat therein, who sped
    Alone and glorious throughout heaven, arrayed
In sapphires and in gold that lit the air.

Then I rejoiced as hoping happy things,
    Who rather should have then discerned how God
    Had haste to make my lady all His own,
Even as it came to pass. And with these stings
    Of sorrow, and with life's most weary load
    I dwell, who fain would be where she is gone.

From the Italian, by Dante Gabriel Rossetti

The Friar of Orders Grey

AUTHOR UNKNOWN

In Hamlet Shakespeare adds a great beauty to this old song. The subtle transposition of a few words, and the beat falling on the first syllable of each line as it is sung by Ophelia, lift it into the precision and ecstasy of poetry. Rossetti, in his modern sequel, follows the master's example. All three versions are given here to illustrate their respective treatment of the pilgrim's return. The phrase "cockle-hat" refers to the shells which were the badge of pilgrims from the Holy Land.

I

It was a Friar of Orders grey
    Walked forth to tell his beads,
And he met with a lady fair
    Clad in a pilgrim's weeds.

'Now Christ thee save, thou reverend Friar,
    I pray thee tell to me,
If ever at yon holy shrine
    My true love thou didst see.'

'And how should I know your true love
    From many another one?'
'O, by his cockle-hat and staff
    And by his sandal shoon.'

'O Lady, he is dead and gone,
    Lady, he's dead and gone,
And at his head a green grass turf
    And at his heels a stone.'

2

SHAKESPEARE

[Hamlet, IV, 5.]

OPHELIA (*sings*):   How should I your true love know
          From another one?
       By his cockle-hat and staff
          And his sandal shoon.

QUEEN: Alas, sweet lady, what imports this song?

OPHELIA: Say you? nay, pray you, mark.
(*sings*)   He is dead and gone, lady,
       He is dead and gone;
    At his head a grass-green turf,
       At his heels a stone.

Oh, Oh!

QUEEN: Nay, but Ophelia—

OPHELIA: Pray you, mark.
(*sings*)   White his shroud as the mountain snow,—
       Larded with sweet flowers;
    Which bewept to the grave did go
       With true-love showers.

3

DANTE GABRIEL ROSSETTI

'How should I your true love know
    From another one?'
'By his cockle-hat and staff
    And his sandal shoon.'

'And what signs have told you now
    That he hastens home?'
'Lo! the spring is nearly gone,
    He is nearly come.'

'For a token is there nought,
    Say, that he should bring?'
'He will bear a ring I gave,
    And another ring.'

'How may I, when he shall ask,
    Tell him who lies there?'
'Nay, but leave my face unveiled
    And unbound my hair.'

'Can you say to me some word
    I shall say to him?'
'Say I'm looking in his eyes
    Though my eyes are dim.'

Ballad of Good Counsel

GEOFFREY CHAUCER

(1 3 4 0 ? - 1 4 0 0)

Flee from the press and dwell with soothfastness;
    Suffice unto thy good, though it be small;
For hoard hath hate, and climbing tickleness,
    Press hath envy, and wealth oft blindeth all;
    Desire no more than thee behoven shall;
Work well thyself that other folk canst lead;
And Truth thee shall deliver, it is no dread.

Tempest thee not all crooked to redress
    In trust of her that turneth as a ball:
Great rest there stands in little busy-ness.
    Beware thou spurnest not against an awl;
    Strive not, as doth the crock against the wall.
Look to thyself, that dauntest others' deed,
And Truth thee shall deliver, it is no dread.

That which is sent, receive in buxomness:
    The wrestling for this world asketh a fall.
Here is no home; here is but wilderness.
    Forth, pilgrim, forth! Forth, beast, out of thy stall!
    Know thy country; look up, thank God of all;
Hold the high way, and let thy ghost thee lead;
And Truth thee shall deliver, it is no dread.

ENVOI

Therefore, thou Vache, leave thine old wretchedness
    Unto the world; and be no longer thrall;
Cry mercy of Him that of His high goodness
    Made thee of nought; and in especial
    Draw unto Him, and pray for each and all,
For thee, and for all others, Heaven's own meed;
And Truth thee shall deliver, it is no dread.

Slightly modernized version. Wordsworth's head-note to The Prioress' Tale.

The Complaint of Chaucer to His Empty Purse

GEOFFREY CHAUCER

> The conventional medieval "complaint" is usually a plea to
> the poet's lady, imploring her pity. In this ballad Chaucer
> parodies the type by complaining to his empty purse. His
> playful plea to King Henry IV brought within four days a
> double pension to Chaucer.

To you, my purse, and to no other wight
    Complain I, for you are my lady dear!
I am so sorry, now that you are light;
    Surely, unless you make me *heavy* cheer,
    I would as lief be laid upon my bier;
For which unto your mercy thus I cry—
Be heavy again, else surely I must die!

Vouchsafe this very day, ere it be night,
    That I of you the blissful sound may hear,
Or see your color like the sunshine bright,
    That for its yellowness had never a peer.

You are my life! ever my heart you steer,
Queen of comfort, and of good company!
Be heavy again, else surely I must die!

Now purse, that are to me my life's one light
    And my savior, down in this dark world here,
To leave this town, O help me through your might,
        Since you will be no more my treasurer;
        For I am shaven as close as is a friar.
But yet I pray unto your courtesy,
Be heavy again, else surely I must die!

ENVOI

O conqueror of our Brut's Albion,
Who that by line and free election
    Are very King, this song to you I send;
    And you who can my every woe amend,
Have mind upon my supplication!

Version by Belle Cooper.

Prologue to The Canterbury Tales

GEOFFREY CHAUCER

The Influences of the Breezy April

Whan that Aprílle with his shoures soote
The droghte of Marche hath percèd to the roote,
And bathèd every veyne in swich licour,
Of which vertú engendred is the flour;
Whan Zephirus eek with his swete breeth
Inspirèd hath in every holt and heeth
The tendre croppes, and the yonge sonne
Hath in the Ram his halfe cours y-ronne,
And smale fowles maken melodye,
That slepen al the night with open yë,
(So priketh hem natúre in hir coráges) :
Than longen folk to goon on pilgrimages

And palmers for to seken straunge strondes
To ferne halwes, couthe in sondry londes;
And specially, from every shires ende
Of Engelond, to Caunterbury they wende,
The holy blisful martir for to seke,
That hem hath holpen, whan that they were seke.

The Poure Persoun

A good man was ther of religioun,
And was a poure PERSOUN of a toun;
But riche he was of holy thoght and werk.
He was also a lernèd man, a clerk,
That Cristes gospel trewely wolde preche;
His parisshens devoutly wolde he teche.
Benigne he was, and wonder diligent,
And in adversitee ful paciënt;
And swich he was y-prevèd ofte sythes.
Ful looth were him to cursen for his tythes,
But rather wolde he yeven, out of doute,
Un-to his poure parisshens aboute
Of his offríng, and eek of his substáunce.
He coude in litel thing han suffisaunce.
Wyd was his parisshe, and houses fer a-sonder,
But he ne lafte nat, for reyn ne thonder,
In siknes nor in meschief, to visyte
The ferreste in his parisshe, muche and lyte,
Up-on his feet, and in his hand a staf.
This noble ensample to his sheep he yaf,
That first he wroghte, and afterward he taughte;
Out of the gospel he tho wordes caughte;
And this figúre he added eek ther-to,
That if gold ruste, what shal iren do?
For if a preest be foul, on whom we truste,
No wonder is a lewed man to ruste;
And shame it is, if a preest take keep,
A [dirty] shepherde and a clene sheep.

Wel oght*e* a preest ensample for to yive,
By his clenness*e*, how that his sheep shold live.
He sette nat his benefic*e* to hyre,
And leet his sheep encombred in the myre,
And ran to London, un-to sëynt Poules,
To seken him a chaunter*ye* for soules,
Or with a bretherheed to been withholde;
But dwelt*e* at hoom, and kepte wel his folde,
So that the wolf ne made it nat miscarie;
He was a shepherd*e* and no mercenarie.
And though he holy wer*e*, and vertuous,
He was to sinful man nat despitous,
Ne of his speche daungerous ne digne,
But in his teching díscreet and benigne.
To drawen folk to heven by fairnesse
By good ensample, waś his bisinesse:
But it wer*e* any person*e* obstinat,
What-so he wer*e*, of heigh or low*e* estat,
Him wold*e* he snibben sharply for the nones.
A bettr*e* preest, I trow*e* that nowher noon is.
He wayted aft*er* no pomp*e* and reverence,
Ne makèd him a spycèd conscience,
But Cristes lor*e*, and his apostles twelve,
He taught*e*, and first he folwed it him-selve.

Prologue to The Second Nun's Tale

[excerpt]

GEOFFREY CHAUCER

Thou maid and mother, daughter of thy Son,
Thou well of mercy, sinful soulës cure
In whom that God, for bounty, chose to wone,
Thou humble and high over every créatúre,
Thou didst so far ennoble our natúre
That no disdain the Maker had of kind
His Son in Blood and Flesh to clothe and wind.

Within the blissful cloister of thy sides
Took mannës shape the Eternal Love and Peace
That of the Trinë compass Lord and guide is
Whom earth and sea and heaven, without cease
For ever praise; and thou, Virgin, spotless,
Bore of thy body, and dweltest maiden pure,
The Creatór of every creatúre.

Assembled is in thee magnificence
With mercy, goodness, and with such pitée
That thou that art the sum of excellence
Not only helpest them that pray to thee
But often time, of thy benignity
Full freely, ere that men thy help beseech
Thou goest before, thy healing hand to reach.

Now help, thou meek and fair and blissful maid,
Me, exiled in this wilderness of gall.
Think on that woman by the well who said
Even the dogs may eat the crumbs, ay, all
That from their lordës table sometime fall;
And though that I, unworthy son of Eve,
Be sinful, yet accept thou my belief.

The Prioress' Tale

GEOFFREY CHAUCER

'Call up him who left half told
The story of Cambuscan bold.'

In the following poem no further deviation from the original has been made than was necessary for the fluent reading and instant understanding of the Author. So much, however, is the language altered since Chaucer's time, especially in pronunciation, that much had to be removed, and its place supplied with as little incongruity as possible. The ancient accent has been retained in a few conjunctions, as *alsò* and *alwày,* from a conviction that such sprinklings of antiquity would be admitted, by persons of taste, to have a graceful accordance with the subject. The fierce bigotry of the Prioress forms a fine background for her tender-hearted sympathies with the Mother and Child; and the mode in which the story is told amply atones for the extravagance of the miracle.

I

O Lord, our Lord! how wondrously, (quoth she)
Thy name in this large world is spread abroad!
For not alone by men of dignity
Thy worship is performed and precious laud.
But by the mouths of children, gracious God!
Thy goodness is set forth; they when they lie
Upon the breast thy name do glorify.

II

Wherefore in praise, the worthiest that I may,
Jesu! of thee, and the white Lily-flower
Which did thee bear, and is a Maid for aye,
To tell a story I will use my power;
Not that I may increase her honor's dower,
For she herself is honor, and the root
Of goodness, next her Son, our soul's best boot.

III

O Mother Maid! O Maid and Mother free!
O bush unburnt! burning in Moses' sight!
That down didst ravish from the Deity,
Through humbleness, the spirit that did alight
Upon thy heart, whence, through that glory's might,
Conceivèd was the Father's sapience,
Help me to tell it in thy reverence!

IV

Lady! thy goodness, thy magnificence,
Thy virtue, and thy great humility,
Surpass all science and all utterance;

For sometimes, Lady! ere men pray to thee
Thou goest before in thy benignity,
The light to us vouchsafing of thy prayer,
To be our guide unto thy Son so dear.

V

My knowledge is so weak, O blissful Queen!
To tell abroad thy mighty worthiness,
That I the weight of it may not sustain;
But as a child of twelve months old or less,
That laboreth his language to express,
Even so fare I; and therefore, I thee pray,
Guide thou my song which I of thee shall say.

VI

There was in Asia, in a mighty town,
'Mong Christian folk, a street where Jews might be,
Assigned to them and given them for their own
By a great Lord, for gain and usury,
Hateful to Christ and to his company;
And through this street who list might ride and wend;
Free was it, and unbarred at either end.

VII

A little school of Christian people stood
Down at the farther end, in which there were
A nest of children come of Christian blood,
That learnèd in that school from year to year
Such sort of doctrine as men usèd there,
That is to say, to sing, and read also,
As little children in their childhood do.

VIII

Among these children was a Widow's son,
A little scholar, scarcely seven years old,
Who day by day unto this school hath gone,

And eke, when he the image did behold
Of Jesu's Mother, as he had been told,
This Child was wont to kneel adown and say
Ave Maria, as he goeth by the way.

IX

This Widow thus her little Son hath taught
Our blissful Lady, Jesu's Mother dear,
To worship aye, and he forgat it not,
For simple infant hath a ready ear.
Sweet is the holiness of youth: and hence
Calling to mind this matter when I may,
Saint Nicholas in my presence standeth aye,
For he so young to Christ did reverence.

X

This little Child, while in the school he sate
His Primer conning with an earnest cheer,
The whilst the rest their anthem-book repeat,
The *Alma Redemptoris* did he hear;
And as he durst he drew him near and near,
And hearkened to the words and to the note,
Till the first verse he learned it all by rote.

XI

This Latin knew he nothing what it said,
For he too tender was of age to know;
But to his comrade he repaired and prayed
That he the meaning of this song would show,
And unto him declare why men sing so;
This oftentimes, that he might be at ease
This Child did him beseech on his bare knees.

XII

His Schoolfellow, who elder was than he,
Answered him thus: 'This song, I have heard say,
Was fashioned for our blissful Lady free;

Her to salute, and also her to pray
To be our help upon our dying day:
If there is more in this, I know it not;
Song do I learn,—small grammar I have got.

XIII

'And is this song fashioned in reverence
Of Jesu's Mother?' said this Innocent;
'Now, certès, I will use my diligence
To con it all ere Christmas-tide be spent;
Although I for my Primer shall be shent,
And shall be beaten three times in an hour
Our Lady I will praise with all my power.'

XIV

His Schoolfellow, whom he had besought,
As they went homeward taught him privily
And then he sang it well and fearlessly,
From word to word according to the note:
Twice in a day it passèd through his throat;
Homeward and schoolward whensoe'er he went,
On Jesu's Mother fixed was his intent.

XV

Through all the Jewry (this before said I)
This little Child, as he came to and fro,
Full merrily then would he sing and cry,
O Alma Redemptoris! high and low.
The sweetness of Christ's Mother pierced so
His heart, that her to praise, to her to pray,
He cannot stop his singing by the way.

XVI

The Serpent, Satan, our first foe, that hath
His wasp's nest in Jew's heart, upswelled—'O woe,
O Hebrew people!' said he in his wrath,

'Is it an honest thing? Shall this be so?
That such a Boy where'er he lists shall go
In your despite, and sing his hymns and saws,
Which is against the reverence of our laws!'

XVII

From that day forward have the Jews conspired
Out of the world this Innocent to chase;
And to this end a Homicide they hired,
That in an alley had a privy place,
And, as the Child 'gan to the school to pace
This cruel Jew him seized, and held him fast
And cut his throat, and in a pit him cast.

XVIII

I say that him into a pit they threw,
A loathsome pit, whence noisome scents exhale;
O cursèd folk! away, ye Herods new!
What may your ill intentions you avail?
Murder will out; certès it will not fail;
Know, that the honor of high God may spread,
The blood cries out on your accursèd deed.

XIX

'O Martyr 'stablished in virginity!
Now may'st thou sing for aye before the throne,
Following the Lamb celestial,' quoth she,
'Of which the great Evangelist, Saint John,
In Patmos wrote, who saith of them that go
Before the Lamb singing continually,
That never fleshly woman they did know.'

XX

Now this poor widow waiteth all that night
After her little Child, and he came not;
For which, by earliest glimpse of morning light,

With face all pale with dread and busy thought,
She at the school and elsewhere him hath sought,
Until thus far she learned, that he had been
In the Jews' street, and there he last was seen.

XXI

With Mother's pity in her breast enclosed
She goeth, as she were half out of her mind,
To every place wherein she hath supposed
By likelihood her little Son to find;
And ever on Christ's Mother meek and kind
She cried, till to the Jewry she was brought,
And him among the accursed Jews she sought.

XXII

She asketh, and she piteously doth pray
To every Jew that dwelleth in that place
To tell her if her child had passed that way;
They all said—Nay; but Jesu of his grace
Gave to her thought, that in a little space
She for her Son in that same spot did cry
Where he was cast into a pit hard by.

XXIII

O thou great God that dost perform thy laud
By mouths of Innocents, lo! here thy might
This gem of chastity, this emerald,
And eke of martyrdom this ruby bright,
There, where with mangled throat he lay upright,
The *Alma Redemptoris* 'gan to sing
So loud that with his voice the place did ring.

XXIV

The Christian folk that through the Jewry went,
Come to the spot in wonder at the thing;
And hastily they for the Provost sent;

Immediately he came, not tarrying,
And praiseth Christ that is our heavenly King,
And eke his Mother, honor of Mankind;
Which done, he bade that they the Jews should bind.

XXV

This Child with piteous lamentation then
Was taken up, singing his song alwày;
And with procession great and pomp of men
To the next Abbey him they bare away;
His Mother swooning by the body lay,
And scarcely could the people that were near
Remove this second Rachel from the bier.

XXVI

Torment and shameful death to every one
This Provost does for those bad Jews prepare
That of this murder wist, and that anon:
Such wickedness his judgments cannot spare,
Who will do evil, evil shall he bear;
Them therefore with wild horses did he draw,
And after that he hung them by the law.

XXVII

Upon his bier this Innocent doth lie
Before the altar while the Mass doth last;
The Abbot with his convent's company
Then sped themselves to bury him full fast;
And, when they holy water on him cast,
Yet spake this Child when sprinkled was the water,
And sang, *O Alma Redemptoris Mater!*

XXVIII

This Abbot, for he was a holy man,
As all Monks are, or surely ought to be,
In supplication to the Child began,

Thus the saying, 'O dear Child! I summon thee
In virtue of the holy Trinity
Tell me the cause why thou dost sing this hymn,
Since that thy throat is cut, as it doth seem.'

XXIX

'My thoat is cut into the bone I trow,'
Said this young Child, 'and by the law of kind
I should have died, yea many hours ago;
But Jesus Christ, as in the books ye find,
Will that his glory last, and be in mind;
And, for the worship of his Mother dear,
Yet may I sing, *O Alma!* loud and clear.

XXX

'This well of mercy, Jesu's Mother sweet,
After my knowledge, I have loved alwày;
And in the hour when I my death did meet
To me she came, and thus to me did say,
"Thou in thy dying sing this holy lay,"
As ye have heard; and soon as I had sung
Methought she laid a grain upon my tongue.

XXXI

'Wherefore I sing, nor can from song refrain,
In honor of that blissful Maiden free,
Till from my tongue off-taken is the grain
And after that thus said she unto me;
"My little Child, then will I come for thee
Soon as the grain from off thy tongue they take;
Be not dismayed, I will not thee forsake!" '

XXXII

This holy Monk, this Abbot—him mean I,
Touched then his tongue, and took away the grain;
And he gave up the ghost full peacefully;

And, when the Abbot had this wonder seen,
His salt tears trickled down like showers of rain;
And on his face he dropped upon the ground,
And still he lay as if he had been bound.

XXXIII

Eke the whole convent on the pavement lay,
Weeping and praising Jesu's Mother dear;
And after that they rose, and took their way,
And lifted up this Martyr from the bier,
And in a tomb of precious marble clear
Enclosed his uncorrupted body sweet.—
Where'er he be, God grant us him to meet.

XXXIV

Young Hew of Lincoln! in like sort laid low
By cursed Jews—thing well and widely known,
For it was done a little while ago—
Pray also thou for us, while here we tarry
Weak sinful folk, that God, with pitying eye,
In mercy would his mercy multiply
On us, for reverence of his Mother Mary!

Grace for Theology

[From *Piers Plowman*]

WILLIAM LANGLAND
(1 3 3 0 ? – 1 4 0 0 ?)

I have threatened Theology a thousand times over;
The more I muse on it the mistier I think it,
And the deeper I dive the darker I find it.
It is no science for subtleties, so much I am certain.
I should hold it idleness if love were not in it;
But because it holds love best I love it the better.
Where love is the leader, grace is never lacking.

31

The Child Jesus to Mary the Rose

JOHN LYDGATE
(1 3 7 0 ? – 1 4 5 1 ?)

My Father above, beholding the meekness
    As dew on roses doth his balm spread,
Sendeth His Ghost, most sovereign of cleanness,
    Into thy breast, ah, Rose of Womanhood!
    When I for man was born in my manhood—
For which, with roses of heavenly influence,
I me rejoice to play in thy presence.

Benign Mother, who first did enclose
    The blessèd bud that sprang out of Jesse,
Thou of Judah the very perfect Rose,
    Chosen of my Father for thine humility
    Without fading, most cleanest to bear me—
For which with roses of chaste innocence
I me rejoice to play in thy presence.

O Mother! Mother! of mercy most abound,
    Fairest Mother that ever was alive,
Though I for man have many a bloody wound,
    Among them all there be roses five,
    Against whose mercy fiends may not strive;
Mankind to save, best roses of defence,
When they me pray for help in thy presence.

To the Virgin

JOHN LYDGATE

Queen of Heaven, of Hell eke Emperess,
Lady of this world, O very lodestar
To mariners 'gainst all mortal distress
In their passage that they do not err;

Thy look of mercy cast down from so far
On all thy servants by chaste compassion,
Grant them good peace, save them from mortal war,
To thy five Joys that have devotion.

Celestial Cypress set upon Syon,
Highest Cedar of perfit holiness,
Carbuncle of charity and green emerald stone,
Whole and unbroken in virginal clearness;
O Sapphire, *loupe* [1] all swelling to repress
On cankered sores and venomous feloun,
In ghostly woundes by their governess,
To thy five Joys that have devotion.

Rod of Aaron, gracious and benign;
Well of all grace and merciful pity,
Where the Holy Ghost list to close and sign
The crystal cloister of thy Virginity;
Balm of Engadi 'gainst all infirmity,
Of folk that languish to tribulation,
Preserve and keep from all adversity,
To thy five Joys that have devotion.

To Mistress Margaret Hussey

JOHN SKELTON
(1 4 6 0 ? - 1 5 2 9)

Merry Margaret,
As midsummer flower,
Gentle as falcon
Or hawk of the tower:
With solace and gladness,
Much mirth and no madness,
All good and no badness,

[1] *loupe*—jewel

So joyously,
So maidenly,
So womanly
Her demeaning
In every thing
Far, far passing
That I can indite,
Or suffice to write,
Of merry Margaret,
As midsummer flower,
Gentle as falcon
Or hawk of the tower:
As patient and still,
And as full of good will
As fair Isaphill;
Coliander,
Sweet pomander,
Good Cassander;
Steadfast of thought,
Well made, well wrought;
Far may be sought,
Ere that ye can find
So courteous, so kind,
As merry Margaret,
This midsummer flower,
Gentle as falcon
Or hawk of the tower.

To a Lady

WILLIAM DUNBAR
(1 4 6 5 ? - 1 5 3 0)

Sweet rose of virtue and of gentleness,
Delightsome lily of rare lustiness,
    Richest in bounty and in beauty clear,

And every virtue that's esteemèd dear,
Except only that you are merciless.

Your garden fair, agleam with crystal dew,
Flaunts flowers fresh of every lovely hue;
    Rose-red and white commingling oft are seen,
    And wholesome herbs on stalks of tender green;
Yet leaf nor flower found I none of rue.

I doubt that March, with his cold blasts so keen,
Has slain this gentle herb I fain would glean;
    Whose piteous death gives to my heart such pain
    That gladly I would plant his root again—
So comforting his leaves to me have been.

Version by Belle Cooper

The Heavenly City

AUTHOR UNKNOWN
(*1 5 t h   C e n t u r y*)

Hierusalem, my happy home,
    When shall I come to thee?
When shall my sorrows have an end?
    Thy joys when shall I see?

O happy harbor of the saints!
    O sweet and pleasant soil!
In thee no sorrow may be found,
    No grief, no care, no toil.

There lust and lucre cannot dwell;
    There envy bears no sway;
There is no hunger, heat, nor cold,
    But pleasure every way.

35

Thy walls are made of precious stones,
    Thy bulwarks diamonds square;
Thy gates are of right orient pearl,
    Exceeding rich and rare.

Thy turrets and thy pinnacles
    With carbuncles do shine;
Thy very streets are paved with gold,
    Surpassing clear and fine.

Ah, my sweet home, Hierusalem,
    Would God I were in thee!
Would God my woes were at an end,
    Thy joys that I might see!

Thy gardens and thy gallant walks
    Continually are green;
There grow such sweet and pleasant flowers
    As nowhere else are seen.

Quite through the streets, with silver sound,
    The flood of life doth flow;
Upon whose banks on every side
    The wood of life doth grow.

There trees forevermore bear fruit,
    And evermore do spring;
There evermore the angels sit,
    And evermore do sing.

Our Lady sings *Magnificat*
    With tones surpassing sweet;
And all the virgins bear their part,
    Sitting about her feet.

Hierusalem, my happy home,
    Would God I were in thee!
Would God my woes were at an end,
    Thy joys that I might see!

From the Latin: URBIS BEATA HIERÙSALEM

His Epitaph

[From *The Pastime of Pleasure*]

STEPHEN HAWES

(? —— - 1 5 2 3)

O mortal folk, you may behoid and see
How I lie here, sometime a mighty knight:
The end of joy and all prosperitee
Is death at last, thorough his course and might:
After the day there cometh the dark night,
For though the day be never so long,
At last the bells ringeth to evensong.

The Ballad of Dead Ladies

FRANCOIS VILLON

(1 4 3 1 - 1 4 6 3 ?)

Tell me now in what hidden way is
    Lady Flora the lovely Roman?
Where's Hipparchia, and where is Thaïs,
    Neither of them the fairer woman?
    Where is Echo, beheld of no man,
Only heard on river and mere,—
    She whose beauty was more than human? . . .
But where are the snows of yester-year?

Where's Héloise, the learnèd nun
    For whose sake Abeillard, I ween
Lost manhood and put priesthood on?
    (From Love he won such dule and teen!)
    And where, I pray you, is the Queen
Who willed that Buridan should steer
    Sewed in a sack's mouth down the Seine? . . .
But where are the snows of yester-year?

37

White Queen Blanche, like a queen of lilies,
    With a voice like any mermaiden,—
Bertha Broadfoot, Beatrice, Alice,
    And Ermengarde the lady of Maine,—
    And that good Joan whom Englishmen
At Rouen doomed and burned her there,—
    Mother of God, where are they then? . . .
But where are the snows of yester-year?

Nay, never ask this week, fair lord,
    Where they are gone, nor yet this year,
Save with this much for an overword,—
    But where are the snows of yester-year?

From the French, by Dante Gabriel Rossetti

The Soul of Dante

MICHELANGELO BUONARROTI
(1475 - 1564)

I

From heaven his spirit came, and robed in clay
    The realms of justice and of mercy trod,
    Then rose a living man to gaze on God,
That he might make the truth as clear as day.
For that pure star that brightened with his ray
    The ill-deserving nest where I was born,
    The whole wide world would be a prize to scorn;
None but his Maker can due guerdon pay.

I speak of Dante, whose high work remains
    Unknown, unhonoured by that thankless brood,
    Who only to just men deny their wage.
Were I but he! Born for like lingering pains,
    Against his exile coupled with his good
    I'd gladly change the world's best heritage!

II

No tongue can tell of him what should be told,
　　For on blind eyes his splendour shines too strong;
　　'Twere easier to blame those who wrought him wrong
Than sound his least praise with a mouth of gold.
He to explore the place of pain was bold,
　　Then soared to God, to teach our souls by song;
　　The gates heaven oped to bear his feet along,
Against his just desire his country rolled.

Thankless I call her, and to her own pain
　　The nurse of fell mischance; for sign take this,
　　That ever to the best she deals more scorn:
Among a thousand proofs let one remain;
　　Though ne'er was fortune more unjust than his,
　　His equal or his better ne'er was born.

From the Italian, by John Addington Symonds

For Inspiration

MICHELANGELO BUONARROTI

The prayers I make will then be sweet indeed,
　　If Thou the spirit give by which I pray;
　　My unassisted heart is barren clay,
Which of its native self can nothing feed;
Of good and pious works Thou art the seed
　　Which quickens where Thou say'st it may;
　　Unless Thou show us then Thine own true way,
No man can find it! Father, Thou must lead!

Do Thou, then, breathe those thoughts into my mind
　　By which such virtue may in me be bred
　　That in Thy holy footsteps I may tread;
The fetters of my tongue do Thou unbind,
　　That I may have the power to sing of Thee
　　And sound Thy praises everlastingly.

From the Italian, by William Wordsworth

A Lyke-Wake Dirge

AUTHOR UNKNOWN

(15th Century)

This ae night, this ae night,
—*Every night and alle,*
Fire and sleet [1] and candle-lighte,
And Christ receive thy saule.

When thou from hence away art past,
—*Every night and alle,*
To Whinny-muir thou com'st at last;
And Christ receive thy saule.

If ever thou gavest hosen and shoon.
—*Every night and alle,*
Sit thee down and put them on;
And Christ receive thy saule.

If hosen and shoon thou ne'er gav'st none
—*Every night and alle,*
The whins shall prick thee to the bare bone;
And Christ receive thy saule.

From Whinny-muir when thou may'st pass,
—*Every night and alle,*
To Bridge o' Dread thou com'st at last;
And Christ receive thy saule.

From Bridge o' Dread when thou may'st pass,
—*Every night and alle,*
To Purgatory fire thou com'st at last;
And Christ receive thy saule.

[1] *sleet,* sometimes emended to *salt* or *fleet.* But *sleet* is preferable, contrasting the winter's night with the fire within; and was preferred by Sir Walter Scott. The poetry of the people is not fettered by philosophy; and if the philologist were to emend some of our nursery rhymes and ballads, half their poetry would be lost.

If ever thou gavest meat or drink,
  —*Every night and alle,*
The fire shall never make thee shrink;
  And Christ receive thy saule.

If meat or drink thou ne'er gav'st none,
  —*Every night and alle,*
The fire will burn thee to the bare bone;
  And Christ receive thy saule.

This ae night, this ae night,
  —*Every night and alle,*
Fire and sleet and candle-light,
  And Christ receive thy saule.

Consider Well

SAINT THOMAS MORE
(1 4 7 8 - 1 5 3 5)

Consider well that both by night and day
  While we most busily provide and care
For our disport, our revel, and our play,
  For pleasant melody and dainty fare,
  Death stealeth on full slily; unaware
He lieth at hand and shall us all surprise,
We wot not when nor, where nor in what wise.

When fierce temptations threat thy soul with loss
  Think on His Passion and the bitter pain,
Think on the mortal anguish of the Cross,
  Think on Christ's blood let out at every vein,
  Think on His precious heart all rent in twain;
For thy redemption think all this was wrought,
Nor be that lost which He so dearly bought.

41

Fortune

SAINT THOMAS MORE

Eye-flattering fortune, look thou never so fair,
Or never so pleasantly begin to smile
As though thou wouldst my ruin all repair;
During my life thou shalt me not beguile.
Trust shall I God, to enter in a while
His haven of heaven, sure and uniform;
Ever after thy calm, look I for a storm.

An Earnest Suit

SIR THOMAS WYATT
(1 5 0 3 ? - 1 5 4 2)

And wilt thou leave me thus?
Say nay, say nay! For shame,
To save thee from the blame
Of all my grief and grame.
And wilt thou leave me thus?
Say nay, say nay.

And wilt thou leave me thus,
That hath loved thee so long
In wealth and woe among?
And is thy heart so strong
As for to leave me thus?
Say nay, say nay.

And wilt thou leave me thus,
That hath given thee my heart,
Never for to depart
Neither for pain nor smart;

And wilt thou leave me thus?
Say nay, say nay.

And wilt thou leave me thus
And have no more pity
Of him that loveth thee?
Alas, thy cruelty!
And wilt thou leave me thus?
Say nay, say nay!

Forget Not Yet the Tried Intent

SIR THOMAS WYATT

Forget not yet the tried intent
Of such a truth as I have meant;
My great travail so gladly spent,
        Forget not yet!

Forget not yet when first began
The weary life ye know, since whan
The suit, the service none tell can,
        Forget not yet!

Forget not yet the great assays,
The cruel wrong, the scornful ways;
The painful patience in delays,
        Forget not yet!

Forget not! O, forget not this,—
How long ago hath been, and is,
The mind that never meant amiss—
        Forget not yet!

Forget not, then, thine own approved,
The which so long hath thee so loved,
Whose steadfast faith yet never moved:
        Forget not this!

Farewell

SIR THOMAS WYATT

What should I say,
    Since faith is dead,
And truth away
    From you is fled?
    Should I be led
        With doubleness?
        Nay, nay, mistress!

I promised you,
    And you promised me,
To be as true,
    As I would be.
    But since I see
        Your double heart,
        Farewell my part!

Though for to take
    It is not my mind,
But to forsake
    One so unkind,
    And as I find
        So will I trust,
        Farewell, unjust!

Can ye say nay,
    But that you said
That I alway
    Should be obeyed?
    And thus betrayed,
        Or that I wist,
        Farewell, unkissed!

Of a Contented Mind

THOMAS, LORD VAUX
(1 5 1 0 - 1 5 5 6)

When all is done and said,
 In the end this shall you find:
He most of all doth bathe in bliss
 That hath a quiet mind;
And, clear from worldly cares,
 To deem can be content
The sweetest time in all his life
 In thinking to be spent.

The body subject is
 To fickle Fortune's power,
And to a million of mishaps
 Is casual every hour;
And death in time doth change
 It to a clod of clay;
Whenas the mind, which is divine,
 Runs never to decay.

Companion none is like
 Unto the mind alone;
For many have been harmed by speech;
 Through thinking, few, or none:
Fear oftentimes restraineth words,
 But makes not thought to cease;
And he speaks best that hath the skill
 When for to hold his peace.

Our wealth leaves us at death,
 Our kinsmen at the grave;
But virtues of the mind unto
 The heavens with us we have:

Wherefore, for Virtue's sake,
   I can be well content
The sweetest time in all my life
   To deem in thinking spent.

Retrospect

[Written in the Tower of London]

CHIDIOCK TICHBORNE
(*Martyred 1587*)

My prime of youth is but a frost of cares,
   My feast of joy is but a dish of pain,
My crop of corn is but a field of tares,
   And all my good is but vain hope of gain.
The day is past, and yet I saw no sun,
   And now I live, and now my life is done.

The spring is past, and yet it hath not sprung;
   The fruit is dead, and yet the leaves are green;
My youth is gone, and yet I am but young;
   I saw the world, and yet I was not seen;
My thread is cut, and yet it is not spun,
   And now I live, and now my life is done.

I sought my death, and found it in my womb;
   I looked for life, and saw it was a shade;
I trod the earth, and knew it was my tomb;
   And now I die, and now I am but made.
The glass is full, and now my glass is run,
   And now I live, and now my life is done.

The Quiet Life

ATTRIBUTED TO WILLIAM BYRD
(1 5 3 8 - 1 6 2 3)

What pleasure have great princes
    More dainty to their choice
Than herdsmen wild, who careless
    In quiet life rejoice?
And, fortune's fate not fearing,
Sing sweet in summer morning?

Their dealings plain and rightful,
    Are void of all deceit;
They never know how spiteful
    It is to kneel and wait
On favorite presumptuous
Whose pride is vain and sumptuous.

All day their flocks each tendeth,
    At night they take their rest,
More quiet than who sendeth
    His ship into the East,
Where gold and pearl are plenty,
But getting very dainty.

For lawyers and their pleading,
    They 'steem it not a straw;
They think that honest meaning
    Is of itself a law,
Whence conscience judgeth plainly;
They spend no money vainly.

O happy who thus liveth!
    Not caring much for gold;
With clothing which sufficeth
    To keep him from the cold.
Though poor and plain his diet,
Yet merry it is, and quiet.

A Song

WILLIAM BYRD

Let not the sluggish sleep
    Close up thy waking eye,
Until with judgement deep
    Thy daily deeds thou try:
He that one sin in conscience keeps
    When he to quiet goes,
More venturous is than he that sleeps
    With twenty mortal foes.

The Forest's Queen

PHILIP MASSINGER
(1 5 8 3 – 1 6 4 0)

Welcome, thrice welcome to this shady green,
Our long-wished Cynthia, the forest's queen!
The trees begin to bud, the glad birds sing
In winter, changed by her into the spring.
    We know to-night,
    Perpetual light
      Dawns from your eye:
    You being near,
    We cannot fear,
      Though death stood by.

From you our swords take edge, our hearts grow bold;
From you in fee their lives your liegemen hold.
These groves your kingdom, and our laws your will;
Smile, and we spare; but, if you frown, we kill.
    Bless then the hour
    That gives the power

In which you may,
At bed and board,
Embrace your lord
    Both night and day.

Welcome, thrice welcome to this shady green,
Our long-wished Cynthia, the forest's queen!

The Maid of Honour

PHILIP MASSINGER

Look on this Maid of Honour, now
Truly honoured in her vow
She pays to heaven vain delight
By day, or pleasure of the night.
She no more thinks of this fair hair
(Favours for great kings to wear)
Must now be shorn; her rich array
Changed into a homely grey.
The dainties with which she was fed,
And her proud flesh pamperèd,
Must not be tasted; from the spring
For wine, cold water we will bring;
And with fasting mortify
The feasts of sensuality.
Her jewels, beads; and she must look
Not in a glass but holy book,
To teach her the ne'er erring way
To immortality. O may
She as she purposes to be
A child new-born to piety
Perséver in it, and good men
With saints and angels say **Amen.**

Rosalind's Madrigal

THOMAS LODGE
(1555 - 1625)

Love in my bosom, like a bee,
    Doth suck his sweet;
Now with his wings he plays with me,
    Now with his feet;
    Within mine eyes he makes his nest,
    His bed amidst my tender breast;
    My kisses are his daily feast;
    And yet he robs me of my rest:
      Ah, wanton, will ye?

And if I sleep, then percheth he
    With pretty flight,
And makes his pillow of my knee
    The livelong night.
    Strike I my lute, he tunes the string;
    He music plays if so I sing;
    He lends me every lovely thing;
    Yet, cruel, he my heart doth sting:
      Whist, wanton, still ye!

Else I with roses every day
    Will whip you hence,
And bind you when you long to play,
    For your offence;
    I'll shut mine eyes to keep you in;
    I'll make you fast it for your sin;
    I'll count your power not worth a pin:
    Alas, what hereby shall I win,
      If he gainsay me?

What if I beat the wanton boy
    With many a rod?
He will repay me with annoy,
    Because a god.

Then, sit thou safely on my knee,
And let thy bower my bosom be;
Lurk in mine eyes; I like of thee;
O Cupid, so thou pity me,
    Spare not, but play thee.

Rosaline

THOMAS LODGE

Like to clear in highest sphere
    Where all imperial glory shines,
Of selfsame colour is her hair
    Whether unfolded or in twines:
        Heigh ho, fair Rosaline!
Her eyes are sapphires set in snow,
    Refining heaven by every wink;
The gods to fear whenas they glow,
    And I do tremble when I think:
        Heigh ho, would she were mine!

Her cheeks are like the blushing cloud
    That beautifies Aurora's face,
Or like the silver crimson shroud
    That Phoebus' smiling looks doth grace.
        Heigh ho, fair Rosaline!
Her lips are like two budded roses
    Whom ranks of lilies neighbor nigh,
Within which bounds she balm incloses
    Apt to entice a deity:
        Heigh ho, would she were mine!

Her neck is like a stately tower
    Where Love himself imprisoned lies,
To watch for glances every hour
    From her divine and sacred eyes:
        Heigh ho, fair Rosaline!

Her paps are centres of delight,
 Her breasts are orbs of heavenly frame,
Where Nature moulds the dew of light
 To feed perfection with the same:
  Heigh ho, would she were mine!

With orient pearl, with ruby red,
 With marble white, with sapphire blue,
Her body every way is fed,
 Yet soft in touch and sweet in view:
  Heigh ho, fair Rosaline!
Nature herself her shape admires;
 The gods are wounded in her sight;
And Love forsakes his heavenly fires,
 And at her eyes his brand doth light:
  Heigh ho, would she were mine!

Then muse not, nymphs, though I bemoan
 The absence of fair Rosaline,
Since for her fair there is fairer none,
 Nor for her virtues so divine:
  Heigh ho, fair Rosaline!
Heigh ho, my heart! would God that she were mine!

Of Rosalind

THOMAS LODGE

Of all chaste birds the Phœnix doth excel,
Of all strong beasts the Lion bears the bell,
Of all sweet flowers the Rose doth sweetest smell,
 Of all fair maids my Rosalind is fairest.

Of all pure metals Gold is purely best,
Of all high trees the Pine hath highest crest,
Of all soft sweets, I like my mistress' breast.
 Of all chaste thoughts my mistress' thoughts are rarest.

Of all proud birds the Eagle pleaseth Jove,
Of pretty fowles Venus likes her Dove,
Of trees Minerva doth the Olive love,
    Of all sweet Nymphs I honour Rosalind.

Of all her gifts her wisdom pleaseth most,
Of all her graces, virtue she doth boast.
For all these gifts my life and joy are lost
    If Rosalind prove cruel and unkind.

A Lover's Protestation

THOMAS LODGE

First shall the heaven want starry light,
    The seas be robbèd of their waves,
The day want sun, the sun want bright,
    The night want shade, the dead men graves,
The April flowers and leaf and tree,
Before I false my faith to thee.

First shall the tops of highest hills
    By humble plains be overpried,
And poets scorn the Muses' quills,
    And fish forsake the water-glide,
And Iris lose her coloured weed
Before I fail thee at thy need.

First direful hate shall turn to peace
    And love relent in deep disdain,
And death his fatal stroke shall cease
    And envy pity every pain,
And pleasure mourn, and sorrow smile
Before I talk of any guile.

First Time shall stay his stayless race,
    And Winter bless his boughs with corn,
And snow bemoisten July's face,
    And Winter, Spring and Summer mourn
Before my pen, by help of Fame,
Cease to recite thy sacred name.

Of the Blessèd Sacrament of the Altar

ROBERT SOUTHWELL
(1 5 6 1 ? - 1 5 9 5)

In paschall feast, the end of ancient rite,
    An entrance was to never-ending grace;
Types to the truth, dim glimpses to the light;
    Performing deed presaging signs did chase;
Christ's final meal was fountain of our good,
For mortal meat He gave immortal food.

That which He gave, He was: O peerless gift!
    Both God and man He was, and both He gave.
He in His hands Himself did truly lift.
    Far off they see Whom in themselves they have.
Twelve did He feed, twelve did their feeder eat.
He made, He dressed, He gave, He was, their meat.

They saw, they heard, they felt Him sitting near.
    Unseen, unfelt, unheard, they Him received;
No diverse thing, though diverse it appear;
    Though senses fail, yet faith is not deceived;
And if the wonder of the work be new,
Believe the work because His word is true.

Here truth believe, belief inviteth Love.
    So sweet a truth Love never yet enjoyed.
What thought can think, what will doth best approve,
    Is here obtained where no desire is void.

The grace, the joy, the treasure here is such,
No wit can wish, nor will embrace so much.

Self-love here cannot crave more than it finds,
  Ambition to no higher worth aspire;
The eagerest famine of most hungry minds
  May fill, yea far exceed their own desire.
In sum, here all is in a sum expressed,
Of much the most, of every good the best.

To ravish eyes here heavenly beauties are;
  To win the ear sweet music's sweetest sound;
To lure the taste the angels' heavenly fare;
  To soothe the scent divine perfumes abound.
To please the touch, He in our hearts doth bed,
Whose touch doth cure the deaf, the dumb, the dead.

Here to delight the wit true wisdom is;
  To woo the will, of every good the choice;
For memory, a mirror showing bliss;
  Here's all that can both sense and soul rejoice;
And if, to all, all this it do not bring,
The fault is in the men, not in the thing.

Though blind men see no light, the sun doth shine.
  Sweet cakes are sweet, though fevered tastes deny it.
Pearls precious are, though trodden on by swine;
  Each truth is true, though all men do not try it;
The best still to the bad doth work the worst
Things bred to bliss do make them more accurst.

The angels' eyes, whom veils cannot deceive,
  Might best disclose what best they do discern;
Men must with sound and silent faith receive
  More than they can by sense or reason learn.
God's power our proofs, His works our wit exceed.
The Doer's might is reason of His deed.

A body is endued with ghostly rights;
 And Nature's work from Nature's law is free.
In heavenly sun lie hid eternal lights,
 Lights clear and near, yet them no eye can see.
Dead forms a never dying life do shroud.
A boundless sea lies in a little cloud.

The God of hosts in slender host doth dwell,
 Yea, God and man with all to either due,
That God who rules the heavens and rifled hell,
 That man whose death did us to life renew:
That God and man that is the angels' bliss,
In form of bread and wine our nurture is.

Whole may His body be in smallest bread,
 Whole in the whole, yea whole in every crumb;
With which, be one or be ten thousand fed,
 All to each one, to all but One doth come;
And though each one as much as all receive,
Not one too much, nor all too little have.

One soul in man is all in every part.
 One face at once in many mirrors shines.
One fearful noise doth make a thousand start;
 One eye at once of countless things defines.
If proofs of one in many, Nature frame,
God may in stranger sort perform the same.

God present is at once in every place,
 Yet God in every place is ever one;
So may there be by gifts of ghostly grace
 One man in many rooms, yet filling none.
Since angels may effects of bodies show,
God, angels' gifts on bodies, may bestow.

A Child My Choice

ROBERT SOUTHWELL

Let folly praise that fancy loves, I praise and love that Child
Whose heart no thought, whose tongue no word, whose hand no deed
      defiled.
I praise Him most, I love Him best, all praise and love is His;
While Him I love, in Him I live, and cannot live amiss.
Love's sweetest mark, laud's highest theme, man's most desirèd light,
To love Him life, to leave Him death, to live in Him delight.
He mine by gift, I His by debt, thus each to other due,
First friend He was, best friend He is, all times will try Him true.
Though young, yet wise; though small, yet strong; though man, yet God
      He is;
As wise He knows, as strong He can, as God He loves to bless.
His knowledge rules, His strength defends, His love doth cherish all;
His birth our joy, His life our light, His death our end of thrall.
Alas! He weeps, He sighs, He pants, yet do His angels sing;
Out of His tears, His sighs and throbs, doth bud a joyful spring.
Almighty Babe, whose tender arms can force all foes to fly,
Correct my faults, protect my life, direct me when I die!

The Burning Babe

ROBERT SOUTHWELL

As I in hoary winter's night stood shivering in the snow,
Surprised I was with sudden heat which made my heart to glow;
And lifting up a fearful eye to view what fire was near,
A pretty Babe all burning bright, did in the air appear;
Who, scorchèd with exceeding heat, such floods of tears did shed
As though His floods would quench His flames with what His tears
      were fed;

57

'Alas!' quoth He, 'but newly born, in fiery heats I fry,
Yet none approach to warm their hearts or feel my fire but I!
My faultless breast the furnace is, the fuel wounding thorns;
Love is the fire and sighs the smoke, the ashes shame and scorns;
The fuel Justice layeth on, and Mercy blows the coals;
The metal in this furnace wrought are men's defilèd souls;
For which, as now on fire I am, to work them to the good,
So will I melt into a bath, to wash them in my blood.'
With this He vanished out of sight, and swiftly shrunk away.
And straight I callèd unto mind that it was Christmas day.

Times Go by Turns

ROBERT SOUTHWELL

The loppèd tree in time may grow again;
    Most naked plants renew both fruit and flower;
The sorriest wight may find release of pain,
    The driest soil suck in some moist'ning shower;
Times go by turns and chances change by course,
From foul to fair, from better hap to worse.

The sea of Fortune doth not ever flow,
    She draws her favors to the lowest ebb;
Her time hath equal times to come and go,
    Her loom doth weave the fine and coarsest web;
No joy so great but runneth to an end,
No hap so hard but may in fine amend.

Not always full of leaf nor ever spring,
    No endless night, yet not eternal day;
The saddest birds a season find to sing,
    The roughest storm a calm may soon allay;
Thus with succeeding turns God tempereth all,
That man may hope to rise, yet fear to fall.

A chance may win that by mischance was lost;
    The net that holds no great, takes little, fish;
In some things all, in all things none are crossed;
    Few all they need, but none have all they wish;
Unmeddled [1] joys here to no man befall,
Who least, hath some; who most, hath never all.

The Shepherd Upon a Hill

AUTHOR UNKNOWN
(*Medieval*)

Can I not sing but hoy
When the jolly shepherd made so much joy.

The shepherd upon a hill he sat,
He had on him his tabard and his hat,
His tarbox, his pipe and his flagat.[2]
His name was called Jolly, Jolly Wat;
For he was a good herdës boy.
    Ut hoy!
For in his pipe he made so much joy.

The shepherd upon a hill was laid,
His dog to his girdle was tied,
He had not slept but a little broyd,[3]
But *Gloria in excelsis* was to him said.
    Ut hoy!
For in his pipe he made so much joy.

The shepherd on a hill he stood,
Round about him his sheep they yode
He put his hand under his hood,
He saw a star as red as blood.
    Ut hoy!
For in his pipe he made so much joy.

[1] *unmeddled*—unmixed   [2] *flagat*—flageolet   [3] *broyd*—a brief time

'Now farewell, Mall, and also Will,
For my love, go ye all still
Unto I come again you till;
And evermore, Will, ring well thy bell.'
Ut hoy!
For in his pipe he made so much joy.

'Now must I go where Christ was born;
Farewell! I come again to-morn.
Dog, keep well my sheep from the corn,
And warn well, warroke,[1] when I blow my horn.'
Ut hoy!
For in his pipe he made so much joy.

The shepherd said anon right:
'I will go see yon marvellous sight
Whereas the angel singeth on height,
And the star that shineth so bright.'
Ut hoy!
For in his pipe he made so much joy.

When Wat to Bethlehem come was,
He sweat; he had gone faster than a pace;
He found Jesu in a simple place,
Between an ox and an ass.
Ut hoy!
For in his pipe he made so much joy.

'Jesu, I offer to thee my pipe,
My skirt, my tarbox and my scrip.
Home to my fellows now will I skip,
And also look unto my sheep.'
Ut hoy!
For in his pipe he made so much joy.

[1] *warroke*—young boy

'Now farewell, mine own herdsman Wat!'—
'Yea, 'fore God, Lady, my name is that!
Lull well Jesu in thy lap;
And farewell, Joseph, in thy round cap!'
    Ut hoy!
For in his pipe he made so much joy.

'Now may I well both hop and sing
For I have been at Christ's bearing.
Home to my fellows now will I fling,
Christ of heaven to His bliss us bring!'
    Ut hoy!
For in his pipe he made so much joy.

To God the Father

HENRY CONSTABLE
(1562 - 1613)

Great God: within whose simple essence, we
    Nothing but that which is Thy Self can find;
    When on Thyself Thou didst reflect Thy mind
Thy thought was God, which took the form of Thee;
And when this God, thus born, Thou lov'st, and He
    Loved Thee again, with passion of like kind,
    As lovers' sighs which meet become one mind,
Both breathed one Spirit of equal deity.
Eternal Father, whence these two do come
    And wil'st the title of my father have,
    An heavenly knowledge in my mind engrave,
That it Thy Son's true Image may become:
    Incense my heart with sighs of holy Love,
    That it the temple of the Spirit may prove.

On the Death of Sir Philip Sidney

HENRY CONSTABLE

Give pardon, blessèd soul, to my bold cries,
If they, importune, interrupt thy song,
Which now with joyful notes thou singest among
The angel-quiristers of the heavenly skies.
Give pardon eke, sweet soul, to my slow eyes,
That since I saw thee now it is so long,
And yet the tears that unto thee belong
To thee as yet they did not sacrifice;
I did not know that thou wert dead before;
I did not feel the grief I did sustain;
The greater stroke astonisheth the more;
Astonishment takes from us sense of pain;
I stood amazed when others' tears begun,
And now begin to weep, when they have done.

Diaphenia

ATTRIBUTED TO HENRY CONSTABLE

Diaphenia, like the daffadowndilly
White as the sun, fair as the lily,
   Heigh ho, how I do love thee!
I do love thee as my lambs
Are belovèd of their dams;
   How blest were I if thou would'st prove me!

Diaphenia, like the spreading roses,
That in thy sweets all sweets encloses,
   Fair sweet, how I do love thee!
I do love thee as each flower
Loves the sun's life-giving power;
   For dead, thy breath to life might move me.

Diaphenia, like to all things blessèd
When all thy praises are expressèd,
    Dear joy, how I do love thee!
As the birds do love the spring,
Or the bees their careful king:
    Then in requite, sweet virgin, love me.

Love's Franciscan

HENRY CONSTABLE

Sweet hand! the sweet yet cruel bow thou art,
From whence as one, five ivory arrows fly,
So with five wounds at once I wounded lie
Bearing in breast the print of every dart.
Saint Francis had the like, yet felt no smart:
Where I in living torments never die;
His wounds were in his hands and feet where I
All these same helpless wounds feel in my heart.
Now as Saint Francis (if a saint) am I.
The bow which shot these shafts a relic is;
I mean the hand, which is the reason why
So many for devotion thee would kiss,
And I thy glove kiss as a thing divine;
Thy arrows quiver, and thy relics shine.

To Saint Catherine

HENRY CONSTABLE

Because thou wast the daughter of a king,
Whose beauty did all Nature's works exceed,
And wisdom wonder to the world did breed,
A Muse might rouse herself on Cupid's wing;
But, sith the graces which from Nature spring

63

Were graced by those which from grace did proceed,
And glory have deserved, my Muse doth need
An angel's feathers when thy praise I sing.
For all in thee became angelical:
An angel's face had angels' purity,
And thou an angel's tongue didst speak withal;
Lo! why thy soul, set free by martyrdom,
Was crowned by God in angels' company,
And angels' hands thy body did entomb.

To Saint Margaret

HENRY CONSTABLE

Fair Amazon of Heaven who tookst in hand
Saint Michael and Saint George to imitate,
And for a tyrant's love transformed to hate
Wast for thy lily faith retained in band,
Alone on foot and with thy naked hand
Thou didst like Michael and his host; and that
For which on horse armed George we celebrate
Whilst thou, like them, a dragon didst withstand.
Behold my soul shut in my body's gaol,
The which the Drake of Hell gapes to devour.
Teach me (O virgin) how thou didst prevail.
Virginity, thou sayest, was all thy aid:
Give me then purity instead of power,
And let my soul, made chaste, pass for a Maid.

To Our Blessèd Lady

HENRY CONSTABLE

In that (O Queen of Queens) thy birth was free
From guilt, which others do of grace bereave,
When in their mothers' womb they life receive,
God, as His sole-borne daughter lovèd thee.

To match thee like thy birth's nobility,
He thee His Spirit for thy spouse did leave,
Of whom thou didst His only Son conceive,
And so was linked to all the Trinity.

Cease then, O queens, who earthly crowns do wear,
To glory in the pomp of worldly things;
If men such high respect unto you bear,
Which daughters, wives, and mothers are of kings,
What honour should unto that Queen be done
Who had your God for Father, Spouse, and Son?

Our Lady's Lullaby

RICHARD VERSTEGAN (ROWLANDS)
(1548-1636)

Upon my lap my Sovereign sits,
And sucks upon my breast;
Meanwhile, His love sustains my life,
And gives my body rest.

    Sing lullaby, my little Boy.
    Sing lullaby, my life's Joy.

When thou hast taken thy repast,
Repose, my Babe, on me;
So may thy Mother and thy Nurse
Thy cradle also be.

    Sing lullaby.

My Babe, my Bliss, my Child, my Choice,
My Fruit, my Flower, and Bud,
My Jesus, and my only Joy,
The Sum of all my good.

    Sing lullaby.

Thy fruit of death from Paradise
Made thee exilèd mourn;
My fruit of life to Paradise
Makes joyful thy return.

Sing lullaby.

The shepherds left their keeping sheep
For joy to see my Lamb;
How may I more rejoice to see
Myself to be the Dam.

Sing lullaby.

Three kings their treasure hither brought
Of incense, myrrh and gold,
The heaven's Treasure and the King
That here they might behold.

Sing lullaby.

One sort an angel did direct;
A star did guide the other;
And all the fairest Son to see
That ever had a mother.

Sing lullaby, my little Boy.
Sing lullaby, my life's Joy.

England's Prayer

WILLIAM BLUNDELL OF CROSBY
(1 5 6 0 – 1 6 3 8)

Sweet Jesus with Thy Mother mild,
Sweet Virgin Mother with thy Child,
Angels and Saints of each degree,
Redress our country's misery.

Give judgment, Lord, twixt them and us,
The balance yet let pity hold,
Let mercy measure their offence
And grace reduce them to Thy fold,
That we, all children of the Spouse,
May live as brethren in Thy house.

Omnia Vincit

AUTHOR UNKNOWN

Fain would I change that note
        To which fond love hath charmed me,
Long, long to sing by rote,
        Fancying that that harmed me:
Yet when this thought doth come,
'Love is the perfect sum
        Of all delight,'
I have no other choice
Either for pen or voice,
        To sing or write.

O Love, they wrong thee much
        That say thy sweet is bitter;
When thy rich fruit is such
        As nothing can be sweeter.
Fair house of joy and bliss,
Where truest pleasure is,
        I do adore thee;
I know thee what thou art,
I serve thee with my heart,
        And fall before thee.

There Is a Lady Sweet and Kind

ATTRIBUTED TO THOMAS FORD
(in one of whose collections of songs it appeared)
(1 5 8 0 - 1 6 4 8)

There is a lady sweet and kind,
Was never face so pleased my mind;
I did but see her passing by,
And yet I love her till I die.

Her gesture, motion, and her smiles,
Her wit, her voice, my heart beguiles,
Beguiles my heart, I know not why,
And yet I love her till I die.

Cupid is wingèd and doth range
Her country, so my love doth change;
But change she earth, or change she sky,
Yet will I love her till I die.

The Triumph of Charis

BEN JONSON
(1 5 7 3 ? - 1 6 3 7)

See the Chariot at hand here of Love,
    Wherein my Lady rideth!
Each that draws is a swan or a dove,
    And well the car Love guideth.
As she goes, all hearts do duty
    Unto her beauty;
And enamoured do wish, so they might
    But enjoy such a sight,
That they still were to run by her side,
Through swords, through seas, whither she would ride.

Do but look on her eyes, they do light
 All that Love's world compriseth!
Do but look on her hair, it is bright
 As Love's star when it riseth!
Do but mark, her forehead's smoother
  Than words that soothe her;
And from her arched brows such a grace
  Sheds itself through the face
As alone there triumphs to the life
All the gain, all the good, of the elements' strife.

Have you seen but a bright lily grow
 Before rude hands have touched it?
Have you marked but the fall of the snow
 Before the soil hath smutched it?
Have you felt the wool of beaver,
  Or swan's down ever?
Have you smelt of the bud of the briar?
  Or the nard in the fire?
Or have tasted the bag of the bee?
O so white! O so soft! O so sweet is she!

The Noble Nature

[From *A Pindaric Ode*]

BEN JONSON

It is not growing like a tree
In bulk, doth make man better be;
Or standing long an oak, three hundred year,
To fall a log at last, dry, bald, and sear;
 A lily of a day
 Is fairer far, in May,
Although it fall and die that night,
It was a plant and flower of Light.
In small proportions we just beauties see;
And in short measures life may perfect be.

Simplex Munditiis

BEN JONSON

Still to be neat, still to be dressed,
As you were going to a feast;
Still to be powdered, still perfumed:
Lady, it is to be presumed,
Though art's hid causes are not found,
All is not sweet, all is not sound.

Give me a look, give me a face,
That makes simplicity a grace;
Robes loosely flowing, hair as free:
Such sweet neglect more taketh me
Than all th' adulteries of art;
They strike mine eyes, but not my heart.

Song

[From *The Masque of Beauty*]

BEN JONSON

The musicians which were placed in the arbours came forth through the mazes
singing this full song, iterated in the closes by two echoes rising out of the fountains.

When Love at first did move
From out of Chaos, brightened
So was the world, and lightened
As now.
    1. Echo—As now!
      2. Echo—As now!

Yield Night, then, to the Light,
As Blackness hath to Beauty:
Which is but the same duty.
It was for Beauty that the world was made,
And where she reigns, Love's lights admit no shade.
    1. Echo—Love's lights admit no shade.
      2. Echo—Admit no shade.

Song of Echo

BEN JONSON

Slow, slow, fresh fount, keep time with my salt tears;
    Yet slower yet; O faintly, gentle springs;
List to the heavy part the music bears,
    Woe weeps out her division when she sings.
        Droop herbs and flowers,
        Fall grief in showers;
        Our beauties are not ours;
          O, I could still,
Like melting snow upon some craggy hill,
        Drop, drop, drop, drop,
Since Nature's pride is now a withered daffodil.

The Sad Shepherd

[Selection]

BEN JONSON

A spring, now she is dead! of what? of thorns,
Briars, and brambles? thistles, burs and docks?
Cold hemlock, yew? the mandrake or the box?
These may grow still; but what can spring beside?
Did not the whole earth sicken when she died?
As if there since did fall one drop of dew,
But what was wept for her! or any stalk
Did bear a flower, or any branch a bloom,
After her wreath was made! In faith, in faith,
You do not fair to put these things upon me,
Which can in no sort be: Earine,
Who had her very being, and her name,
With the first knots or buddings of the spring,
Born with the primrose, or the violet,
Or earliest roses blown; when Cupid smiled;

And Venus led the Graces out to dance,
And all the flowers and sweets in Nature's lap
Leaped out, and made their solemn conjuration,
To last but while she lived! Do not I know
How the veil wither'd the same day? how Dove,
Dean, Eye, and Erwash, Idel, Snite and Soare,
Each broke his urn, and twenty waters more,
That swelled proud Trent, shrunk themselves dry? that since
No sun or moon, or other cheerful star,
Look'd out of Heaven, but all the cope was dark,
As it were hung so for her exequies!
And not a voice or sound to ring her knell
But of that dismal pair, the screeching-owl,
And buzzing hornet! Hark! hark! hark! the foul
Bird! how she flutters with her wicked wings!
Peace! you shall hear her screech.

> *Cla.* Good Karolin, sing,
Help to divert this phant'sie.
> *Kar.* All I can.

(*Karolin, the kind shepherd, sings*)

Though I am young and cannot tell
Either what death or love is well,
        Yet I have heard they both bear darts,
        And both do aim at human hearts.
And then again, I have been told
Love wounds with heat, as death with cold;
        So that I fear they do but bring
        Extremes to touch, and mean one thing.
As in a ruin we it call
One thing to be blown up, or fall
        Or to our end, like way may have
        By a flash of lightning, or a wave;
So love's inflamèd shaft or brand
May kill as soon as death's cold hand,
        Except love's fires the virtue have
        To fright the frost out of the grave.

The Picture of Her Mind

[From the Elegy on the Lady Venetia Digby, Wife of Sir Kenelm Digby]

BEN JONSON

Painter, you're come, but may be gone,
   Now I have better thought thereon,
   This work I can perform alone;
   And give you reasons more than one.

*   *   *   *   *

You could make shift to paint an eye,
   An eagle towering in the sky,
   The sun, sea, or soundless pit;
   But these are *like* a mind, not *it*.

No, to express this mind to sense,
   Would ask a heaven's intelligence;
   Since nothing can report that flame,
   But what's of kin to whence it came.

*   *   *   *   *

There, high exalted in the sphere,
   As it another nature were,
   It moveth all; and makes a flight
   As circular as infinite.

Whose notions when it will express
   In speech, it is with that excess
   Of grace, and music to the ear,
   As what it spoke, it planted there.

The voice so sweet, the words so fair,
   As some soft chime had stroked the air;
   And though the sound were parted thence,
   Still left an echo in the sense.

73

But that a mind so rapt, so high,
    So swift, so pure, should yet apply
    Itself to us, and come so nigh
    Earth's grossness; there's the how and why.

Is it because it sees us dull,
    And sunk in clay here, it would pull
    Us forth, by some celestial sleight,
    Up to her own sublimèd height?

Or hath she here, upon the ground,
    Some Paradise or palace found,
    In all the bounds of beauty, fit
    For her t' inhabit? There is it.

Thrice happy house, that hast receipt
    For this so lofty form, so streight,
    So polish'd, perfect, round and even,
    As it slid moulded off from Heaven.

Not swelling like the ocean proud,
    But stooping gently, as a cloud,
    As smooth as oil poured forth, and calm
    As showers, and sweet as drops of balm.

Smooth, soft, and sweet, in all a flood,
    Where it may run to any good:
    And where it stays, it there becomes
    A nest of odorous spice and gums.

In action, wingèd as the wind;
    In rest, like spirits left behind
    Upon a bank, or field of flowers,
    Begotten by the wind and showers.

In thee, fair mansion, let it rest,
    Yet know, with what thou art possest,
    Thou, entertaining in thy breast
    But such a mind, mak'st God thy guest.

The Lady Venetia Digby

[Her Relation to the Saints]

(*Sera quidem tanto struitur medicina dolore.*)

BEN JONSON

'Twere time that I died too, now she is dead
Who was my Muse, and life of all I said.

    Dare I profane, so irreligious be,
To greet or grieve her soft euthanasy!
So sweetly taken to the court of bliss,
As spirits had stolen her spirit in a kiss,
From off her pillow and deluded bed:
And left her lovely body unthought dead. . . .

    Saints, Martyrs, Prophets, with those Hierarchies
Arch-Angels, Principalities,
The Dominations, Virtues, and the Powers,
The Thrones, the Cherubs, and Seraphic bowers,
That, planted round, there sing before the Lamb
A new song to His praise, and great I AM:
And she doth know, out of the shade of death,
What 'tis to enjoy an everlasting breath!
To have her captived spirit freed from flesh,
And, on her innocence, a garment fresh
And white as that put on: and in her hand
With bough of palm, a crownèd victress stand. . . .

    There all the happy souls that ever were,
Shall meet with gladness in one theatre:
And each shall know there one another's face,
By beatific virtue of the place.
There shall the brother with the sister walk,
And sons and daughters with their parents talk:
But all of God. They still shall have to say,
But make him All in All their Theme that day:

That happy day that never shall see night,
Where He will be all beauty to the sight:
Wine or delicious fruits unto the taste:
A music in the ears will ever last:
Unto the scent a spicery or balm:
And to the touch a flower like soft as palm.
He will all glory, all perfection be,
God in the Union and the Trinity!
That holy, great, and glorious mystery,
Will there revealèd be in majesty!
By light and comfort of Spiritual grace!
The vision of Our Saviour, face to face. . . .

A Hymn to God the Father

BEN JONSON

Hear me, O God!
　　A broken heart
　　Is my best part:
Use still thy rod,
That I may prove,
　　Therein, Thy love.

If Thou hadst not
　　Been stern to me,
　　But left me free,
I had forgot
　　Myself and Thee.

For, sin's so sweet,
　　As minds ill-bent
　　Rarely repent,
Unless they meet
　　Their punishment.

Who more can crave
 Than Thou hast done?
 Thou gav'st a Son
To free a slave,
 First made of nought,
 With all since bought.

Sin, death, and hell
 His glorious Name
 Quite overcame;
Yet I rebel,
 And slight the same.

But, I'll come in
 Before my loss
 Me farther toss;
As sure to win
 Under His cross.

An Epitaph on Salathiel Pavy, a Child of Queen Elizabeth's Chapel

BEN JONSON

Weep with me, all you that read
 This little story;
And know, for whom a tear you shed
 Death's self is sorry.
'Twas a child that so did thrive
 In grace and feature,
As heaven and nature seemed to strive
 Which owned the creature.
Years he numbered scarce thirteen
 When fates turned cruel,
Yet three filled zodiacs had he been
 The stage's jewel;

And did act, what now we moan,
    Old men so duly,
As, sooth, the Parcæ thought him one,
    He played so truly.
So by error, to his fate
    They all consented;
But viewing him since, alas too late,
    They have repented,
And have sought, to give new birth,
    In baths to steep him;
But being so much too good for earth,
    Heaven vows to keep him.

The Assumption

SIR JOHN BEAUMONT
(1 5 8 3 - 1 6 2 7)

Who is she that ascends so high,
Next the Heavenly King,
Round about whom Angels fly
And her praises sing?

Who is she that, adorned with light,
Makes the sun her robe,
At whose feet the queen of night
Lays her changing globe?

To that crown direct thine eye,
Which her head attires;
There thou mayst her name descry
Writ in starry fires.

This is she who in pure womb
Heaven's Prince remained;
Therefore in no earthly tomb
Can she be contained.

Heaven she was, which held that fire
Whence the world took light,
And to Heaven doth now aspire
Flames with flames t'unite.

Of My Dear Son, Gervase Beaumont

SIR JOHN BEAUMONT

Dear Lord, receive my son, whose winning love
To me was like a friendship, far above
The course of nature or his tender age;
Whose looks could all my bitter griefs assuage;
Let his pure soul, ordained seven years to be
In that frail body which was part of me,
Remain my pledge in Heaven, as sent to show
How to this port at every step I go.

Of Sir Philip Sidney

SIR JOHN BEAUMONT

He left two children, who for virtue, wit,
Beauty, were loved of all,—thee and his writ:
Two was too few; yet death hath from us took
Thee, a more faultless issue than his book,
Who, now the only living thing we have
From him, we'll see, shall never find a grave
As thou hast done. Alas, would it might be
That books their sexes had, as well as we,
That we might see this married to its worth,
And many poems like itself bring forth.

Lines on the Tombs in Westminster

FRANCIS BEAUMONT

(1 5 8 4 – 1 6 1 6)

Mortality, behold and fear!
What a change of flesh is here!
Think how many royal bones
Sleep within this heap of stones;
Here they lie had realms and lands,
Who now want strength to stir their hands;
Where from their pulpits sealed with dust
They preach, 'In greatness is no trust.'
Here's an acre sown indeed
With the richest royal'st seed
That the earth did e'er suck in,
Since the first man died for sin;
Here the bones of birth have cried,
'Though gods they were, as men they died.'
Here are sands, ignoble things,
Dropt from the ruined sides of kings.
Here's a world of pomp and state,
Buried in dust, once dead by fate.

Three Songs

[From *The Masque of the Inner Temple*]

FRANCIS BEAUMONT

I

Song for a Dance

Shake off your heavy trance!
    And leap into a dance
Such as no mortals use to tread:
    Fit only for Apollo
To play to, for the Moon to lead,
    And all the Stars to follow!

II

The Masquers Called Away

We should stay longer if we durst:
    Away! Alas that he that first
Gave Time wild wings to fly away—
    Hath no power to make him stay!
And though these games must needs be played,
I would this pair, when they are laid,
    And not a creature nigh 'em,
Could catch his scythe, as he doth pass,
And clip his wings, and break his glass,
    And keep him ever by 'em.

III

Bridal Song

Peace and silence be the guide
    To the man and to the bride!
If there be a joy new
In marriage, let it fall on you,
    That all the world may wonder!
If we should stay, we should do worse,
And turn our blessing to a curse
    By keeping you asunder.

The Examination of His Mistress' Perfections

FRANCIS BEAUMONT

Though by thy bounteous favor I be in
A paradise, where I may freely taste
Of all the virtuous pleasures which thou hast,
I, wanting knowledge, must, in all my bliss,
Err with my parents, and ask what it is.
    My faith saith 'tis not Heaven; and I dare swear,
If it be Hell, no pain of sense is there.

Wert thou but fair, and no whit virtuous,
Thou wert no more to me but a fair house
Haunted with spirits, from which men do them bless,
And no man will half furnish to possess:
Or, hadst thou worth wrapped in a rivelled skin,
'Twere inaccessible. Who durst go in
To find it out? For sooner would I go
To find a pearl covered with hills of snow;
'Twere buried virtue, and thou might'st me move
To reverence the tomb, but not to love,—
No more than dotingly to cast mine eye
Upon the urn where Lucrece' ashes lie.

But thou art fair and sweet, and every good
That ever yet durst mix with flesh and blood:
The Devil ne'er saw in his fallen state
An object whereupon to ground his hate
So fit as thee; all living things but he
Love thee; how happy, then, must that man be
Whom from amongst all creatures thou dost take!
Is there a hope beyond it? Can he make
A wish to change thee for? This is my bliss,
Let it run on now: I know what it is.

On the Life of Man

FRANCIS BEAUMONT

Like to the falling of a star,
Or as the flights of eagles are,
Or like the fresh spring's gaudy hue,
Or silver drops of morning dew;
Or like the wind that chafes the flood,
Or bubbles which on water stood:
Even such is man, whose borrowed light
Is straight called in and paid to night:

The wind blows out, the bubble dies,
The spring intombed in autumn lies;
The dew's dried up, the star is shot,
The flight is past, and man forgot.

Our Blood and State

[From *The Contention of Ajax and Ulysses*]

JAMES SHIRLEY

(*1 5 9 4 ? - 1 6 6 6*)

The glories of our blood and state
    Are shadows, not substantial things;
There is no armour against fate;
    Death lays his icy hand on kings.
        Sceptre and crown
        Must tumble down,
And in the dust be equal made
With the poor crooked scythe and spade.

Some men with swords may reap the field,
    And plant fresh laurels where they kill;
But their strong nerves at last must yield,
    They tame but one another still.
        Early or late,
        They stoop to fate,
And must give up their murmuring breath
When they, pale captives, creep to death.

The garlands wither on your brow,
    Then boast no more your mighty deeds;
Upon death's purple altar now
    See where the victor-victim bleeds.
        Your heads must come
        To the cold tomb;
Only the actions of the just
Smell sweet, and blossom in their dust.

Death, the Conqueror

[From *Cupid and Death*]

JAMES SHIRLEY

Victorious men of earth! no more
    Proclaim how wide your empires are!
Though you bind in every shore
    And your triumphs reach as far
      As night or day,
    Yet you, proud monarchs! must obey,
And mingle with forgotten ashes when
Death calls ye to the crowd of common men.

Devouring Famine, Plague, and War,
    Each able to undo mankind,
Death's servile emissaries are;
    Nor to these alone confined,
      He hath at will
    More quaint and subtle ways to kill:
A smile or kiss, as he will use the art,
Shall have the cunning skill to break a heart.

Upon Scarlet and Blush-Coloured Ribbands, Given by Two Ladies

JAMES SHIRLEY

Let other servants boast a snowy glove,
    Or glory in their mistress' hair,
    Or think they straight immortal prove,
      If they once obtain to wear
A ring enamelled, by her finger blest,
    Wherein the rainbow is expressed,
    In whose circle Cupid dwelling,
Doth offer a sweet posy to their smelling.

Not all the orient beauties that embrace
    Fair Venus' neck, nay, grant that she
    Deign to disfurnish her own face
      And bestow her mole on me,—
Not this, nor those are half so rich, so fair
    As these two silken ribbands are;
    Favours Juno might have given
The Graces, on her wedding day in heaven.

Mysterious colours, carrying more than show!
    For you express in your rich dye
    Rare virtues, which the owners owe,[1]
      Constant love, and modesty:
To which when I prove false, my blood be curst,
    To satisfy the injured first;
    Shame be next reward, and then
I forfeit blush and scarlet back again.

A Hymn

JAMES SHIRLEY

O fly, my Soul! What hangs upon
      Thy drooping wings,
      And weighs them down
With love of gaudy mortal things?

The Sun is now i' the east: each shade
      As he doth rise
      Is shorter made,
That earth may lessen to our eyes.

O be not careless then and play
      Until the Star of Peace
Hide all his beams in dark recess!
Poor pilgrims needs must lose their way
When all the shadows do increase.

[1] *owe*—own

Love's Victories

[From *Cupid and Death*]

JAMES SHIRLEY

Though little be the god of Love,
Yet his arrows mighty are,
And his victories above
What the valiant reach by war.
Nor are his limits with the sky;
O'er the Milky Way he'll fly
And sometimes wound a deity.
Apollon once the Python slew,
But a keener arrow flew
From Daphne's eye, and made a wound
For which the god no balsam found.
One smile of Venus, too, did more
On Mars than armies could before.
If a warm fit thus pull him down,
How will she ague-shake him with a frown!
Thus Love can fiery spirits tame,
And, when he please, cold rocks inflame.

The Commonwealth of Birds

JAMES SHIRLEY

Listen, gallants, to my words,
I sing the Commonwealth of Birds.
A Buzzard doth command the town;
Gulls are brethren of the gown;
Great, but not Moguls they be,
Of the land, and not the sea.

There is, in every ward of these,
Widgeons placed for deputies:
The citizens have merry lives;
They Cuckoos are, who take to wives,
  Pretty Parrots, Blackbirds, Rails,
  Many of them pure Wagtails.

Each parish constable is a Daw;
Wry-neck, watchmen with club law,
Who, taking any Owls by night,
Straight convey them to the Kite,
  Who keeps the Counter, and indeed
  Knows on Poultry how to feed.

Diverse gentlemen there are,
A Robin-red-breast and a Stare;
Canary birds are not a few;
Rooks have crept among them too;
  Dunghill Cocks, that will be beat;
  Godwits, only good to eat.

Would you know the lawyers? These
Are a nest of Goldfinches:
But few men there are that know
The Physician from a Crow;
  Yet Bitter many of them are,
  And the good, like Black-swans, rare.

If any chance to ask of me,
Where this Commonwealth should be,
I answer, 'tis above the Moon,
'Twas mine by revelation;
  There the Larks are, and we shall
  See them, when the sky doth fall.

Cupid Ungodded

JAMES SHIRLEY

Why how now, Cupid, grown so wild?
So great a tyrant, and a child?
What wert thou but an empty shade,
Until our superstition made
Thee first a god, blind, young, to be
A soft and harmless deity?
Our fancy gave that rich pair
Of wings, to wanton in the air;
Thy gaudy quiver, and thy bow,
And golden shafts we did bestow,
But for no other exercise
Than to kill bees, or butterflies.

    But since thou hast employed thy darts
Only to wound thy makers' hearts,
And that thy wings serve but to fly
From lovers, when they bleeding die;
Thy blindness used but to invite
Our pity, till we lose our sight;
Thy weakness, not through want of years,
But from the surfeit of our tears;
Stoop to the justice of thy fate,—
We can unmake, that did create.

    And first give back, ingrateful thing,
To us, that made, thy glorious wing:
Those painted feathers thou shalt find
Contemned, and tossed by every wind,
Till wandering in some night, they are
The mark of a prodigious star,
And blasted: these the world shall name
The spotted wings of evil fame.
Next, give thy arrows back, which we
Did mean for love, not cruelty.
That rich enamelled bow is mine;

Come, that gay quiver too resign,
And shining belt: these will I burn,
And keep their ashes in some urn,
Till opened on that solemn day
When men to souls sad requiems pay;
Lovers shall curse, and sigh, and make
A new litany for thy sake.
        But thou art still alive; and be;
To murder, were to pity thee.
Know, wretch, thou shalt not die, before
I see thee begging at some door!
And, taken for a vagrant, stript,
Then by a furious beedle whipt,
No more with roses, but with thorn:
To all this world thus made a scorn;
        I'll give thee eyes, before we part,
        To see thy shame, and break thy heart.

To the Excellent Pattern of Beauty and Virtue, Lady Elizabeth, Countess of Ormond

JAMES SHIRLEY

Madam,

Were you but only great, there are some men
Whose heat is not the Muses', nor their pen
Steered by chaste truth, could flatter you in prose,
Or glorious verse, but I am none of those.
I never learned that trick of court to wear
Silk at the cost of flattery; or make dear
My pride, by painting a great lady's face
When she had done't before, and swear the grace
Was Nature's; anagram upon her name,
And add to her no virtue, my own shame.
I would not make this lord a god, then try
How to commit new court idolatry;

And when he dies, hang on his silent hearse
Wet elegies, and haunt his ghost inverse.
These, some hold witty, thriving garbs, but I
Choose to my loss a modest poesy,
And place my genius upon subjects fit
For imitation, rather than hold wit;
And such are you, who both in name and blood
Born great, have learned this lesson to be good.

Armed with this knowledge, madam, I not fear
To hold fair correspondence with the year,
And bring my gift, hearty, as you are fair,
A servant's wish, for all my wealth is prayer,
Which with the year thus enters. May you be
Still the same flowing goodness that we see.

In your most noble lord be happy still,
And heaven chain your hearts into one will;
Be rich in your two darlings of the spring,
Which as it waits, perfumes their blossoming,
The growing pledges of your love, and blood;
And may that unborn blessing timely bud,
The chaste and noble treasure of your womb,
Your own, and the age's expectation come;
And when your days and virtues have made even,
Die late, beloved of earth, and change for heaven.

The Martyrdom of Father Campion

HENRY WALPOLE, JESUIT
(*Martyred 1595*)

England, look up! Thy soil is stained with blood,
Thou hast made martyrs many of thine own.
If thou hadst Grace, their deaths would do thee good.
The seed will take, which in such blood is sown,
And Campion's learning, fertile so before,
Thus watered too, must needs of force be more.

All Europe wonders at so rare a man.
England is filled with rumour of his end.
London must needs, for it was present then
When constantly three saints their lives did spend.
The streets, the stones, the steps, they hale them by,
Proclaim the cause, for which these martyrs die.

The Tower says, the truth he did defend.
The Bar bears witness of his guiltless mind.
Tyburn doth tell, he made a patient end.
In every gate his martyrdom we find.
In vain you wrought, that would obscure his name,
For heaven and earth will still record the same.

His quartered limbs shall join with joy again,
And rise a body brighter than the sun.
Your bloody malice tortured him in vain,
For every wrench some glory hath him won.
And every drop of blood which he did spend
Hath reaped a joy, which never shall have end.

Nox Nocti Indicat Scientiam

WILLIAM HABINGTON

(1 6 0 5 - 1 6 6 4)

When I survey the bright
Celestial sphere,
So rich with jewels hung, that night
Doth like an Ethiop bride appear:

My soul her wings doth spread
And heavenward flies,
The Almighty's mysteries to read
In the large volumes of the skies.

For the bright firmament
        Shoots forth no flame
So silent, but is eloquent
        In speaking the Creator's name.

No unregarded star
        Contracts its light
Into so small a character,
        Removed far from our human sight,

But if we steadfast look
        We shall discern
In it, as in some holy book,
        How man may heavenly knowledge learn.

It tells the conqueror
        That far-stretched pow'r,
Which his proud dangers traffic for,
        Is but the triumph of an hour,

That from the farthest North,
        Some nation may,
Yet undiscovered, issue forth,
        And o'er his new-got conquest sway;

Some nation yet shut in
        With hills of ice
May be let out to scourge his sin,
        Till they shall equal him in vice.

And then they likewise shall
        Their ruin have;
For as yourselves your empires fall,
        And every kingdom hath a grave.

Thus those celestial fires,
        Though seeming mute,
The fallacy of our desires
        And all the pride of life, confute:—

For they have watched since first
 The world had birth;
And found sin in itself accurst,
 And nothing permanent on earth.

To Roses in the Bosom of Castara

WILLIAM HABINGTON

Ye blushing virgins happy are
In the chaste nunnery of her breasts,
For he'd profane so chaste a fair
Whoe'er should call them Cupid's nests.

Transplanted thus, how bright ye grow,
How rich a perfume do ye yield!
In some close garden, cowslips so
Are sweeter than i' th' open field.

In those white cloisters live secure
From the rude blasts of wanton breath,
Each hour more innocent and pure,
Till you shall wither into death.

Then that which living gave you room
Your glorious sepulchre shall be.
There wants no marble for a tomb,
Whose breast hath marble been to me.

Song

SIR WILLIAM DAVENANT
(1 6 0 6 – 1 6 6 8)

The lark now leaves his wat'ry nest,
 And, climbing, shakes his dewy wings,
He takes this window for the East,
 And to implore your light he sings:

'Awake, awake! The morn will never rise
Till she can dress her beauty at your eyes.'

The merchant bows unto the seaman's star,
    The ploughman from the sun his season takes;
But still the lover wonders what they are
    Who look for day before his mistress wakes.
'Awake, awake! Break through your veils of lawn!
Then draw your curtains, and begin the dawn.'

Praise and Prayer

SIR WILLIAM DAVENANT

Praise is devotion fit for mighty minds,
    The diff'ring world's agreeing sacrifice;
Where Heaven divided faiths united finds:
    But Prayer in various discord upward flies.

For Prayer the ocean is where diversely
    Men steer their course, each to a sev'ral coast;
Where all our interests so discordant be
    That half beg winds by which the rest are lost.

By Penitence when we ourselves forsake,
    'Tis but in wise design on piteous Heaven;
In Praise we nobly give what God may take,
    And are, without a beggar's blush, forgiven.

To a Mistress Dying

SIR WILLIAM DAVENANT

LOVER: Your beauty, ripe and calm and fresh
        As eastern summers are,
    Must now, forsaking time and flesh,
        Add light to some small star.

PHILOSOPHER: Whilst she yet lives, were stars decayed,
                 Their light by hers relief might find;
           But Death will lead her to a shade
                 Where Love is cold and Beauty blind.

LOVER: Lovers, whose priests all poets are,
                 Think every mistress, when she dies,
           Is changed at least into a star:
                 And who dares doubt the poets wise?

PHILOSOPHER: But ask not bodies doomed to die
                 To what abode they go;
           Since Knowledge is but Sorrow's spy,
                 It is not safe to know.

Wishes for the Supposed Mistress

RICHARD CRASHAW

(1 6 1 2 ? - 1 6 4 9)

Whoe'er she be—
That not impossible She
That shall command my heart and me;

Where'er she lie,
Locked up from mortal eye,
In shady leaves of destiny:

Till that ripe birth
Of studied Fate stand forth,
And teach her fair steps to our earth;

Till that divine
Idea take a shrine
Of crystal flesh, through which to shine:

—Meet you her, my Wishes,
Bespeak her to my blisses,
And be ye called my absent kisses.

I wish her Beauty,
That owes not all its duty
To gaudy tire, or glistering shoe-tie:

Something more than
Taffeta or tissue can,
Or rampant feather, or rich fan.

*   *   *   *

A Face, that's best
By its own beauty drest,
And can alone commend the rest:

A Face, made up
Out of no other shop
Than what Nature's white hand sets ope.

Sydneian showers
Of sweet discourse, whose powers
Can crown old Winter's head with flowers.

Soft silken hours,
Open suns, shady bowers;
'Bove all, nothing within that lowers.

Whate'er delight
Can make day's forehead bright
Or give down to the wings of night.

Days, that need borrow
No part of their good-morrow
From a fore-spent night of sorrow.

Days, that in spite
Of darkness, by the light
Of a clear mind, are day all night.

Life, that dares send
A challenge to his end,
And when it comes, say, 'Welcome, friend!'

I wish her store
Of worth may leave her poor
Of wishes; and I wish—no more.

—Now, if Time knows
That Her, whose radiant brows
Weave them a garland of my vows;

Her, that dares be
What these lines wish to see:
I seek no further, it is She.

'Tis She, and here,
Lo! I unclothe and clear
My wishes' cloudy character.

Such worth as this is,
Shall fix my flying wishes,
And determine them to kisses.

Let her full glory,
My fancies, fly before ye;
Be ye my fictions—but her story.

Christ Crucified

RICHARD CRASHAW

Thy restless feet cannot go
    For us and our eternal good,
As they were ever wont. What though
    They swim, alas! in their own flood?

Thy hands to give Thou canst not lift,
    Yet will Thy hand still giving be;
It gives, but O, itself's the gift!
    It gives though bound, though bound 'tis free!

97

A Song of Divine Love

RICHARD CRASHAW

Lord, when the sense of thy sweet grace
Sends up my soul to seek thy face,
Thy blessèd eyes breed such desire
I die in love's delicious fire.
O love, I am thy sacrifice.
Be still triumphant, blessèd eyes.
Still shine on me, fair suns, that I
Still may behold though still I die.

Though still I die, I live again,
Still longing so to be still slain;
So gainful is such loss of breath,
I die even in desire of death.
Still live in me this loving strife
Of living death and dying life:
For while thou sweetly slayest me,
Dead to myself, I live in Thee.

A Hymn Sung as by the Shepherds
[From *The Holy Nativity*]

RICHARD CRASHAW

We saw Thee in Thy balmy nest,
    Young Dawn of our Eternal Day!
We saw Thine eyes break from their east
    And chase the trembling shades away.
We saw Thee; and we blest the sight;
We saw Thee by Thine own sweet light.

'Poor World,' said I, 'what wilt thou do
    To entertain this starry Stranger?
Is this the best thou canst bestow—
    A cold and not too cleanly manger?

Contend, the powers of heaven and earth,
To fit a bed for this huge birth!'

'Proud World,' said I, 'cease your contest,
  And let the mighty Babe alone.'
The phoenix builds the phoenix' nest;
  Love's architecture is his own;
The Babe Whose birth embraves this morn
Made His own bed e'er He was born.

I saw the curled drops, soft and slow,
  Come hovering o'er the place's head;
Offering their whitest sheets of snow
  To furnish the fair Infant's bed.
'Forbear,' said I; 'be not too bold;
Your fleece is white, but 'tis too cold.'

I saw the obsequious Seraphim
  Their rosy fleece of fire bestow;
For well they now can spare their wing,
  Since Heaven itself lies here below.
'Well done,' said I; 'but are you sure
Your down, so warm, will pass for pure?'

No, no, your King's not yet to seek
  Where to repose His royal head;
See, see, how soon His new-bloomed cheek
  'Twixt's mother's breasts is gone to bed!
'Sweet choice!' said we; 'no way but so,
Not to lie cold, yet sleep in snow.'

CHORUS

She sings Thy tears asleep, and dips
  Her kisses in Thy weeping eye;
She spreads the red leaves of Thy lips,
  That in their buds yet blushing lie;
She 'gainst those mother diamonds tries
The points of her young eagle's eyes.

Welcome! though not to those gay flies,
    Gilded i' th' beams of earthly kings;
Slippery souls in smiling eyes,
    But to poor shepherds, homespun things,
Whose wealth's their flock, whose wit to be
Well-read in their simplicity.

Yet when young April's husband-showers
    Shall bless the fruitful Maia's bed,
We'll bring the first-born of her flowers,
    To kiss Thy feet, and crown Thy head:
To Thee, dread Lamb, Whose love must keep
The shepherds more than they the sheep.

To Thee, meek Majesty, soft King
    Of simple graces and sweet loves,
Each of us his lamb will bring,
    Each his pair of silver doves:
Till burnt at last, in fire of Thy fair eyes,
Ourselves become our own best sacrifice!

The Flaming Heart

[Upon the Book and Picture of the Seraphical Saint Teresa.
She is Usually Expressed with a Seraphim Beside Her.]

RICHARD CRASHAW

Well-meaning readers, you that come as friends
And catch the precious name this piece pretends,
Make not too much haste to admire
That fair-cheeked fallacy of fire.
That is a seraphim, they say,
And this the great Teresia.
Readers, be ruled by me, and make
Here a well-placed and wise mistake:
You must transpose the picture quite,
And spell it wrong to read it right;

Read him for her, and her for him,
And call the saint the seraphim.

    Painter, what didst thou understand
To put her dart into his hand?
See, even the years and size of him
Shows this the mother-seraphim.
This is the mistress-flame; and duteous, he
Her happy fireworks, here, comes down to see.
O, most poor-spirited of men!
Had thy cold pencil kissed her pen,
Thou couldst not so unkindly err
To show us this faint shade for her.
Why, man, this speaks pure mortal frame;
And mocks with female frost love's manly flame.
One wouldst suspect thou meantst to paint
Some weak, inferior woman-saint.
But had thy pale-faced purple took
Fire from the burning cheeks of that bright book,
Thou wouldst on her have heaped up all
That could be found seraphical;
Whate'er this youth of fire wears fair,
Rosy fingers, radiant hair,
Glowing cheek, and glistering wings,
All those fair and flagrant things,
But, before all, that fiery dart
Had filled the hand of this great heart.
Do then, as equal right requires:
Since his the blushes be, and hers the fires,
Resume and rectify thy rude design;
Undress thy seraphim into mine;
Redeem this injury of thy art;
Give him the veil, give her the dart,
Give him the veil that he may cover
The red cheeks of the rivalled lover;
Ashamed that our world now can show
Nests of new seraphim here below.
Give her the dart, for it is she,

Fair youth, shoots both thy shaft and thee.
Say, all ye wise and well-pierced hearts
That live and die amidst her darts,
What is't your tasteful spirits do prove
In that rare life of her and Love?
Say and bear witness: sends she not
A seraphim at every shot?
What magazines of immortal arms there shine!
Heaven's great artillery in each love-spun line.
Give then the dart to her who gives the flame;
Give him the veil who gives the shame.

      But if it be the frequent fate
Of worst faults to be fortunate;
If all's prescription, and proud wrong
Hearken not to an humble song;
For all the gallantry of him,
Give me the suffering seraphim.
His be the bravery of all those bright things,
The glowing cheeks, the glistering wings;
The rosy hand, the radiant dart;
Leave her alone the flaming heart.
Leave her that, and thou shalt leave her
Not one loose shaft, but Love's whole quiver;
For in Love's field was never found
A nobler weapon than a wound.
Love's passives are his activ'st part;
The wounded is the wounding heart.
O, heart! the equal poise of Love's both parts,
Big alike with wound and darts,
Live in these conquering leaves! live all the same;
And walk through all tongues one triumphant flame!
Live here, great heart; and love, and die, and kill,
And bleed, and wound; and yield and conquer still!
Let this immortal life where'er it comes
Walk in a crowd of loves and martyrdoms;
Let mystic deaths wait on 't; and wise souls be
The love-slain witnesses of this life of thee.

O, sweet incendiary! show here thy art
Upon this carcass of a hard cold heart;
Let all thy scattered shafts of light that play
Among the leaves of thy large books of day,
Combined against this breast, at once break in
And take away from me myself and sin!
This gracious robbery shall thy bounty be,
And my best fortunes such fair spoils of me.
O, thou undaunted daughter of desires!
By all thy dower of lights and fires,
By all the eagle in thee, all the dove,
By all thy lives and deaths of love,
By thy large draughts of intellectual day,
And by thy thirsts of love more large than they,
By all thy brim-filled bowls of fierce desire,
By thy last morning's draught of liquid fire,
By the full kingdom of that final kiss
That seized thy parting soul and sealed thee His,
By all the heavens thou hast in Him,
Fair sister of the seraphim,
By all of Him we have in thee:
Leave nothing of myself in me!
Let me so read thy life that I
Unto all life of mine may die!

The Guest

[From *Christ Church Manuscript*]

AUTHOR UNKNOWN
(*After 1620*)

Yet if his majesty, our sovereign lord,
    Should of his own accord
    Friendly himself invite,
And say, 'I'll be your guest to-morrow night,'

How should we stir ourselves, call and command
All hands to work! 'Let no man idle stand!

'Set me fine Spanish tables in the hall,
    See they be fitted all;
    Let there be room to eat,
And order taken that there want no meat.
See every sconce and candlestick made bright,
That without tapers they may give a light.

'Look to the presence: are the carpets spread,
    The dazie o'er the head,
    The cushions in the chairs,
And all the candles lighted on the stairs?
Perfume the chambers, and in any case
Let each man give attendance in his place.'

Thus if the King were coming would we do,
    And 'twere good reason too;
    For 'tis a duteous thing
To show all honour to an earthly king,
And after all our travail and our cost,
So he be pleased, to think no labour lost.

But at the coming of the King of Heaven
    All's set at six and seven:
    We wallow in our sin,
Christ can not find a chamber in the inn.
We entertain Him always like a stranger,
And, as at first, still lodge Him in the manger.

Silence Invoked

RICHARD FLECKNOE
(*17th Century*)

Stillborn Silence, thou that art
Floodgate of the deeper heart;

Offspring of a heavenly kind,
Frost o' the mouth and thaw o' the mind;

Secrecy's confident, and he
Who makes religion mystery;

Admiration's speakingest tongue,—
Leave thy desert shades among

Reverend hermits' hallowed cells,
Where retiredest Devotion dwells;

With thy enthusiasms come,
Seize this maid, and strike her dumb.

The Magdalen

SIR EDWARD SHERBURNE
(*1618 – 1702*)

The proud Egyptian queen, her Roman guest,
 (T'express her love in height of state and pleasure)
With pearl dissolved in gold, did feast,
 Both food and treasure.

And now (dear Lord!) Thy lover, on the fair
 And silver tables of Thy feet, behold!
Pearl, in her tears and in her hair,
 Offers Thee gold.

On a Drop of Dew

ANDREW MARVELL

(1 6 2 1 - 1 6 7 8)

See how the Orient dew
 Shed from the bosom of the Morn
 Into the blowing roses,
Yet careless of its mansion new,
For the clear region where 'twas born,
 Round in its self encloses:
 In its little globe's extent
Frames, as it can, its native element.
 How it the purple flow'r does slight,
  Scarce touching where it lies
But gazing back upon the skies,
  Shines with a mournful light,
   Like its own tear,
Because so long divided from the sphere.
 Restless it roules, and unsecure,
 Trembling, lest it grow impure;
 Till the warm sun pity its pain
And to the skies exhale it back again.
  So the soul, that drop, that ray,
Of the clear fountain of Eternal day,
(Could it within the human flow'r be seen)
 Rememb'ring still its former height,
 Shuns the sweet leaves and blossoms green,
 And, recollecting its own light,
Does in its pure and circling thoughts express
The greater heaven in an heaven less.
 In how coy a figure wound,
Every way it turns away;
(So the world-excluding round)
Yet receiving in the day.
Dark beneath, but bright above,
Here disdaining, there in love.

How loose and easie hence to go;
How girt and ready to ascend;
Moving but on a point below,
It all about does upwards bend.
Such did the manna's sacred dew distil,
White and entire, although congeal'd and chill;
Congealed on earth; but does, dissolving, run
Into the glories of the almighty sun.

Song for St. Cecilia's Day

JOHN DRYDEN

(1 6 3 1 – 1 7 0 0)

From harmony, from heavenly harmony,
    This universal frame began:
When Nature underneath a heap
        Of jarring atoms lay,
    And could not heave her head,
The tuneful voice was heard from high:
    'Arise, ye more than dead.'
Then cold and hot and moist and dry
In order to their stations leap,
    And music's power obey.
From harmony, from heavenly harmony,
    This universal frame began;
    From harmony to harmony
Through all the compass of the notes it ran,
The diapason closing full in man.

What passion cannot music raise and quell?
        When Jubal struck the chorded shell,
His listening brethren stood around,
        And, wondering, on their faces fell
To worship that celestial sound.

Less than a god they thought there could not dwell
    Within the hollow of that shell
    That spoke so sweetly and so well.
What passion cannot music raise and quell?

    The trumpet's loud clangor
        Excites us to arms,
    With shrill notes of anger
        And mortal alarms.
    The double double double beat
        Of the thundering drum
        Cries: Hark! the foes come;
Charge, charge, 'tis too late to retreat!

    The soft complaining flute
        In dying notes discovers
        The woes of hopeless lovers,
Whose dirge is whispered by the warbling lute.

      Sharp violins proclaim
Their jealous pangs and desperation,
Fury, frantic indignation,
Depth of pains and height of passion
      For the fair, disdainful dame.

But oh! what art can teach,
What human voice can reach
      The sacred organ's praise?
Notes inspiring holy love,
Notes that wing their heavenly ways
      To mend the choirs above.

Orpheus could lead the savage race,
And trees unrooted left their place,
    Sequacious of the lyre;
But bright Cecilia raised the wonder higher.

When to her organ vocal breath was given,
An angel heard, and straight appeared—
    Mistaking earth for heaven.

GRAND CHORUS

As from the power of sacred lays
    The spheres began to move,
And sung the great Creator's praise
    To all the blest above;
So when the last and dreadful hour
This crumbling pageant shall devour,
The trumpet shall be heard on high,
The dead shall live, the living die,
And Music shall untune the sky.

Alexander's Feast; or, The Power of Music

[A Song in Honour of St. Cecilia's Day]

JOHN DRYDEN

'Twas at the royal feast for Persia won
        By Philip's warlike son:
    Aloft in awful state
    The godlike hero sate
        On his imperial throne;
His valiant peers were placed around;
Their brows with roses and with myrtles bound
    (So should desert in arms be crowned).
The lovely Thais, by his side,
Sate like a blooming Eastern bride,
In flower of youth and beauty's pride.
        Happy, happy, happy pair!
            None but the brave,
            None but the brave,
        None but the brave deserves the fair.

CHORUS

Happy, happy, happy pair!
   None but the brave,
   None but the brave,
None but the brave deserves the fair.

Timotheus, placed on high amid the tuneful quire,
With flying fingers touched the lyre;
   The trembling notes ascend the sky,
   And heavenly joys inspire
   The song began from Jove,
   Who left his blissful seats above
   (Such is the power of mighty love).
   A dragon's fiery form belied the god;
   Sublime on radiant spires he rode,
   When he to fair Olympia pressed;
   And while he sought her snowy breast,
   Then round her slender waist he curled,
And stamped an image of himself, a sovereign of the world.
   —The listening crowd admire the lofty sound,
   'A present deity,' they shout around;
   'A present deity,' the vaulted roofs rebound.
      With ravished ears
      The monarch hears,
      Assumes the god,
      Affects to nod,
And seems to shake the spheres.

CHORUS

      With ravished ears
      The monarch hears,
      Assumes the god,
      Affects to nod,
   And seems to shake the spheres.

The praise of Bacchus then the sweet musician sung,
Of Bacchus ever fair and ever young.

The jolly god in triumph comes;
Sound the trumpets, beat the drums;
 Flushed with a purple grace
 He shows his honest face.
Now give the hautboys breath; he comes, he comes.
 Bacchus, ever fair and young,
  Drinking joys did first ordain;
 Bacchus' blessings are a treasure,
 Drinking is the soldier's pleasure;
  Rich the treasure,
  Sweet the pleasure,
 Sweet is pleasure after pain.

CHORUS

 Bacchus' blessings are a treasure,
 Drinking is the soldier's pleasure;
  Rich the treasure,
  Sweet the pleasure,
 Sweet is pleasure after pain.

Soothed with the sound, the king grew vain;
 Fought all his battles o'er again;
And thrice he routed all his foes, and thrice he slew the slain.
 The master saw the madness rise,
 His glowing cheeks, his ardent eyes;
 And while he heaven and earth defied,
 Changed his hand, and checked his pride.
  He chose a mournful Muse,
  Soft pity to infuse;
 He sung Darius great and good,
  By too severe a fate,
 Fallen, fallen, fallen, fallen,
  Fallen from his high estate,
 And weltering in his blood;
 Deserted at his utmost need
 By those his former bounty fed!

On the bare earth exposed he lies,
With not a friend to close his eyes.
With downcast looks the joyless victor sate,
.Revolving in his altered soul
  The various turns of chance below;
And, now and then, a sigh he stole,
  And tears began to flow.

CHORUS

Revolving in his altered soul
  The various turns of chance below;
And, now and then, a sigh he stole,
  And tears began to flow.

The mighty master smiled to see
That love was in the next degree:
'Twas but a kindred sound to move,
For pity melts the mind to love.
  Softly sweet in Lydian measures,
  Soon he soothed his soul to pleasures.
War, he sung, is toil and trouble;
Honor but an empty bubble;
  Never ending, still beginning,
Fighting still, and still destroying;
  If the world be worth thy winning,
Think, O think it worth enjoying:
  Lovely Thais sits beside thee,
  Take the good the gods provide thee.
The many rend the skies with loud applause;
So Love was crowned, but Music won the cause.
  The prince, unable to conceal his pain,
    Gazed on the fair
    Who caused his care,
  And sighed and looked, sighed and looked,
  Sighed and looked, and sighed again;
At length, with love and wine at once oppressed,
The vanquished victor sunk upon her breast.

CHORUS

The prince, unable to conceal his pain,
    Gazed on the fair
    Who caused his care,
And sighed and looked, sighed and looked,
  Sighed and looked, and sighed again;
At length, with love and wine at once oppressed,
The vanquished victor sunk upon her breast.

Now strike the golden lyre again;
A louder yet, and yet a louder strain.
Break his bands of sleep asunder,
And rouse him, like a rattling peal of thunder.
    Hark, hark, the horrid sound
      Has raised up his head;
      As awaked from the dead,
    And amazed, he stares around.
'Revenge, revenge,' Timotheus cries,
    'See the Furies arise;
    See the snakes that they rear,
    How they hiss in their hair,
And the sparkles that flash from their eyes!
    Behold a ghastly band,
    Each a torch in his hand!
Those are Grecian ghosts, that in battle were slain,
      And unburied remain
      Inglorious on the plain;
      Give the vengeance due
      To the valiant crew.
Behold how they toss their torches on high,
    How they point to the Persian abodes,
    And glittering temples of their hostile gods.'
The princes applaud with a furious joy;
And the king seized a flambeau with zeal to destroy;
    Thais led the way,
    To light him to his prey,
And, like another Helen, fired another Troy.

CHORUS

And the king seized a flambeau with zeal to destroy;
 Thais led the way,
 To light him to his prey,
And, like another Helen, fired another Troy.

 —Thus, long ago,
Ere heaving bellows learned to blow,
 While organs yet were mute,
 Timotheus, to his breathing flute
 And sounding lyre,
Could swell the soul to rage, or kindle soft desire.
 At last divine Cecilia came
 Inventress of the vocal frame;
The sweet enthusiast, from her sacred store,
 Enlarged the former narrow bounds,
 And added length to solemn sounds,
With Nature's mother-wit, and arts unknown before.
 Let old Timotheus yield the prize,
  Or both divide the crown:
 He raised a mortal to the skies;
  She drew an angel down.

GRAND CHORUS

 At last divine Cecilia came,
 Inventress of the vocal frame;
The sweet enthusiast, from her sacred store,
 Enlarged the former narrow bounds,
 And added length to solemn sounds,
With Nature's mother-wit, and arts unknown before.
 Let old Timotheus yield the prize,
  Or both divide the crown:
 He raised a mortal to the skies;
  She drew an angel down.

Veni, Creator Spiritus

JOHN DRYDEN

Creator Spirit, by whose aid
The world's foundations first were laid,
Come visit every pious mind,
Come pour thy joys on human-kind;
From sin and sorrow set us free,
And make thy temples worthy thee.

O source of uncreated light,
The Father's promised Paraclete!
Thrice holy fount, thrice holy fire,
Our hearts with heavenly love inspire;
Come, and thy sacred unction bring,
To sanctify us while we sing.

Plenteous of grace, descend from high,
Rich in thy seven-fold energy!
Thou strength of His Almighty hand,
Whose power does heaven and earth command!
Proceeding Spirit, our defense,
Who dost the gifts of tongues dispense,
And crown'st thy gift with eloquence!

Refine and purge our earthly parts;
But, O, inflame and fire our hearts!
Our frailties help, our vice control,
Submit the senses to the soul;
And when rebellious they are grown,
Then lay thy hand and hold them down.

Chase from our minds the infernal foe,
And peace, the fruit of love, bestow;
And, lest our feet should step astray,
Protect and guide us in the way.

Make us eternal truths receive,
And practise all that we believe;
Give us thyself, that we may see
The Father, and the Son, by thee.

Immortal honour, endless fame,
Attend the Almighty Father's name;
The Saviour Son be glorified,
Who for lost man's redemption died;
And equal adoration be,
Eternal Paraclete, to thee.

THE
EIGHTEENTH,
NINETEENTH,
AND
TWENTIETH
CENTURIES

Universal Prayer

ALEXANDER POPE
(1 6 8 8 - 1 7 4 4)

Father of all! in every age,
    In every clime adored,
By saint, by savage, and by sage,
    Jehovah, Jove, or Lord!

Thou Great First Cause, least understood,
    Who all my sense confined
To know but this, that Thou art good,
    And that myself am blind!

Yet gave me, in this dark estate,
    To see the good from ill;
And, binding nature fast in fate,
    Left free the human will.

What conscience dictates to be done,
    Or warns me not to do,
This teach me more than hell to shun,
    That, more than heav'n pursue.

What blessings Thy free bounty gives,
    Let me not cast away;
For God is paid when man receives,
    To enjoy is to obey.

Yet not to earth's contracted span
    Thy goodness let me bound,
Or think Thee Lord alone of man,
    When thousand worlds are round.

Let not this weak, unknowing hand
    Presume Thy bolts to throw,
And deal damnation round the land
    On each I judge Thy foe.

If I am right, Thy grace impart
Still in the right to stay;
If I am wrong, oh, teach my heart
To find the better way!

Save me alike from foolish pride,
And impious discontent,
At aught Thy wisdom has denied,
Or aught Thy goodness lent.

Teach me to feel another's woe,
To hide the fault I see;
That mercy I to others show,
That mercy show to me.

Mean though I am, not wholly so,
Since quickened by Thy breath;
O lead me wheresoe'er I go,
Through this day's life or death.

This day be bread and peace my lot:
All else beneath the sun,
Thou knowest if best bestowed or not,
And let Thy will be done.

To Thee, whose temple is all space,—
Whose altar, earth, sea, skies,—
One chorus let all beings raise!
All nature's incense rise!

Eloisa's Prayer for Abelard

ALEXANDER POPE

May one kind grave unite each hapless name,
And graft my love immortal on thy fame!
Then, ages hence, when all my woes are o'er,
When this rebellious heart shall beat no more:

If ever chance two wand'ring lovers brings
To Paraclete's white walls and silver springs,
O'er the pale marble shall they join their heads,
And drink the falling tears each other sheds;
Then sadly say, with mutual pity moved,
'O may we never love as these have loved!'
From the full choir, when loud hosannas rise,
And swell the pomp of dreadful sacrifice,
Amid that scene if some relenting eye
Glance on the stone where our cold relics lie,
Devotion's self shall steal a thought from Heaven,
One human tear shall drop, and be forgiven.
And sure if fate some future bard shall join
In sad similitude of griefs to mine,
Condemned whole years in absence to deplore
And image charms he must behold no more,—
Such if there be, who loves so long, so well,
Let him our sad, our tender story tell;
The well-sung woes will soothe my pensive ghost;
He best can paint them who shall feel them most.

A Paraphrase on Thomas à Kempis

ALEXANDER POPE
[Done by the author at twelve years old]

Speak, gracious Lord, oh speak; Thy servant hears:
　　For I'm Thy servant and I'll still be so:
Speak words of comfort in my willing ears;
　　And since my tongue is in Thy praises slow,
And since that Thine all rhetoric exceeds,
Speak Thou in words, but let me speak in deeds!

Nor speak alone, but give me grace to hear
　　What Thy celestial sweetness does impart;

Let it not stop when entered at the ear,
 But sink, and take deep rooting in my heart.
As the parched earth drinks rain (but grace afford)
With such a gust will I receive Thy word.

Nor with the Israelites shall I desire
 Thy heavenly word by Moses to receive,
Lest I should die; but Thou who didst inspire
 Moses himself, speak Thou, that I may live.
Rather with Samuel I beseech with tears,
Speak, gracious Lord, oh speak; Thy servant hears.

Lines from an Essay on Man

ALEXANDER POPE

Know then thyself, presume not God to scan;
The proper study of mankind is man.
Placed on this isthmus of a middle state,
A being darkly wise, and rudely great;
With too much knowledge for the sceptic side,
With too much weakness for the stoic's pride,
He hangs between; in doubt to act, or rest;
In doubt to deem himself a God, or beast;
In doubt his mind or body to prefer;
Born but to die, and reasoning but to err;
Alike in ignorance, his reason such,
Whether he thinks too little, or too much;
Chaos of thought and passion, all confused;
Still by himself abused, or disabused;
Created half to rise, and half to fall;
Great lord of all things, yet a prey to all;
Sole judge of truth, in endless error hurled:
The glory, jest, and riddle of the world!

Ode on Solitude

ALEXANDER POPE

Happy the man whose wish and care
A few paternal acres bound,
Content to breathe his native air
   In his own ground.

Whose herds with milk, whose fields with bread,
Whose flocks supply him with attire;
Whose trees in summer yield him shade,
   In winter fire.

Blest, who can unconcernedly find
Hours, days, and years glide soft away
In health of body, peace of mind;
   Quiet by day,

Sound sleep by night; study and ease
Together mixed, sweet recreation,
And innocence, which most doth please,
   With meditation.

Thus let me live, unseen, unknown;
Thus unlamented let me die;
Steal from the world, and not a stone
   Tell where I lie.

The Dying Christian to His Soul

ALEXANDER POPE

Vital spark of heavenly flame!
Quit, O quit this mortal frame!
Trembling, hoping, lingering, flying,
O the pain, the bliss of dying!

Cease, fond Nature, cease thy strife,
And let me languish into life!

Hark! they whisper; angels say,
'Sister spirit, come away!'
What is this absorbs me quite?
Steals my senses, shuts my sight,
Drowns my spirits, draws my breath?
Tell me, my soul, can this be death?

The world recedes; it disappears!
Heaven opens my eyes, my ears
With sounds seraphic ring.
Lend, lend your wings! I mount! I fly!
O Grave! where is thy victory?
O Death! where is thy sting?

Rise, Crowned with Light

[From *The Messiah*]

ALEXANDER POPE

Rise, crowned with light, imperial Salem, rise!
Exalt thy towering head and lift thine eyes.
See heaven its sparkling portals wide display,
And break upon thee in a flood of day.

See a long race thy spacious courts adorn,
See future sons, and daughters yet unborn,
In crowding ranks on every side arise,
Demanding life, impatient for the skies.

See barbarous nations at thy gates attend,
Walk in thy light, and in thy temple bend:
See thy bright altars thronged with prostrate kings,
While every land its joyous tribute brings.

The seas shall waste, the skies to smoke decay,
Rocks fall to dust, and mountains melt away;
But fixed His word, His saving power remains;
Thy realm shall last, thy own Messiah reigns.

A Canadian Boat Song

[Written on the River St. Lawrence]

THOMAS MOORE
(1 7 7 9 – 1 8 5 2)

Faintly as tolls the evening chime
Our voices keep tune and our oars keep time.
Soon as the woods on shore look dim,
We'll sing at St. Anne's our parting hymn.
Row, brothers, row, the stream runs fast,
The Rapids are near and the daylight's past.

Why should we yet our sail unfurl?
There is not a breath the blue wave to curl;
But, when the wind blows off the shore,
Oh! sweetly we'll rest our weary oar.
Blow, breezes, blow, the stream runs fast,
The Rapids are near and the daylight's past.

Utawa's tide! this trembling moon
Shall see us float over thy surges soon.
Saint of this green isle! hear our prayers,
Oh, grant us cool heavens and favoring airs.
Blow, breezes, blow, the stream runs fast,
The Rapids are near and the daylight's past.

At the Mid Hour of Night

THOMAS MOORE

At the mid hour of night, when stars are weeping, I fly
To the lone vale we loved, when life shone warm in thine eye;
    And I think oft, if spirits can steal from the regions of air,
    To revisit past scenes of delight, thou wilt come to me there,
And tell me our love is remember'd, even in the sky.

Then I sing the wild song it once was rapture to hear!
When our voices commingling breath'd like one on the ear;
    And, as Echo far off through the vale my sad orison rolls,
    I think, O my love! 'tis thy voice from the Kingdom of Souls,
Faintly answering still the notes that once were so dear.

I Wish I Was by That Dim Lake

THOMAS MOORE

I wish I was by that dim Lake
Where sinful souls their farewell take
Of this vain world, and half-way lie
In death's cold shadow, ere they die.
There, there, far from thee,
Deceitful world, my home should be;
Where, come what might of gloom and pain,
False hope should ne'er deceive again.

The lifeless sky, the mournful sound
Of unseen waters falling round;
The dry leaves, quiv'ring o'er my head,
Like man, unquiet ev'n when dead!
These, ay, these shall wean
My soul from life's deluding scene,
And turn each thought, o'ercharg'd with gloom,
Like willows, downward towards the tomb.

As they, who to their couch at night
Would win repose, first quench the light,
So must the hopes, that keep this breast
Awake, be quenched, ere it can rest.
Cold, cold, this heart must grow,
Unmoved by either joy or woe,
Like freezing founts, where all that's thrown
Within their current turns to stone.

Sound the Loud Timbrel

THOMAS MOORE

"And Miriam the prophetess, the sister of Aaron, took a timbrel in her hand; and all the women went out after her with
timbrels and with dances."—*Exod. xv, 20.*

"And it came to pass, that in the morning watch the Lord
looked unto the host of the Egyptians through the pillar of
fire and of cloud, and troubled the host of the Egyptians."
—*Exod. xiv, 24.*

Sound the loud Timbrel o'er Egypt's dark sea!
Jehovah has triumphed—his people are free.
Sing—for the pride of the Tyrant is broken,
 His chariots, his horsemen, all splendid and brave—
How vain was their boast, for the Lord hath but spoken,
 And chariots and horsemen are sunk in the wave.
Sound the loud Timbrel o'er Egypt's dark sea;
Jehovah has triumphed—his people are free!

Praise to the Conqueror, praise to the Lord!
His word was our arrow, his breath was our sword.—
Who shall return to tell Egypt the story
 Of those she sent forth in the hour of her pride?
For the Lord hath looked out from his pillar of glory,
 And all her brave thousands are dashed in the tide.
Sound the loud Timbrel o'er Egypt's dark sea;
Jehovah has triumphed—his people are free!

127

The Stricken Deer

THOMAS MOORE

Come, rest in this bosom, my own stricken deer,
Though the herd have fled from thee, thy home is still here;
Here still is the smile, that no cloud can o'ercast,
And a heart and a hand all thine own to the last.

O, what was love made for, if 'tis not the same
Through joy and through torment, through glory and shame?
I know not, I ask not, if guilt's in that heart,
I but know that I love thee, whatever thou art.

Thou hast called me thy Angel in moments of bliss,
And thy Angel I'll be, 'mid the horrors of this,—
Through the furnace, unshrinking, thy steps to pursue,
And shield thee, and save thee—or perish there too!

The Minstrel Boy

THOMAS MOORE

The Minstrel Boy to the war is gone,
    In the ranks of death you'll find him;
His father's sword he has girded on,
    And his wild harp slung behind him.—
'Land of song!' said the warrior-bard,
    'Though all the world betrays thee,
One sword at least thy rights shall guard,
    One faithful harp shall praise thee!'

The Minstrel fell!—but the foeman's chain
    Could not bring his proud soul under;
The harp he loved ne'er spoke again,
    For he tore its chords asunder;

And said, 'No chains shall sully thee,
    Thou soul of love and bravery!
Thy songs were made for the pure and free,
    They shall never sound in slavery.'

Child's Song

[From a Masque]

THOMAS MOORE

I have a garden of my own,
    Shining with flowers of every hue;
I loved it dearly while alone,
    But I shall love it more with you;
And there the golden bees will come,
    In summer-time at break of morn,
And wake us with their busy hum
    Around the Siha's fragrant thorn.

I have a fawn from Aden's land,
    On leafy buds and berries nurst;
And you shall feed him from your hand,
    Though he may start with fear at first.
And I will lead you where he lies
    For shelter in the noontide heat;
And you may touch his sleeping eyes,
    And feel his little silvery feet.

Echo

THOMAS MOORE

How sweet the answer Echo makes
    To music at night,
When roused by lute or horn, she wakes,
And far away, o'er lawns and lakes,
    Goes answering light.

Yet Love hath echoes truer far,
    And far more sweet,
Than e'er beneath the moonlight's star,
Of horn, or lute, or soft guitar,
    The songs repeat.

'Tis when the sigh, in youth sincere,
    And only then,—
The sigh that's breathed for one to hear,
Is by that one, that only dear,
    Breathed back again!

The Two Streams

THOMAS MOORE

I saw, from yonder silent cave,
    Two Fountains running, side by side,
The one was Memory's limpid wave,
    The other cold Oblivion's tide.
'O Love!' said I, in thoughtless mood,
    As deep I drank of Lethe's stream,
'Be all my sorrows in this flood
    Forgotten like a vanished dream!'

But who could bear that gloomy blank,
    Where joy was lost as well as pain?
Quickly of Memory's fount I drank,
    And brought the past all back again;
And said, 'O Love, whate'er my lot,
    Still let this soul to thee be true—
Rather than have one bliss forgot,
    Be all my pains remembered too!'

Oft in the Stilly Night

THOMAS MOORE

Oft, in the stilly night,
    Ere slumber's chain has bound me,
Fond Memory brings the light
    Of other days around me;
        The smiles, the tears
        Of boyhood's years,
    The words of love then spoken;
        The eyes that shone,
        Now dimmed and gone,
    The cheerful hearts now broken!
Thus, in the stilly night,
    Ere slumber's chain has bound me,
Sad Memory brings the light
    Of other days around me.

When I remember all
    The friends so linked together,
I've seen around me fall,
    Like leaves in wintry weather,
        I feel like one
        Who treads alone
    Some banquet-hall deserted,
        Whose lights are fled,
        Whose garlands dead,
    And all but he departed!
Thus, in the stilly night,
    Ere slumber's chain has bound me,
Sad Memory brings the light
    Of other days around me.

Soggarth Aroon

JOHN BANIM
(1 7 9 8 – 1 8 4 2)

Am I the slave they say,
    Soggarth aroon,[1]
Since you did show the way,
    Soggarth aroon,
Their slave no more to be,
While they would work with me
Old Ireland's slavery,
    Soggarth aroon!

* * * * *

Who, in the winter's night,
    Soggarth aroon,
When the cold blast did bite,
    Soggarth aroon,
Came to my cabin door,
And, on the earthen floor,
Knelt by me, sick and poor,
    Soggarth aroon?

Who, on the marriage day,
    Soggarth aroon,
Made the poor cabin gay,
    Soggarth aroon?
And did both laugh and sing,
Making our hearts to ring,
At the poor christening,
    Soggarth aroon?

Who, as friend only met,
    Soggarth aroon,
Never did flout me yet,
    Soggarth aroon?

[1] *Soggarth*—priest (cf. *sacerdos*)

And when my heart was dim
Gave, while his eye did brim—
What should I give to him,
   Soggarth aroon?

Och, you and only you,
   Soggarth aroon!
And for this I was true to you,
   Soggarth aroon;
In love they'll never shake,
When for Old Ireland's sake
We a true part did take,
   Soggarth aroon!

Gone in the Wind

JAMES CLARENCE MANGAN
(1 8 0 3 - 1 8 4 9)

Solomon! where is thy throne? It is gone in the wind.
Babylon! where is thy might? It is gone in the wind.
Like the swift shadows of Noon, like the dreams of the Blind,
Vanish the glories and pomps of the earth in the wind.

Man! canst thou build upon aught in the pride of thy mind?
Wisdom will teach thee that nothing can tarry behind;
Though there be thousand bright actions embalmed and enshrined,
Myriads and millions of brighter are snow in the wind.

Solomon! where is thy throne? It is gone in the wind.
Babylon! where is thy might? It is gone in the wind.
All that the genius of Man hath achieved and designed
Waits for its hour to be dealt with as dust by the wind.

Pity thou, reader! the madness of poor Humankind,
Raving of Knowledge,—and Satan so busy to blind!
Raving of Glory,—like me,—for the garlands I bind
(Garlands of song) are but gathered, and—strewn in the wind!

The Nameless One

JAMES CLARENCE MANGAN

Roll forth, my song, like the rushing river
    That sweeps along to the mighty sea;
God will inspire me while I deliver
    My soul to thee!

Tell thou the world, when my bones lie whitening
    Amid the last homes of youth and eld,
That there once was one whose veins ran lightning
    No eye beheld.

Tell how his boyhood was one drear night-hour,
    How shone for him, through his griefs and gloom,
No star of all heaven sends to light our
    Path to the tomb.

Roll on, my song, and to after-ages
    Tell how, disdaining all earth can give,
He would have taught men from wisdom's pages
    The way to live.

And tell how trampled, derided, hated,
    And worn by weakness, disease and wrong,
He fled for shelter to God, who mated
    His soul with song.

With song which alway, sublime or vapid,
    Flowed like a rill in the morning beam,
Perchance not deep, but intense and rapid—
    A mountain stream.

Tell how this Nameless, condemned for years long
    To herd with demons from hell beneath,
Saw things that made him, with groans and tears, long
        For even death.

Go on to tell how, with genius wasted,
    Betrayed in friendship, befooled in love,
With spirit shipwrecked, and young hopes blasted,
        He still, still strove;

Till, spent with toil, dreeing death for others,
    (And some whose hands should have wrought for him,
If children live not for sires and mothers),
        His mind grew dim.

And he fell far through that pit abysmal,
    The gulf and grave of Maginn and Burns,
And pawned his soul for the devil's dismal
        Stock of returns.

But yet redeemed it in days of darkness,
    Mid shapes and signs of the final wrath,
When death, in hideous and ghastly starkness,
        Stood on his path.

And tell how now, amid wreck and sorrow,
    And want, and sickness, and houseless nights,
He bides in calmness the silent morrow
        That no ray lights.

And lives he still, then? Yes! Old and hoary
    At thirty-nine, from despair and woe,
He lives, enduring what future story
        Will never know.

Him grant a grave to, ye pitying noble,
    Deep in your bosoms! There let him dwell!
He, too, had tears for all souls in trouble,
        Here and in hell.

The Dawning of the Day

JAMES CLARENCE MANGAN

'Twas a balmy summer morning,
         Warm and early,
      Such as only June bestows;
Everywhere the earth adorning,
         Dews lay pearly
      In the lily-bell and rose.
Up from each green-leafy bosk and hollow
   Rose the blackbird's pleasant lay;
And the soft cuckoo was sure to follow:
   'Twas the dawning of the day!

Through the perfumed air the golden
         Bees flew round me;
      Bright fish dazzled from the sea,
Till medreamt some fairy olden-
         World spell bound me
      In a trance of witcherie.
Steeds pranced round anon with stateliest housings,
   Bearing riders prankt in rich array,
Like flushed revelers after wine-carousings:
   'Twas the dawning of the day!

Then a strain of song was chanted,
         And the lightly
      Floating sea-nymphs drew anear.
Then again the shore seemed haunted
         By hosts brightly
      Clad, and wielding sword and spear!
Then came battle shouts—an onward rushing—
   Swords, and chariots, and a phantom fray.
Then all vanished: the bright skies were blushing
   In the dawning of the day!

Cities girt with glorious gardens,
　　　Whose immortal
　　Habitants in robes of light
Stood, methought, as angel-wardens
　　　Nigh each portal,
　　Now arose to daze my sight.
Eden spread around, revived and blooming;
　　When—lo! as I gazed, all passed away:
I saw but black rocks and billows looming
　　In the dim chill dawn of day!

St. Patrick's Hymn Before Tarah

JAMES CLARENCE MANGAN

At Tarah to-day, in this awful hour,
　　I call on the Holy Trinity:
Glory to Him who reigneth in power,
The God of the elements, Father and Son
And Paraclete Spirit, which Three are the One,
　　The ever-existing Divinity!

At Tarah to-day I call on the Lord,
　　On Christ, the omnipotent Word,
Who came to redeem us from death and sin
　　　Our fallen race:
　　　And I put and I place
The virtue that lieth and liveth in
　　His incarnation lowly,
　　His baptism pure and holy,
His life of toil and tears and affliction,
His dolorous death—His crucifixion,
His burial, sacred and sad and lone,
　　His resurrection to life again,
His glorious ascension to Heaven's high throne,

And lastly, His future dread
    And terrible coming to judge all men—
Both the living and dead . . .

At Tarah to-day I put and I place
    The virtue that dwells in the seraphim's love,
And the virtue and grace
        That are in the obedience
        And unshaken allegiance
    Of all the archangels and angels above,
And in the hope of the resurrection
To everlasting reward and election.
And in the prayers of the fathers of old,
And in the truths the prophets foretold,
And in the Apostles' manifold preachings,
And in the confessors' faith and teachings;
And in the purity ever dwelling
    Within the immaculate Virgin's breast,
And in the actions bright and excelling
    Of all good men, the just and the blest.

At Tarah to-day, in this fateful hour,
I place all heaven within its power,
And the sun with its brightness,
And the snow with its whiteness,
And fire with all the strength it hath,
And lightning with its rapid wrath,
And the winds with their swiftness along their path,
And the sea with its deepness,
And the rocks with their steepness,
And the earth with its darkness,—
        All these I place,
    By God's almighty help and grace,
Between myself and the powers of darkness.

      At Tarah to-day
      May God be my stay!

May the strength of God now nerve me!
May the power of God preserve me!
May God the Almighty be near me!
May God the Almighty espy me!
May God the Almighty hear me!
May God give me eloquent speech!
May the arm of God protect me!
May the wisdom of God direct me!
May God give me power to teach and to preach!

May the shield of God defend me!
May the host of God attend me,
  And ward me,
  And guard me
Against the wiles of demons and devils,
Against the temptations of vices and evils,
Against the bad passions and wrathful will
 Of the reckless mind and the wicked heart,—
Against every man who designs me ill,
 Whether leagued with others or plotting apart!

 In this hour of hours,
 I place all those powers
 Between myself and every foe
 Who threaten my body and soul
  With danger or dole,
To protect me against the evils that flow
From lying soothsayers' incantations,
From the gloomy laws of the Gentile nations,
From heresy's hateful innovations,
From idolatry's rites and invocations.
 Be these my defenders,
 My guards against every ban—
And spell of smiths, and Druids, and women;
In fine, against every knowledge that renders
The light Heaven sends us dim in
 The spirit and soul of man!

May Christ, I pray,
Protect me to-day
Against poison and fire,
Against drowning and wounding;
That so, in His grace abounding,
I may earn the preacher's hire!

Christ as a light
Illumine and guide me!
Christ as a shield o'ershadow and cover me!
Christ be under me!—Christ be over me!
Christ be beside me,
On the left hand and right!
Christ be before me, behind me, about me;
Christ this day be within and without me!

Christ, the lowly and meek,
Christ the All-Powerful be
In the heart of each to whom I speak,
In the mouth of each who speaks to me!
In all who draw near me,
To see me or hear me!

At Tarah to-day, in this awful hour,
I call on the Holy Trinity!
Glory to Him who reigneth in power,
The God of the elements, Father and Son
And Paraclete Spirit, which Three are the One,
The ever-existing Divinity!

Salvation dwells with the Lord,
With Christ, the omnipotent Word.
From generation to generation
Grant us, O Lord, thy grace and salvation!

King Cahal Mór of the Wine-red Hand

JAMES CLARENCE MANGAN

I walked entranced
Through a land of Morn:
The sun, with wondrous excess of light,
Shone down and glanced
Over seas of corn
And lustrous gardens aleft and right.
Even in the clime
Of resplendent Spain,
Beams no such sun upon such a land;
But it was the time,
'Twas in the reign
Of Cahal Mór of the Wine-red Hand.

Anon stood nigh
By my side a man
Of princely aspect and port sublime.
Him queried I—
'Oh, my Lord and Khan,
What clime is this, and what golden time?'
Then he—'The clime
Is a clime to praise,
The clime is Erin's, the green and bland;
And it is the time,
These be the days
Of Cahal Mór of the Wine-red Hand.'

Then saw I thrones
And circling fires,
And a Dome rose near me, as by a spell,
Whence flowed the tones
Of silver lyres,
And many voices in wreathèd swell;

And their thrilling chime
Fell on mine ears
As the heavenly hymn of an angel-band—
'It is now the time,
These be the years
Of Cahal Mór of the Wine-red Hand.'

I sought the hall,
And behold!—a change
From light to darkness, from joy to woe!
Kings, nobles, all,
Looked aghast and strange;
The minstrel group sat in dumbest show!
Had some great crime
Wrought this dread amaze,
This terror? None seemed to understand
'Twas then the time,
We were in the days
Of Cahal Mór of the Wine-red Hand.

I again walked forth;
But lo! the sky
Showed flecked with blood, and an alien sun
Glared from the north,
And there stood on high,
Amid his shorn beams, a skeleton!
And it was by the stream
Of the castled Maine,
One Autumn eve, in the Teuton's land,
That I dreamed this dream
Of the time and reign
Of Cahal Mór of the Wine-red Hand.

Eileen Aroon

GERALD GRIFFIN
(1 8 0 3 – 1 8 4 0)

When like the early rose,
   Eileen Aroon!
Beauty in childhood blows,
   Eileen Aroon!
When, like a diadem,
Buds blush around the stem,
Which is the fairest gem?—
   Eileen Aroon!

Is it the laughing eye,
   Eileen Aroon!
Is it the timid sigh,
   Eileen Aroon!
Is it the tender tone,
Soft as the string'd harp's moan?
Oh, it is truth alone,—
   Eileen Aroon!

When like the rising day,
   Eileen Aroon!
Love sends his early ray,
   Eileen Aroon!
What makes his dawning glow,
Changeless through joy or woe?
Only the constant know:—
   Eileen Aroon!

I knew a valley fair,
   Eileen Aroon!
I knew a cottage there,
   Eileen Aroon!

143

Far in that valley's shade
I knew a gentle maid,
Flower of a hazel glade,—
     Eileen Aroon!

Who in the song so sweet?
     Eileen Aroon!
Who in the dance so fleet?
     Eileen Aroon!
Dear were her charms to me,
Dearer her laughter free,
Dearest her constancy,—
     Eileen Aroon!

Were she no longer true,
     Eileen Aroon!
What should her lover do?
     Eileen Aroon!
Fly with his broken chain
Far o'er the sounding main,
Never to love again,—
     Eileen Aroon!

Youth must with time decay,
     Eileen Aroon!
Beauty must fade away,
     Eileen Aroon!
Castles are sack'd in war,
Chieftains are scatter'd far,
Truth is a fixèd star,—
     Eileen Aroon!

I Love My Love in the Morning

GERALD GRIFFIN

I love my Love in the morning,
 For she like morn is fair—
Her blushing cheek its crimson streak,
 Its clouds her golden hair,
Her glance its beam so soft and kind,
 Her tears, its dewy showers,
And her voice the tender whispering wind
 That stirs the early bowers.

I love my Love in the morning,
 I love my Love at noon;
For she is bright as the lord of light,
 Yet mild as Autumn's moon.
Her beauty is my bosom's sun,
 Her faith my fostering shade,
And I will love my darling one
 Till ever the sun shall fade.

I love my Love in the morning,
 I love my Love at even;
Her smile's soft play is like the ray
 That lights the western heaven.
I loved her when the sun was high,
 I loved her when he rose;
But best of all when evening's sigh
 Was murmuring at its close.

The Bells of Shandon

FRANCIS MAHONY (FATHER PROUT)
(1 8 0 4 - 1 8 6 6)

With deep affection,
And recollection,
I often think of
    The Shandon bells,
Whose sounds so wild would,
In the days of childhood,
Fling around my cradle
    Their magic spells—
On this I ponder
Where'er I wander,
And thus grow fonder,
    Sweet Cork, of thee;
With the bells of Shandon,
That sound so grand on
The pleasant waters
    Of the River Lee.

I have heard bells chiming
Full many a clime in,
Tolling sublime in
    Cathedral shrine;
While at a glib rate
Brass tongues would vibrate—
But all their music
    Spoke nought to thine;
For memory dwelling
On each proud swelling
Of the belfry knelling
    Its bold notes free,
Made the bells of Shandon
Sound far more grand on

The pleasant waters
    Of the River Lee.

I have heard bells tolling
Old Adrian's mole in,
Their thunder rolling
    From the Vatican,
And cymbals glorious,
Swinging uproarious
In the gorgeous turrets
    Of Notre Dame;
But thy sounds were sweeter
Than the dome of Peter
Flings o'er the Tiber,
    Pealing solemnly.
Oh, the bells of Shandon
Sound far more grand on
The pleasant waters
    Of the River Lee.

There's a bell in Moscow,
While on tower and kiosko
In Saint Sophia
    The Turkman gets,
And loud in air,
Calls men to prayer
From the tapering summits
    Of tall minarets.
Such empty phantom
I freely grant them,
But there's an anthem
    More dear to me—
'Tis the bells of Shandon,
That sound so grand on
The pleasant waters
    Of the River Lee.

The Song of the Western Men

ROBERT STEPHEN HAWKER
(1 8 0 3 - 1 8 7 5)

A good sword and a trusty hand!
    A merry heart and true!
King James's men shall understand
    What Cornish lads can do!

And have they fixed the where and when?
    And shall Trelawny die?
Here's twenty thousand Cornish men
    Will know the reason why!

Out spake their captain brave and bold,
    A merry wight was he:
'If London Tower were Michael's hold,
    We'd set Trelawny free!

'We'll cross the Tamar, land to land,
    The Severn is no stay,
With "one and all," and hand in hand;
    And who shall bid us nay?

'And when we come to London Wall,
    A pleasant sight to view,
Come forth! come forth! ye cowards all,
    Here's men as good as you.'

Trelawny he's in keep and hold,
    Trelawny he may die;
But here's twenty thousand Cornish bold
    Will know the reason why!

A Christ-Cross Rhyme

ROBERT STEPHEN HAWKER

Christ His Cross shall be my speed!
Teach me, Father John, to read,
That in Church on Holy day
I may chant the psalm and pray.

Let me learn, that I may know
What the shining windows show:
Where the lovely Lady stands,
With that bright Child in her hands.

Teach me letters, A, B, C,
Till that I shall able be
Signs to know and words to frame,
And to spell sweet Jesus' Name.

Then, dear Master, will I look
Day and night in that fair book
Where the tales of saints are told,
With their pictures, all in gold.

Teach me, Father John, to say
Vesper-verse and Matin-lay;
So when I to God shall plead,
Christ His Cross shall be my speed.

Aishah Shechinah

ROBERT STEPHEN HAWKER

A shape, like folded light, embodied air,
    Yet wreathed with flesh, and warm;
All that of Heaven is feminine and fair,
    Moulded in visible form.

She stood, the Lady Shechinah of Earth,
  A chancel for the sky;
Where woke, to breath and beauty, God's own birth,
  For men to see Him by.

Round her, too pure to mingle with the day,
  Light, that was Life, abode;
Folded within her fibres meekly lay
  The link of boundless God.

So linked, so blent, that when, with pulse fulfilled,
  Moved but that infant Hand,
Far, far away, His conscious Godhead thrilled,
  And stars might understand.

Lo! where they pause, with intergathering rest,
  The Threefold and the One!
And lo! He binds them to her orient breast,
  His Manhood girded on.

The Zone, where two glad worlds forever meet,
  Beneath that bosom ran:
Deep in that womb, the conquering Paraclete
  Smote Godhead on to man!

Sole scene among the stars, where, yearning, glide
  The Threefold and The One:
Her God upon her lap, the Virgin-Bride,
  Her awful Child: her Son.

'Are They Not All Ministering Spirits?'

ROBERT STEPHEN HAWKER

We see them not—we cannot hear
    The music of their wing—
Yet know we that they sojourn near,
    The Angels of the spring!

They glide along this lovely ground
    When the first violet blows;
Their graceful hands have just unbound
    The zone of yonder rose!

I gather it for thy dear breast,
    From stain and shadow free;
That which an Angel's touch hath blest
    Is meet, my love, for thee!

'I am the Resurrection and the Life,' saith the Lord!

ROBERT STEPHEN HAWKER

We stood beside an opening grave,
By fair Morwenna's walls of grey:
Our hearts were hushed—the God who gave
Had called a sister-soul away.
    Hark! what wild tones around us float:
    The chanting cuckoo's double note!

We uttered there the solemn sound—
'Man that is born from flesh of Eve,
The banished flower of Eden's ground,
Hath but a little time to live';—
    And still, amid each pausing word,
    The strange cry of that secret bird.

'Ashes to ashes—dust to dust'—
The last farewell we sadly said.
Our mighty hope—our certain trust—
The resurrection of the dead.
  Again, all air, it glides around,
  A voice!—the spirit of a sound.

A doctrine dwells in that deep tone;
A truth is borne on yonder wing;
Long years! long years! the note is known—
The blessèd messenger of spring!
  Thus saith that pilgrim of the skies:
  'Lo! all that dieth shall arise!'

Rejoice! though dull with wintry gloom
Love's sepulchre and sorrow's night,
The sun shall visit depth and tomb
A season of eternal light!
  Like the glad bosom of the rose,
  The mound shall burst—the grave inclose!

Yea! soothed by that unvarying song
What generations here have trod!
What winds have breathed that sound along,
Fit signal of the changeless God!
  Hark! yet again the echoes float,
  The chanting cuckoo's double note!

The Silent Tower of Bottreaux

ROBERT STEPHEN HAWKER

Tintadgel bells ring o'er the tide,
The boy leans on his vessel's side;
He hears that sound, and dreams of home
Soothe the wild orphan of the foam.
 'Come to thy God in time!'
 Thus saith their pealing chime:
 'Youth, manhood, old age past,
 Come to thy God at last.'

But why are Bottreaux' echoes still?
Her Tower stands proudly on the hill;
Yet the strange chough that home hath found,
The lamb lies sleeping on the ground.
 'Come to thy God in time!'
 Should be her answering chime:
 'Come to thy God at last!'
 Should echo on the blast.

The ship rode down with courses free,
The daughter of a distant sea:
Her sheet was loose, her anchor stored,
The merry Bottreaux bells on board.
 'Come to thy God in time!'
 Rung out Tintadgel chime:
 'Youth, manhood, old age past,
 Come to thy God at last!'

The pilot heard his native bells
Hang on the breeze in fitful swells;
'Thank God!' with reverent brow he cried,
'We'll make the shore with evening's tide.'
 'Come to thy God in time!'
 It was his marriage chime:
 'Youth, manhood, old age past,'
 His bell must ring at last.

'Thank God, thou whining knave! on land,
But thank, at sea, the steersman's hand'—
The captain's voice above the gale—
'Thank the good ship and ready sail.'
　　　'Come to thy God in time!'
　　　Sad grew the boding chime:
　　　'Come to thy God at last!'
　　　Boomed heavy on the blast.

Uprose the sea! as if it heard
The mighty Master's signal-word:
What thrills the captain's whitening lip?
The death-groans of his sinking ship.
　　　'Come to thy God in time!'
　　　Swung deep the funeral chime:
　　　'Grace, mercy, kindness past,
　　　Come to thy God at last!'

Long did the rescued pilot tell—
When grey hairs o'er his forehead fell,
While those around would hear and weep—
That fearful judgment of the deep.
　　　'Come to thy God in time!'
　　　He read his native chime:
　　　'Youth, manhood, old age past,'
　　　His bell rang out at last.

Still when the storm of Bottreaux' waves
Is wakening in his weedy caves:
Those bells, that sullen surges hide,
Peal their deep notes beneath the tide:
　　　'Come to thy God in time!'
　　　Thus saith the ocean chime:
　　　'Storm, billow, whirlwind past,
　　　Come to thy God at last!'

Morwennæ Statio

ROBERT STEPHEN HAWKER

My Saxon shrine! the only ground
    Wherein this weary heart hath rest:
What years the birds of God have found
    Along thy walls their sacred nest!
The storm—the blast—the tempest shock,
    Have beat upon these walls in vain;
She stands—a daughter of the rock—
    The changeless God's eternal fane.

Firm was their faith, the ancient bands,
    The wise of heart in wood and stone;
Who reared, with stern and trusting hands,
    These dark grey towers of days unknown:
They filled these aisles with many a thought,
    They bade each nook some truth reveal:
The pillared arch its legends brought,
    A doctrine came with roof and wall.

Huge, mighty, massive, hard, and strong,
    Were the choice stones they lifted then;
The vision of their hope was long,
    They knew their God, those faithful men.
They pitched no tent for change or death.
    No home to last man's shadowy day;
There! there! the everlasting breath
    Would breathe whole centuries away.

See now, along that pillared aisle,
    The graven arches, firm and fair;
They bend their shoulders to the toil,
    And lift the hollow roof in air.
A sign! beneath the ship we stand,
    The inverted vessel's arching side;

Forsaken—when the fisher-band
    Went forth to sweep a mightier tide.

Pace we the ground! our footsteps tread
    A cross—the builder's holiest form:
That awful couch, where once was shed
    The blood, with man's forgiveness warm.
And here, just where His mighty breast
    Throbbed the last agony away,
They bade the voice of worship rest,
    And white-robed Levites pause and pray.

Mark! the rich rose of Sharon's bowers
    Curves in the paten's mystic mould:
The lily, lady of the flowers,
    Her shape must yonder chalice hold.
Types of the Mother and the Son,
    The twain in this dim chancel stand;
The badge of Norman banners, one
    And one a crest of English land.

How all things glow with life and thought,
    Where'er our faithful fathers trod!
The very ground with speech is fraught,
    The air is eloquent of God.
In vain would doubt or mockery hide
    The buried echoes of the past;
A voice of strength, a voice of pride,
    Here dwells amid the storm and blast.

Still points the tower, and pleads the bell;
    The solemn arches breathe in stone;
Window and wall have lips to tell
    The mighty faith of days unknown.
Yea! flood, and breeze, and battle-shock
    Shall beat upon this church in vain:
She stands, a daughter of the rock,
    The changeless God's eternal fane.

Datur Hora Quieti

ROBERT STEPHEN HAWKER

To the MS. of this poem is the following note:—'Why do you wish the burial to be at five o'clock?' 'Because it was the time at which he used to leave work.'

'At eve should be the time,' they said,
To close their brother's narrow bed:
'Tis at that pleasant hour of day
The labourer treads his homeward way.

His work was o'er, his toil was done,
And therefore with the set of sun,
To wait the wages of the dead,
We laid our hireling in his bed.

The Pillar of the Cloud

JOHN HENRY NEWMAN
(1 8 0 1 – 1 8 9 0)

Lead, Kindly Light, amid the encircling gloom
        Lead Thou me on!
The night is dark, and I am far from home—
        Lead Thou me on!
Keep Thou my feet; I do not ask to see
The distant scene—one step enough for me.

I was not ever thus, nor pray'd that Thou
        Shouldst lead me on.
I loved to choose and see my path, but now
        Lead Thou me on!
I loved the garish day, and, spite of fears,
Pride ruled my will: remember not past years.

157

So long Thy power hath blest me, sure it still
    Will lead me on,
O'er moor and fen, o'er crag and torrent, till
    The night is gone;
And with the morn those angel faces smile
Which I have loved long since, and lost awhile.

Angel

JOHN HENRY NEWMAN

My work is done,
    My task is o'er,
        And so I come,
        Taking it home;
For the crown is won.
    Alleluia,
    For evermore.

My Father gave
    In charge to me
        This child of earth
        E'en from its birth,
To serve and save,
    Alleluia,
    And saved is he.

This child of clay
    To me was given,
        To rear and train
        By sorrow and pain
In the narrow way,
    Alleluia,
    From earth to heaven.

The Elements

[A Tragic Chorus]

JOHN HENRY NEWMAN

Man is permitted much
    To scan and learn
    In Nature's frame:
Till he well-nigh can tame
Brute mischiefs and can touch
Invisible things, and turn
All warring ills to purposes of good.
    Thus, as a god below,
    He can control,
And harmonize, what seems amiss to flow
    As severed from the whole
    And dimly understood.

But o'er the elements
    One Hand alone,
    One Hand has sway
What influence day by day
    In straiter belt prevents
    The impious Ocean, thrown
Alternate o'er the ever-sounding shore?
    Or who has eye to trace
    How the Plague came?
Forerun the doublings of the Tempest's race?
    Or the Air's weight and flame
    On a set scale explore?

    Thus God has willed
That man, when fully skilled
Still gropes in twilight dim;

Encompassed all his hours
By fearfullest powers
Inflexible to him.
That so he may discern
His feebleness.
And e'en for earth's success
To Him in wisdom turn,
Who holds for us the Keys of either home,
Earth and the world to come.

Snapdragon

[A Riddle for a Flower Book]

JOHN HENRY NEWMAN

I am rooted in the wall
Of buttressed tower or ancient hall;
Prisoned in an art-wrought bed,
Cased in mortar, cramped with lead;
Of a living stock alone
Brother of the lifeless stone.

Else unprized, I have my worth
On the spot that gives me birth;
Nature's vast and varied field
Braver flowers than me will yield,
Bold in form and rich in hue,
Children of a purer dew;
Smiling lips and winning eyes
Meet for earthly paradise.

Choice are such,—and yet thou knowest
Highest he whose lot is lowest.
They, proud hearts, a home reject
Framed by human architect;

Humble—I can bear to dwell
Near the pale recluse's cell,
And I spread my crimson bloom,
Mingled with the cloister's gloom.

Life's gay gifts and honours rare,
Flowers of favour! win and wear!
Rose of beauty, be the queen
In pleasure's ring and festive scene.
Ivy, climb and cluster, where
Lordly oaks vouchsafe a stair.
Vaunt, fair Lily, stately dame,
Pride of birth and pomp of name.
Miser Crocus, starved with cold,
Hide in earth thy timid gold.
Travelled Dahlia, freely boast
Knowledge brought from foreign coast.
Pleasure, wealth, birth, knowledge, power,
These have each an emblem flower;
So for me alone remains
Lowly thought and cheerful pains.

Be it mine to set restraint
On roving wish and selfish plaint;
And for man's drear haunts to leave
Dewy morn and balmy eve.
Be it mine the barren stone
To deck with green life not its own.
So to soften and to grace
Of human works the rugged face.
Mine, the Unseen to display
In the crowded public way,
Where life's busy arts combine
To shut out the Hand Divine.

Ah! no more a scentless flower,
By approving Heaven's high power,

Suddenly my leaves exhale
Fragrance of the Syrian gale.
Ah! 'tis timely comfort given
By the answering breath of Heaven!
May it be! then well might I
In College cloister live and die.

My Lady Nature and Her Daughters

JOHN HENRY NEWMAN

Ladies, well I deem, delight
In comely tire to move;
Soft, and delicate, and bright,
Are the robes they love.
Silks, where hues alternate play,
Shawls, and scarfs, and mantles gay,
Gold, and gems, and crispèd hair,
Fling their light o'er lady fair.
'Tis not waste, nor sinful pride,
—Name them not, nor fault beside,—
But her very cheerfulness
Prompts and weaves the curious dress
While her holy thoughts still roam
Mid birth-friends and scenes of home.
Pleased to please whose praise is dear,
Glitters she? she glitters there;—
And she has a pattern found her
In Nature's glowing world around her.

Nature loves, as lady bright,
In gayest guise to shine,
All forms of grace, all tints of light,
Fringe her robe divine.
Sun-lit heaven, and rainbow cloud,
Changeful main, and mountain proud,

Branching tree, and meadow green,
All are decked in broidered sheen.
Not a bird on bough-propped tower,
Insect slim, nor tiny flower,
Stone, nor spar, nor shell of sea,
But is fair in its degree.
'Tis not pride, this vaunt of beauty;
Well she 'quits her trust of duty;
And, amid her gorgeous state,
Bright, and bland, and delicate,
Ever beaming from her face
Praise of a Father's love we trace.

Ladies, shrinking from the view
        Of the prying day,
In tranquil diligence pursue
        Their heaven-appointed way.
Noiseless duties, silent cares,
Mercies lighting unawares,
Modest influence working good,
Gifts, by the keen heart understood,
Such as viewless spirits might give,
These they love, in these they live.—
Mighty Nature speeds her through
Her daily toils in silence too:
Calmly rolls her giant spheres,
Sheds by stealth her dew's kind tears;
Cheating sage's vexed pursuit,
Churns the sap, matures the fruit,
And, her deft hand still concealing,
Kindles motion, life, and feeling.

Ladies love to laugh and sing,
        To rouse the chord's full sound,
Or to join the festive ring
        Where dancers gather round.
Not a sight so fair on earth,

As a lady's graceful mirth;
Not a sound so chasing pain,
As a lady's thrilling strain.—
Nor is Nature left behind
In her lighter moods of mind;
Calm her duties to fulfil,
In her glee a prattler still.
Bird and beast of every sort
Hath its antic and its sport;
Chattering brook, and dancing gnat,
Subtle cry of evening bat,
Moss uncouth, and twigs grotesque,
These are Nature's picturesque.

Where the birth of Poesy?
      Its fancy and its fire?
Nature's earth, and sea, and sky,
      Fervid thoughts inspire.
Where do wealth and power find rest,
When hopes have failed, or toil oppressed?
Parks, and lawns, and deer, and trees,
Nature's work, restore them ease.—
Rare the rich, the gifted rare.—
Where shall work-day souls repair,
Unennobled, unrefined,
From the rude world and unkind?
Who shall friend their lowly lot?
High-born Nature answers not.
Leave her in her starry dome,
Seek we lady-lighted home.
Nature 'mid the spheres bears sway,
Ladies rule where hearts obey.

Monks

(*With lines on hinges to fit it*)

JOHN HENRY NEWMAN

Why, dear Cousin,
            why
Ask for verses,
when a poet's
fount of song is
            dry?
Or, if aught be
            there,
Harsh and chill, it
ill may touch the
hand of lady
            fair.
Who can perfumed waters
            bring
From a convent
            spring?

'Monks in the olden
            time,
'They were rhymesters?'—
they were rhymesters,
but in Latin
            rhyme.
Monks in the days of
            old
Lived in secret,
in the Church's
kindly-sheltering
            fold.
No bland meditators
            they

Of a courtly
            lay.

'They had visions
            bright?'—
They had visions,
yet not sent in
slumbers soft and
            light.
No! a lesson
            stern.
First by vigils,
fast, and penance
theirs it was to
            learn.
This their soul-ennobling
            gain,
Joys wrought out by
            pain.

'When from home they
            stirr'd,
Sweet their voices?'—
Still, a blessing
closed their merriest
            word;
And their gayest
            smile
Told of musings
solitary
and the hallowed
            aisle.
'Songsters?'—Hark! they answer!
            round
Plaintive chantings
            sound!

Grey his cowlèd
vest,
Whose strong heart has
pledged his service
to the cloister
blest.
Duly garbed is
he,
As the frost-work
gems the branches
of yon stately
tree.
'Tis a danger-thwarting
spell,
And it fits me
well!

Angelic Guidance

JOHN HENRY NEWMAN

Are these the tracks of some unearthly Friend,
His foot-prints, and his vesture-skirts of light,
Who, as I talk with men, conforms aright
Their sympathetic words, or deeds that blend
With my hid thought;—or stoops him to attend
My doubtful-pleading grief,—or blunts the might
Of ill I see not;—or in dreams of night
Figures the scope, in which what is will end?
Were I Christ's own, then fitly might I call
That vision real; for to the thoughtful mind
That walks with Him, He half unveils His face;
But, when on earth-stained souls such tokens fall,
These dare not claim as theirs what there they find,
Yet, not all hopeless, eye His boundless grace.

Substance and Shadow

JOHN HENRY NEWMAN

They do but grope in learning's pedant round,
    Who on the fantasies of sense bestow
    An idol substance, bidding us bow low
Before those shades of being which are found,
Stirring or still, on man's brief trial-ground;
    As if such shapes and moods, which come and go,
    Had aught of Truth or Life in their poor show,
To sway or judge, and skill to sane or wound.
Son of immortal seed, high-destined Man!
Know thy dread gift,—a creature, yet a cause:
Each mind is its own centre, and it draws
Home to itself, and moulds in its thought's span
All outward things, the vassals of its will,
Aided by Heaven, by earth unthwarted still.

England

JOHN HENRY NEWMAN

Tyre of the West, and glorying in the name
    More than in Faith's pure name!
O trust not crafty fort nor rock renowned
    Earned upon hostile ground;
Wielding Trade's master-keys, at thy proud will
To lock or loose its waters, England! trust not still.

Dread thine own powers! Since haughty Babel's prime,
    High towers have been man's crime.
Since her hoar age, when the huge moat lay bare,
    Strongholds have been man's snare.
Thy nest is in the crags; ah! refuge frail!
Mad counsel in its hour, or traitors will prevail.

He who scanned Sodom for His righteous men
  Still spares thee for thy ten;
But, should vain tongues the Bride of Heaven defy,
  He will not pass thee by;
For, as earth's kings welcome their spotless guest,
So gives He them by turn, to suffer or be blest.

The Patient Church

JOHN HENRY NEWMAN

  Bide thou thy time!
Watch with meek eyes the race of pride and crime,
Sit in the gate, and be the heathen's jest,
  Smiling and self-possest.
O thou, to whom is pledged a victor's sway,
  Bide thou the victor's day!

  Think on the sin
That reaped the unripe seed, and toiled to win
Foul history-marks at Bethel and at Dan;
  No blessing, but a ban;
Whilst the wise Shepherd hid his heaven-told fate,
  Nor recked a tyrant's hate.

  Such loss is gain;
Wait the bright Advent that shall loose thy chain!
E'en now the shadows break, and gleams divine
  Edge the dim distant line.
When thrones are trembling, and earth's fat ones quail,
  True Seed! thou shalt prevail!

The Sign of the Cross

JOHN HENRY NEWMAN

Whene'er across this sinful flesh of mine,
  I draw the Holy sign,
All good thoughts stir within me, and renew
  Their slumbering strength divine;
Till there springs up a courage high and true
  To suffer and to do.

And who shall say, but hateful spirits around,
  For their brief hour unbound,
Shudder to see, and wail their overthrow?
  While on far heathen ground
Some lonely Saint hails the fresh odour, though
  Its source he cannot know.

Progress of Unbelief

JOHN HENRY NEWMAN

Now is the Autumn of the Tree of Life;
  Its leaves are shed upon the unthankful earth,
Which lets them whirl, a prey to the winds' strife,
  Heatless to store them for the months of dearth.
  Men close the door, and dress the cheerful hearth,
Self-trusting still; and in his comely gear
Of precept and of rite, a household Baal rear.

But I will out amid the sleet, and view
  Each shrivelling stalk and silent-falling leaf.
Truth after truth, of choicest scent and hue,
  Fades, and in fading stirs the Angels' grief,
  Unanswered here; for she, once pattern chief
Of faith, my Country, now gross-hearted grown,
Waits but to burn the stem before her idol's throne.

The Queen of Seasons

[A Song for an Inclement May]

JOHN HENRY NEWMAN

All is divine
      which the Highest has made,
Through the days that He wrought,
      till the day when He stayed;
Above and below,
      within and around,
From the centre of space,
      to its uttermost bound.

In beauty surpassing
      the Universe smiled,
On the morn of its birth,
      like an innocent child,
Or like the rich bloom
      of some delicate flower;
And the Father rejoiced
      in the work of His power.

Yet worlds brighter still,
      and a brighter than those,
And a brighter again,
      He had made, had He chose;
And you never could name
      that conceivable best,
To exhaust the resources
      the Maker possessed.

But I know of one work
      of His Infinite Hand,
Which special and singular
      ever must stand;

171

So perfect, so pure,
      and of gifts such a store,
That even Omnipotence
      ne'er shall do more.

The freshness of May,
      and the sweetness of June,
And the fire of July
      in its passionate noon,
Munificent August,
      September serene,
Are together no match
      for my glorious Queen.

O Mary, all months
      and all days are thine own,
In thee lasts their joyousness,
      when they are gone;
And we give to thee May,
      not because it is best,
But because it comes first,
      and is pledge of the rest.

Valentine to a Little Girl

JOHN HENRY NEWMAN

Little maiden, dost thou pine
For a faithful Valentine?
Art thou scanning timidly
Every face that meets thine eye?
Art thou fancying there may be
Fairer face than thou dost see?
Little maiden, scholar mine,
Wouldst thou have a Valentine?

Go and ask, my little child,
Ask the Mother undefiled:
Ask, for she will draw thee near,
And will whisper in thine ear:—
'Valentine! the name is good;
  For it comes of lineage high,
  And a famous family:
And it tells of gentle blood,
Noble blood,—and nobler still,
  For its owner freely poured
Every drop there was to spill
  In the quarrel of his Lord.
Valentine! I know the name,
Many martyrs bear the same;
And they stand in glittering ring
Round their warrior God and King,—
  Who before and for them bled,—
  With their robes of ruby red,
And their swords of cherub flame.'

Yes! there is a plenty there,
Knights without reproach or fear,—
Such St. Denys, such St. George,
  Martin, Maurice, Theodore,
  And a hundred thousand more;
  Guerdon gained and warfare o'er,
By that sea without a surge,
And beneath the eternal sky,
  And the beatific Sun,
   In Jerusalem above,
  Valentine is every one;
Choose from out that company
   Whom to serve, and whom to love.

St. Philip in Himself

[A Song]

JOHN HENRY NEWMAN

The holy Monks, concealed from men,
 In midnight choir, or studious cell,
In sultry field, or wintry glen,
 The holy Monks, I love them well.

The Friars too, the zealous band
 By Dominic or Francis led,
They gather, and they take their stand
 Where foes are fierce, or friends have fled.

And then the unwearied Company,
 Which bears the Name of Sacred might,
The Knights of Jesus, they defy
 The fiend,—full eager for the fight.

Yet there is one I more affect
 Than Jesuit, Hermit, Monk, or Friar,
'Tis an old man of sweet aspect,
 I love him more, I more admire.

I know him by his head of snow,
 His ready smile, his keen full eye,
His words which kindle as they flow,
 Save he be rapt in ecstasy.

He lifts his hands, there issues forth
 A fragrance virginal and rare,
And now he ventures to our North
 Where hearts are frozen as the air.

He comes, by grace of his address,
    By the sweet music of his face,
And his low tones of tenderness,
    To melt a noble, stubborn race.

O sainted Philip, Father dear,
    Look on thy little ones, that we
Thy loveliness may copy here,
    And in the eternal Kingdom see.

Guardian Angel

JOHN HENRY NEWMAN

My oldest friend, mine from the hour
    When first I drew my breath;
My faithful friend, that shall be mine,
    Unfailing, till my death;

Thou hast been ever at my side:
    My Maker to thy trust
Consigned my soul, what time He framed
    The infant child of dust.

No beating heart in holy prayer,
    No faith, informed aright,
Gave me to Joseph's tutelage,
    Or Michael's conquering might.

Nor patron Saint, nor Mary's love,
    The dearest and the best,
Has known my being, as thou hast known,
    And blest, as thou hast blest,

Thou wast my sponsor at the font;
    And thou, each budding year,
Didst whisper elements of truth
    Into my childish ear.

And when, ere boyhood yet was gone,
    My rebel spirit fell,
Ah! thou didst see, and shudder too,
    Yet bear each deed of Hell.

And then in turn, when judgements came,
    And scared me back again,
Thy quick soft breath was near to soothe
    And hallow every pain.

Oh! who of all thy toils and cares
    Can tell the tale complete,
To place me under Mary's smile,
    And Peter's royal feet!

And thou wilt hang about my bed,
    When life is ebbing low;
Of doubt, impatience, and of gloom,
    The jealous sleepless foe.

Mine, when I stand before the Judge;
    And mine, if spared to stay
Within the golden furnace, till
    My sin is burned away.

And mine, O Brother of my soul,
    When my release shall come;
Thy gentle arms shall lift me then,
    Thy wings shall waft me home.

Fifth Choir of Angelicals

[From *The Dream of Gerontius*]

JOHN HENRY NEWMAN

Praise to the Holiest in the height
And in the depth be praise:
In all His words most wonderful;
Most sure in all His ways.

O loving wisdom of our God!
When all was sin and shame,
A second Adam to the fight
And to the rescue came.

O wisest love! that flesh and blood
Which did in Adam fail,
Should strive afresh against the foe,
Shouldst strive and should prevail;

And that a higher gift than grace
Should flesh and blood refine,
God's Presence and His very Self,
And Essence all-divine.

O generous love! that He who smote
In man for man the foe,
The double agony in man
For man should undergo;

And in the garden secretly,
And on the cross on high,
Should teach His brethren and inspire
To suffer and to die.

The Celestial Country

J. M. NEALE
(1 8 1 8 – 1 8 6 6)

The style of this translation from the 12th-century poem by
Bernard of Cluny is so clearly of the 19th century that it seemed
better to place it here rather than in the period of the original.

The world is very evil,
    The times are waxing late;
Be sober and keep vigil,
    The Judge is at the gate—
The Judge that comes in mercy,
    The Judge that comes with might,
To terminate the evil,
    To diadem the right.
When the just and gentle Monarch
    Shall summon from the tomb,
Let men, the guilty, tremble,
    For Man, the God, shall doom!

*   *   *   *   *

For thee, O dear, dear Country!
    Mine eyes their vigils keep;
For very love, beholding
    Thy happy name, they weep.
The mention of thy glory
    Is unction to the breast,
And medicine in sickness,
    And love, and life, and rest.

O one, O only Mansion!
    O Paradise of Joy!
Where tears are ever banished,
    And smiles have no alloy,
Beside thy living waters
    All plants are, great and small,

The cedar of the forest,
    The hyssop of the wall;
With jaspers glow thy bulwarks,
    Thy streets with emeralds blaze,
The fardius and the topaz
    Unite in thee their rays;
Thine ageless walls are bonded
    With amethyst unpriced;
Thy Saints build up its fabric,
    And the corner-stone is **CHRIST**.

The Cross is all thy splendour,
    The Crucified thy praise;
His laud and benediction
    Thy ransomed people raise:
'*Jesus, the Gem of Beauty,*
    True GOD and Man,' they sing,
'*The never-failing Garden,*
    The ever-golden Ring;
The Door, the Pledge, the Husband,
    The Guardian of his Court;
The Day-star of Salvation,
    The Porter and the Port!'

Thou hast no shore, fair ocean!
    Thou hast no time, bright day!
Dear fountain of refreshment
    To pilgrims far away!
Upon the Rock of Ages
    They raise thy holy tower;
Thine is the victor's laurel,
    And thine the golden dower!

Thou feel'st in mystic rapture,
    O Bride that know'st no guile,
The Prince's sweetest kisses,
    The Prince's loveliest smile;

Unfading lilies, bracelets
    Of living pearl thine own;
The LAMB is ever near thee,
    The Bridegroom thine alone.
The Crown is He to guerdon,
    The Buckler to protect,
And He himself the Mansion,
    And He the Architect.

The only art thou needest—
    Thanksgiving for thy lot;
The only joy thou seekest—
    The Life where Death is not.
And all thine endless leisure,
    In sweetest accents, sings
The ill that was thy merit,
    The wealth that is thy King's!

Jerusalem the Golden,
    With milk and honey blest,
Beneath thy contemplation
    Sink heart and voice oppressed.
I know not, O I know not,
    What social joys are there!
What radiancy of glory,
    What light beyond compare!
And when I fain would sing them,
    My spirit fails and faints;
And vainly would it image
    The assembly of the Saints.

They stand, those halls of Syon,
    Conjubilant with song,
And bright with many an angel,
    And all the martyr throng:
The Prince is ever in them,
    The daylight is serene:

The pastures of the blessèd
    Are decked in glorious sheen.

There is the throne of David,
    And there, from care released,
The song of them that triumph,
    The shout of them that feast:
And they who, with their leader,
    Have conquered in the fight,
For ever and for ever
    Are clad in robes of white!

O holy, placid harp-notes
    Of that eternal hymn!
O sacred, sweet refection,
    And peace of Seraphim!
O thirst, for ever ardent,
    Yet evermore content!
O true peculiar vision
    Of God cunctipotent!

Ye know the many mansions
    For many a glorious name,
And divers retributions
    That divers merits claim;
For midst the constellations
    That deck our earthly sky,
This star than that is brighter—
    And so it is on high.

Jerusalem the glorious!
    The glory of the Elect!
O dear and future vision
    That eager hearts expect!
Even now by faith I see thee,
    Even here thy walls discern;

To thee my thoughts are kindled,
 And strive, and pant, and yearn.

Jerusalem the onely,
 That look'st from heaven below,
In thee is all my glory,
 In me is all my woe;
And though my body may not,
 My spirit seeks thee fain,
Till flesh and earth return me
 To earth and flesh again.

O none can tell thy bulwarks,
 How gloriously they rise!
O none can tell thy capitals
 Of beautiful device!
Thy loveliness oppresses
 All human thought and heart;
And none, O peace, O Syon,
 Can sing thee as thou art!

New mansion of new people,
 Whom God's own love and light
Promote, increase, make holy,
 Identify, unite!
Thou City of the Angels!
 Thou City of the Lord!
Whose everlasting music
 Is the glorious decachord!

And there the band of Prophets
 United praise ascribes,
And there the twelvefold chorus
 Of Israel's ransomed tribes,
The lily-beds of virgins,
 The roses' martyr-glow,

The cohort of the Fathers
    Who kept the Faith below.

And there the Sole-Begotten
    Is Lord in regal state—
He, Judah's mystic Lion,
    He, Lamb Immaculate.
O fields that know no sorrow!
    O state that fears no strife!
O princely bowers! O land of flowers!
    O realm and home of Life!

Exult, O dust and ashes!
    The LORD shall be thy part;
His only, His for ever,
    Thou shalt be, and thou art!
Exult, O dust and ashes!
    The LORD shall be thy part;
His only, His for ever,
    Thou shalt be, and thou art!

The Cherwell Waterlily

FREDERICK W. FABER
(1 8 1 4 - 1 8 6 3)

There is a well, a willow-shaded spot,
Cool in a noon-tide gleam,
With rushes nodding in the little stream,
And blue forget-me-not

Set in thick tufts along the bushy marge
With big bright eyes of gold;
And glorious water plants like fans unfold,
Their blossoms strange and large.

That wondering boy, young Hylas, did not find
Beauties so rich and rare,
Where swallow-wort and bright maiden's hair
And dog-grass richly twined.

A sloping bank ran round it like a crown,
Whereon a purple cloud
Of dark wild hyacinths, a fairy crowd
Had settled softly down.

And dreaming sounds of never-ending bells,
From Oxford's holy towers
Came down the stream, and went among the flowers,
And died in little swells.

My God, How Wonderful Thou Art

FREDERICK W. FABER

My God, how wonderful Thou art,
    Thy majesty how bright,
How beautiful Thy mercy-seat,
    In depths of burning light!

How dread are Thine eternal years,
    O everlasting Lord,
By prostrate spirits day and night
    Incessantly adored!

How wonderful, how beautiful,
    The sight of Thee must be,
Thine endless wisdom, boundless power,
    And awful purity!

O how I fear Thee, living God,
    With deepest, tenderest fears,

And worship Thee with trembling hope,
    And penitential tears!

Yet I may love Thee too, O Lord,
    Almighty as Thou art,
For Thou hast stooped to ask of me
    The love of my poor heart.

The Shadow of the Rock

FREDERICK W. FABER

The Shadow of the Rock!
    Stay, Pilgrim! stay!
Night treads upon the heels of day;
There is no other resting-place this way.
    The Rock is near.
    The well is clear.
Rest in the Shadow of the Rock.

The Shadow of the Rock!
    The desert wide
Lies round thee like a trackless tide,
In waves of sand forlornly multiplied.
    The sun is gone.
    Thou art alone.
Rest in the Shadow of the Rock.

The Shadow of the Rock!
    All come alone,
All, ever since the sun hath shone,
Who travelled by this road have come alone.
    Be of good cheer,
    A home is here.
Rest in the Shadow of the Rock.

The Shadow of the Rock!
Night veils the land:
How the palms whisper as they stand!
How the well tinkles faintly through the sand!
Cool water take
Thy thirst to slake,
Rest in the Shadow of the Rock.

The Shadow of the Rock!
Abide! Abide!
This Rock moves ever at thy side,
Pausing to welcome thee at eventide.
Ages are laid
Beneath its shade.
Rest in the Shadow of the Rock.

The Shadow of the Rock!
Always at hand,
Unseen it cools the noon-tide land,
And quells the fire that flickers in the sand.
It comes in sight
Only at night.
Rest in the Shadow of the Rock.

The Shadow of the Rock!
Mid skies storm-riven
It gathers shadows out of heaven,
And holds them o'er us all night cool and even.
Through the charmed air
Dew falls not there.
Rest in the Shadow of the Rock.

The Shadow of the Rock!
To angel's eyes
This Rock its shadow multiplies,
And at this hour in countless places lies.

One Rock, one Shade,
O'er thousands laid.
Rest in the Shadow of the Rock.

The Shadow of the Rock!
To weary feet,
That have been diligent and fleet,
The sleep is deeper and the shade more sweet.
O weary! rest,
Thou art sore pressed.
Rest in the Shadow of the Rock.

The Shadow of the Rock!
Thy bed is made;
Crowds of tired souls like thine are laid
This night beneath the self-same placid shade.
They who rest here
Wake with heaven near.
Rest in the Shadow of the Rock.

The Shadow of the Rock!
Pilgrim! sleep sound;
In night's swift hours with silent bound
The Rock will put thee over leagues of ground,
Gaining more way
By night than day.
Rest in the Shadow of the Rock.

The Shadow of the Rock!
One day of pain
Thou scarce wilt hope the Rock to gain,
Yet there wilt sleep thy last sleep on the plain;
And only wake
In heaven's day-break.
Rest in the Shadow of the Rock.

A Ballad of Sarsfield

AUBREY THOMAS DE VERE
(1 8 1 4 - 1 9 0 2)

Sarsfield went out the Dutch to rout,
    And to take and break their cannon;
To Mass went he at half-past three,
    And at four he crossed the Shannon.

Tirconnel slept. In dream his thoughts
    Old fields of victory ran on;
And the chieftains of Thomond in Limerick's towers
    Slept well by the banks of Shannon.

He rode ten miles and he crossed the ford,
    And couched in the wood and waited;
Till, left and right, on marched in sight
    That host which the true men hated.

'Charge!' Sarsfield cried; and the green hill-side
    As they charged replied in thunder;
They rode o'er the plain and they rode o'er the slain
    And the rebel rout lay under.

The spark flashed out—like a sailor's shout
    The sound into heaven ascended;
The hosts of the sky made to earth reply,
    And the thunders twain were blended!

Sarsfield went out the Dutch to rout,
    And to take and break their cannon;—
A century after, Sarsfield's laughter
    Was echoed from Dungannon.

Sorrow

AUBREY THOMAS DE VERE

Count each affliction, whether light or grave,
   God's messenger sent down to thee; do thou
   With courtesy receive him; rise and bow;
And, ere his shadow pass thy threshold, crave
Permission first his heavenly feet to lave;
   Then lay before him all thou hast; allow
   No cloud of passion to usurp thy brow,
Or mar thy hospitality; no wave
Of mortal tumult to obliterate
   Thy soul's marmoreal calmness. Grief should be
Like joy, majestic, equable, sedate;
   Confirming, cleansing, raising, making free;
Strong to consume small troubles; to commend
Great thoughts, grave thoughts, thoughts lasting to the end.

Evening Melody

AUBREY THOMAS DE VERE

O that the pines which crown yon steep
   Their fires might ne'er surrender!
O that yon fervid knoll might keep,
   While lasts the world, its splendor!

Pale poplars on the breeze that lean,
   And in the sunset shiver,
O that your golden stems might screen
   For aye yon glassy river!

That yon white bird on homeward wing
   Soft-sliding without motion,

And now in blue air vanishing
　　Like snow-flake lost in ocean,

Beyond our sight might never flee,
　　Yet forward still be flying;
And all the dying day might be
　　Immortal in its dying!

Pellucid thus in saintly trance,
　　Thus mute in expectation,
What waits the earth? Deliverance?
　　Ah no! Transfiguration!

She dreams of that 'New Earth' divine,
　　Conceived of seed immortal;
She sings 'Not mine the holier shrine,
　　Yet mine the steps and portal!'

Coleridge

AUBREY THOMAS DE VERE

His eyes saw all things in the symmetry
Of true and just proportion; and his ear
　　That inner tone could hear
Which flows beneath the outer: therefore he
Was as a mighty shell, fashioning all
The winds to one rich sound, ample and musical.

Yet dim that eye with gazing upon heaven;
Wearied with vigils, and the frequent birth
　　Of tears when turned to earth:
Therefore, though farthest ken to him was given,
　　Near things escaped him: through them—as a gem
Diaphanous—he saw; and therefore saw not them.

Moreover, men whom sovereign wisdom teaches
That God not less in humblest forms abides
    That those the great veil hides,
Such men a tremour of bright reverence reaches;
And thus, confronted ever with high things,
Like Cherubim they hide their eyes between their wings.

No loftier, purer soul than this hath ever
With awe revolved the planetary page,
    From infancy to age,
Of Knowledge; sedulous and proud to give her
The whole of his great heart for her own sake;
For what she is; not what she does, or what can make.

And mighty Voices from afar came to him:
Converse of trumpets held by cloudy forms,
    And speech of choral storms:
Spirits of night and noontide bent to woo him:
He stood the while, lonely and desolate
As Adam, when he ruled the world, yet found no mate.

His loftiest thoughts were but like palms uplifted,
Aspiring, yet in supplicating guise;
    His sweetest songs were sighs:
Adown Lethean streams his spirit drifted,
Under Elysian shades from poppied bank
With Amaranths massed in dark luxuriance dank.

Coleridge, farewell! that great and grave transition
Which may not Priest, or King, or Conqueror spare,
    And yet a Babe can bear,
Has come to thee. Through life a goodly vision
Was thine; and time it was thy rest to take.
Soft be the sound ordaining thy sleep to break—
When thou art walking, wake me, for my Master's sake!

Implicit Faith

AUBREY THOMAS DE VERE

Of all great Nature's tones that sweep
    Earth's resonant bosom, far or near,
Low-breathed or loudest, shrill or deep,
    How few are grasped by mortal ear.

Ten octaves close our scale of sound:
    Its myriad grades, distinct or twined,
Transcend our hearing's petty bound,
    To us as colours to the blind.

In Sound's unmeasured empire thus
    The heights, the depths alike we miss;
Ah, but in measured sound to us
    A compensating spell there is!

In holy music's golden speech
    Remotest notes to notes respond:
Each octave is a world; yet each
    Vibrates to worlds its own beyond.

Our narrow pale the vast resumes;
    Our seashell whispers of the sea:
Echoes are ours of angel-plumes
    That winnow far infinity!

—Clasp thou of Truth the central core!
    Hold fast that centre's central sense!
An atom there shall fill thee more
    Than realms on Truth's circumference.

That cradled Saviour, mute and small,
    Was God—is God while worlds endure!
Who holds Truth truly holds it all
    In essence, or in miniature.

Know what thou know'st! He knoweth much
    Who knows not many things: and he
Knows most whose knowledge hath a touch
    Of God's divine simplicity.

The Divine Presence

AUBREY THOMAS DE VERE

All but unutterable Name!
    Adorable, yet awful sound!
Thee can the sinful nations frame
    Save with their foreheads on the ground?

Soul-searching and all-cleansing Fire;
    To see Thy countenance were to die:
Yet how beyond the bound retire
    Of Thy serene immensity?

Thou mov'st beside us, if the spot
    We change—a noteless, wandering tribe;
The orbits of our life and thought
    In Thee their little arcs describe.

In their dead calm, at cool of day,
    We hear Thy voice, and turn, and flee:
Thy love outstrips us on our way!
    From Thee, O God, we fly—to Thee.

Spring Flowers from Ireland

[On receiving an early crocus and some violets
in a second letter from Ireland]

DENIS FLORENCE MCCARTHY

(1 8 1 7 - 1 8 8 2)

Within the letter's rustling fold
    I find, once more—a glad surprise:
A tiny little cup of gold—
    Two lovely violet eyes;—
A cup of gold with emeralds set,
    Once filled with wine from happier spheres;
Two little eyes so lately wet
    With spring's delicious dewy tears.

Oh! little eyes that wept and laughed,
    Now bright with smiles, with tears now dim;
Oh! little cup that once was quaffed
    By fay-queens fluttering round thy rim.
I press each silken fringe's fold—
    Sweet little eyes, once more ye shine;
I kiss thy lip, oh! cup of gold,
    And find thee full of memory's wine.

Within their violet depths I gaze,
    And see, as in the camera's gloom,
The Island with its belt of bays,
    Its chieftained heights all capped with broom;
Which, as the living lens it fills,
    Now seems a giant charmed to sleep—
Now a broad shield embossed with hills,
    Upon the bosom of the deep.

There by the gentler mountain's slope—
    That happiest year of many a year,
That first swift year of love and hope—
    With her then dear and ever dear,
I sat upon the rustic seat—
    The seat an agèd bay-tree crowns—
And saw outspreading from our feet
    The golden glory of the Downs.

The furze-crowned heights, the glorious glen,
    The white-walled chapel glistening near,
The house of God, the homes of men,
    The fragrant hay, the ripening ear;
There, where there seemed nor sin, nor crime,
    There in God's sweet and wholesome air—
Strange book to read at such a time—
    We read of Vanity's false Fair.

We read the painful pages through—
    Perceiving the skill, admired the art,
Felt them if true, not wholly true—
    A truer truth was in our heart.
Save fear and love of One, hath proved
    The sage, how vain is all below;
And one was there who feared and loved,
    And one who loved that she was so.

The vision spreads, the memories grow,
    Fair phantoms crowd the more I gaze.
Oh! cup of gold, with wine o'erflow,
    I'll drink to those departed days:
And when I drain the golden cup
    To them, to those, I ne'er can see,
With wine of hope I'll fill it up,
    And drink to days that yet may be.

I've drunk the future and the past,
 Now for a draught of warmer wine—
One draught the sweetest and the last—
 Lady, I'll drink to thee and thine.
These flowers that to my breast I fold,
 Into my very heart have grown—
To thee I drain the cup of gold,
 And think the violet eyes thine own.

Preludes

COVENTRY PATMORE
(1 8 2 3 – 1 8 9 6)

I

Unthrift

Ah, wasteful woman, she who may
 On her sweet self set her own price,
Knowing man cannot choose but pay,
 How has she cheapened Paradise;
How given for nought her priceless gift,
 How spoiled the bread and spilled the wine,
Which, spent with due, respective thrift,
 Had made brutes men, and men divine.

II

The Attainment

You love? that's high as you shall go;
 For 'tis as true as Gospel text,
Not noble then is never so,
 Either in this world or the next.

The Married Lover

COVENTRY PATMORE

Why, having won her, do I woo?
    Because her spirit's vestal grace
Provokes me always to pursue,
    But, spirit-like, eludes embrace;
Because her womanhood is such
    That, as on court-days subjects kiss
The Queen's hand, yet so near a touch
    Affirms no mean familiarness;
Nay, rather marks more fair the height
    Which can with safety so neglect
To dread, as lower ladies might,
    That grace could meet with disrespect;
Thus she with happy favor feeds
    Allegiance from a love so high
That thence no false conceit proceeds
    Of difference bridged, or state put by;
Because, although in act and word
    As lowly as a wife can be,
Her manners, when they call me lord,
    Remind me 'tis by courtesy;
Not with her least consent of will,
    Which would my proud affection hurt,
But by the noble style that still
    Imputes an unattained desert;
Because her gay and lofty brows,
    When all is won which hope can ask,
Reflect a light of hopeless snows
    That bright in virgin ether bask;
Because, though free of the outer court
    I am, this Temple keeps its shrine
Sacred to Heaven; because, in short,
    She's not and never can be mine.

The Spirit's Epochs

COVENTRY PATMORE

Not in the crises of events,
    Of compassed hopes, or fears fulfilled,
Or acts of gravest consequence,
    Are life's delight and depth revealed.
The day of days was not the day;
    That went before, or was postponed;
The night Death took our lamp away
    Was not the night on which we groaned.
I drew my bride, beneath the moon,
    Across my threshold; happy hour!
But, ah, the walk that afternoon
    We saw the water-flags in flower!

Magna Est Veritas

COVENTRY PATMORE

Here, in this little Bay,
Full of tumultuous life and great repose,
Where, twice a day,
The purposeless, glad ocean comes and goes,
Under high cliffs, and far from the huge town,
I sit me down.
For want of me the world's course will not fail,
When all its work is done, the lie shall rot;
The truth is great, and shall prevail,
When none cares whether it prevail or not.

The Toys

COVENTRY PATMORE

My little Son, who looked from thoughtful eyes
And moved and spoke in quiet grown-up wise,
Having my law the seventh time disobeyed,
I struck him, and dismissed
With hard words and unkissed,
His Mother, who was patient, being dead.
Then, fearing lest his grief should hinder sleep,
I visited his bed,
But found him slumbering deep,
With darkened eyelids, and their lashes yet ·
From his late sobbing wet.
And I, with moan,
Kissing away his tears, left others of my own;
For on a table drawn beside his head
He had put within his reach
A box of counters and a red-veined stone,
A piece of glass abraded by the beach,
And six or seven shells,
A bottle with bluebells,
And two French copper coins, ranged there with careful art,
To comfort his sad heart.
So when that night I prayed
To God, I wept, and said:
Ah, when at last we lie with trancèd breath,
Not vexing Thee in death,
And Thou rememberest of what toys
We made our joys,
How weakly understood,
Thy great commanded good,
Then, fatherly not less
Than I whom Thou hast moulded from the clay,
Thou'lt leave Thy wrath, and say,
'I will be sorry for their childishness.'

Arbor Vitæ

COVENTRY PATMORE

With honeysuckle, over-sweet, festooned;
With bitter ivy bound;
Terraced with funguses unsound;
Deformed with many a boss
And closèd scar, o'ercushioned deep with moss;
Bunched all about with pagan mistletoe;
And thick with nests of the hoarse bird
That talks, but understands not his own word;
Stands, and so stood a thousand years ago,
A single tree.
Thunder has done its worst among its twigs,
Where the great crest yet blackens, never pruned,
But in its heart, alway
Ready to push new verdurous boughs, whene'er
The rotting saplings near it fall and leave it air,
Is all antiquity and no decay.
Rich, though rejected by the forest-pigs,
Its fruit, beneath whose rough, concealing rind
They that will break it find
Heart-succouring savour of each several meat,
And kernelled drink of brain-renewing power,
With bitter condiment and sour,
And sweet economy of sweet,
And odours that remind
Of haunts of childhood and a different day.
Beside this tree.
Praising no Gods nor blaming, sans a wish,
Sits, Tartar-like, the Time's civility,
And eats its dead-dog off a golden dish.

The Azalea

COVENTRY PATMORE

There, where the sun shines first
Against our room,
She trained the gold Azalea, whose perfume
She, Spring-like, from her breathing grace dispersed.
Last night the delicate crests of saffron bloom,
For this their dainty likeness watched and nurst,
Were just at point to burst.
At dawn I dreamed, O God, that she was dead,
And groaned aloud upon my wretched bed,
And waked, ah, God, and did not waken her,
But lay, with eyes still closed,
Perfectly bless'd in the delicious sphere
By which I knew so well that she was near,
My heart to speechless thankfulness composed.
Till 'gan to stir
A dizzy somewhat in my troubled head—
It *was* the azalea's breath, and she *was* dead!
The warm night had the lingering buds disclosed.
And I had fallen asleep with to my breast
A chance-found letter pressed
In which she said,
'So, till to-morrow eve, my Own, adieu!
Parting's well-paid with soon again to meet,
Soon in your arms to feel so small and sweet,
Sweet to myself that am so sweet to you!'

If I Were Dead

COVENTRY PATMORE

'If I were dead, you'd sometimes say, "Poor Child!"'
The dear lips quivered as they spake,
And the tears brake
From eyes which, not to grieve me, brightly smiled.
Poor Child, poor Child!
I seem to hear your laugh, your talk, your song.
It is not true that Love will do no wrong.
Poor Child!
And did you think, when you so cried and smiled,
How I, in lonely nights, should lie awake,
And of those words your full avengers make?
Poor Child, poor Child!
And now, unless it be
That sweet amends thrice told are come to thee,
O God, have Thou *no* mercy upon me!
Poor Child!

Saint Valentine's Day

COVENTRY PATMORE

Well dost thou, Love, thy solemn Feast to hold
        In vestal February;
Not rather choosing out some rosy day
From the rich coronet of the coming May,
When all things meet to marry!
        O, quick prævernal Power
That signal'st punctual through the sleepy mould
The Snowdrop's time to flower,
Fair as the rash oath of virginity
Which is first-love's first cry;

O, Baby Spring,
That flutterest sudden 'neath the breast of Earth
A month before the birth;
Whence is the peaceful poignancy,
The joy contrite,
Sadder than sorrow, sweeter than delight,
That burthens now the breath of everything,
Though each one sighs as if to each alone
The cherished pang were known?
At dusk of dawn, on his dark spray apart,
With it the Blackbird breaks the young Day's heart;
In evening's hush
About it talks the heavenly-minded Thrush;
The hill with like remorse
Smiles to the Sun's smile in his westering course;
The fisher's drooping skiff
In yonder sheltering bay;
The choughs that call about the shining cliff;
The children, noisy in the setting ray;
Own the sweet season, each thing as it may;
Thoughts of strange kindness and forgotten peace
In me increase;
And tears arise
Within my happy, happy Mistress' eyes,
And, lo, her lips, averted from my kiss,
Ask from Love's bounty, ah, much more than bliss!
      Is't the sequestered and exceeding sweet
Of dear Desire electing his defeat?
Is't the waked Earth now to yon purpling cope
Uttering first-love's first cry,
Vainly renouncing, with a Seraph's sigh,
Love's natural hope?
Fair-meaning Earth, foredoom'd to perjury!
Behold, all amorous May,
With roses heaped upon her laughing brows,
Avoids thee of thy vows!
Were it for thee, with that warm bosom near,

To abide the sharpness of the Seraph's sphere?
Forget thy foolish words;
Go to her summons gay,
Thy heart with dead, winged Innocencies filled,
Ev'n as a nest with birds
After the old ones by the hawk are killed.
    Well dost thou, Love, to celebrate
The noon of thy soft ecstasy,
Or e'er it be too late,
Or e'er the Snowdrop die!

To the Body

COVENTRY PATMORE

Creation's and Creator's crowning good;
Wall of infinitude;
Foundation of the sky,
In Heaven forecast
And longed for from eternity,
Though laid the last;
Reverberating dome,
Of music cunningly built home
Against the void and indolent disgrace
Of unresponsive space;
Little, sequestered pleasure-house
For God and for His Spouse;
Elaborately, yea, past conceiving, fair,
Since, from the graced decorum of the hair,
Ev'n to the tingling, sweet
Soles of the simple, earth-confiding feet,
And from the inmost heart
Outwards unto the thin
Silk curtains of the skin,
Every least part

Astonished hears
And sweet replies to some like region of the spheres;
Formed for a dignity prophets but darkly name,
Lest shameless men cry 'Shame!'
So rich with wealth concealed
That Heaven and Hell fight chiefly for this field;
Clinging to everything that pleases thee
With indefectible fidelity;
Alas, so true
To all thy friendships that no grace
Thee from thy sin can wholly disembrace;
Which thus 'bides with thee as the Jebusite,
That, maugre all God's promises could do,
The chosen People never conquered quite;
Who therefore lived with them,
And that by formal truce and as of right,
In metropolitan Jerusalem.
For which false fealty
Thou needs must, for a season, lie
In the grave's arms, foul and unshriven;
Albeit, in Heaven,
Thy crimson-throbbing Glow
Into its old abode aye pants to go,
And does with envy see
Enoch, Elijah, and the Lady, she
Who left the roses in her body's lieu.
O, if the pleasures I have known in thee
But my poor faith's poor first-fruits be,
What quintessential, keen, ethereal bliss
Then shall be his
Who has thy birth-time's consecrating dew
For death's sweet chrism retain'd,
Quick, tender, virginal, and unprofaned!

A Legend

ADELAIDE ANNE PROCTOR
(1 8 2 5 - 1 8 6 4)

I

The Monk was preaching: strong his earnest word;
   From the abundance of his heart he spoke,
And the flame spread,—in every soul that heard
   Sorrow and love and good resolve awoke:—
The poor lay Brother, ignorant and old,
   Thanked God that he had heard such words of gold.

II

'Still let the glory, Lord, be thine alone,'—
   So prayed the Monk, his heart absorbed in praise:
Thine be the glory: if my hands have sown
   The harvest ripened in Thy mercy's rays,
It was Thy blessing, Lord, that made my word
   Bring light and love to every soul that heard.

III

'O Lord, I thank Thee that my feeble strength
   Has been so blest; that sinful hearts and cold
Were melted at my pleading,—knew at length
   How sweet Thy service and how safe Thy fold:
While souls that loved Thee saw before them rise
   Still holier heights of loving sacrifice.'

IV

So prayed the Monk: when suddenly he heard
   An Angel speaking thus: 'Know, O my Son,
The words had all been vain, but hearts were stirred,
   And saints were edified, and sinners won,
By his, the poor lay Brother's humble aid
   Who sat upon the pulpit stair and prayed.'

Give Me Thy Heart

ADELAIDE ANNE PROCTOR

With echoing steps the worshippers
Departed one by one;
The organ's pealing voice was stilled,
The vesper hymn was done;
The shadows fell from roof and arch,
Dim was the incensed air,
One lamp alone with trembling ray,
Told of the Presence there!

In the dark church she knelt alone;
Her tears were falling fast;
'Help, Lord,' she cried, 'the shades of death
Upon my soul are cast!
Have I not shunned the path of sin
And chosen the better part?'
What voice came through the sacred air?
'My child, give me thy heart!

'For I have loved thee with a love
No mortal heart can show;
A love so deep, My Saints in Heaven
Its depths can never know:
When pierced and wounded on the Cross,
Man's sin and doom were Mine,
I loved thee with undying love;
Immortal and divine.'

In awe she listened, and the shade
Passed from her soul away;
In low and trembling voice she cried,
'Lord, help me to obey!

Break Thou the chains of earth, O Lord,
That bind and hold my heart;
Let it be Thine and Thine alone,
Let none with Thee have part!'

The Shrine

DIGBY MACKWORTH DOLBEN
(1 8 4 8 - 1 8 6 7)

There is a shrine whose golden gate
    Was opened by the hand of God;
It stands serene, inviolate,
    Though millions have its pavement trod;
As fresh as when the first sunrise
Awoke the lark in Paradise.

'Tis compassed with the dust and toil
    Of common days, yet should there fall
A single speck, a single soil
    Upon the whiteness of its wall,
The angels' tears in tender rain
Would make the temple theirs again.

Without, the world is tired and old,
    But, once within the enchanted door,
The mists of time are backward rolled,
    And creeds and ages are no more;
But all the human-hearted meet
In one communion vast and sweet.

I enter—all is simply fair,
    Nor incense-clouds, nor carven throne;
But in the fragrant morning air
    A gentle lady sits alone;
My mother—ah! whom should I see
Within, save ever only thee?

He Would Have His Lady Sing

DIGBY MACKWORTH DOLBEN

Sing me the men ere this
Who, to the gate that is
A cloven pearl unrapt,
The big white bars between
With dying eyes have seen
The sea of jasper, lapt
About with crystal sheen;

And all the far pleasance
Where linkèd Angels dance,
With scarlet wings that fall
Magnificial, or spread
Most sweetly overhead,
In fashion musical
Of cadenced lutes instead.

Sing me that town they saw
Withouten fleck or flaw,
Aflame, more fine than glass
Of fair Abbayes the boast,
More glad than wax of cost
Doth make at Candlemas
The Lifting of the Host:

Where many Knights and Dames,
With new and wondrous names,
One great Laudate psalm
Go singing down the street;—
'Tis peace upon their feet,
In hand 'tis pilgrim palm
Of Goddës Land so sweet:—

Where Mother Mary walks
In silver lily stalks,
Star-tired, moon-bedight;
Where Cicely is seen,
With Dorothy in green,
And Magdalen all white,
The Maidens of the Queen.

Sing on—the Steps untrod,
The Temple that is God,
Where incense doth ascend,
Where mount the cries and tears
Of all the dolorous years,
With moan that ladies send
Of durance and sore fears:

And Him who sitteth there,
The Christ of purple hair,
And great eyes deep with ruth,
Who is of all things fair
That shall be or that were,
The sum, and very truth.
Then add a little prayer,

That since all these be so,
Our Liege, who doth us know,
Would fend from Sathanas,
And bring us, of His grace,
To that His joyous place;
So we the Doom may pass,
And see Him in the Face.

A Prayer

DIGBY MACKWORTH DOLBEN

From falsehood and error,
From darkness and terror,
From all that is evil,
From the power of the devil,
From the fire and the doom,
From the judgment to come
Sweet Jesu, deliver
Thy servants forever.

The April of the Ages

DIGBY MACKWORTH DOLBEN

Beautiful, O beautiful—
    In all the mountain passes,
The plenteous dowers of April showers
    Which every Spring amasses,
To bring about through Summer drought
    The blossoming of the grasses.

Beautiful, O beautiful—
    The April of the ages,
Which sweetly brought its showers of thought
    To poets and to sages,
Now stored away our thirst to stay
    In ever-dewy pages.

Flowers for the Altar

DIGBY MACKWORTH DOLBEN

I

Tell us, tell us, holy shepherds,
    What at Bethlehem you saw.—
'Very God of Very God
    Asleep amid the straw.'

Tell us, tell us, all ye faithful,
    What this morning came to pass
At the awful elevation
    In the Canon of the Mass.—

'Very God, of Very God,
    By whom the worlds were made,
In silence and in helplessness
    Upon the Altar laid.'

Tell us, tell us, wondrous Jesu,
    What has drawn Thee from above
To the manger and the Altar.
    All the silence answers—Love.

II

Through the roaring streets of London
    Thou art passing, hidden Lord,
Uncreating, Consubstantial,
    In the seventh Heaven adored.

As of old the ever-Virgin
    Through unconscious Bethlehem
Bore Thee, not in glad procession,
    Jewelled robe and diadem;

Not in pomp and not in power,
    Onward to Nativity,
Shrined but in the tabernacle
    Of her sweet Virginity.

Still thou goest by in silence,
    Still the world cannot receive,
Still the poor and weak and weary
    Only, worship and believe.

'Strange, All-absorbing Love'

DIGBY MACKWORTH DOLBEN

Strange, all-absorbing Love, who gatherest
Unto Thy glowing all my pleasant dew,
Then delicately my garden waterest,
Drawing the old, to pour it back anew:

In the dim glitter of the dawning hours
'Not so' I said, 'but still those drops of light,
Heart-shrined among the petals of my flowers,
Shall hold the memory of the starry night.

'So fresh, no need of showers shall there be.'
Ah, senseless gardener! must it come to pass
That 'neath the glaring noon thou shouldest see
Thine earth become as iron, His heavens as brass?

Nay rather, O my Sun, I will be wise,
Believe in Love which may not yet be seen,
Yield Thee my earth-drops, call Thee from the skies,
In soft return, to keep my bedding green.

So when the bells at Vesper-tide shall sound,
And the dead ocean o'er my garden flows,
Upon the Golden Altar may be found
Some scarlet berries and a Christmas rose.

After Reading Homer

DIGBY MACKWORTH DOLBEN

Happy the man, who on the mountain-side
Bending o'er fern and flower his basket fills;
Yet he will never know the outline-power,
The awful Whole of the Eternal Hills.

So some there are who never feel the strength
In thy blind eyes, majestic and complete,
Which conquers those who motionlessly sit,
O dear divine old Giant, at thy feet.

The Garden

DIGBY MACKWORTH DOLBEN

There is a garden, which I think He loves
    Who loveth all things fair;
And once the Master of the flowers came
    To teach love-lessons there.

He touched my eyes, and in the open sun
    They walked, the Holy Dead,
Trailing their washen robes across the turf,
    An aureole round each head.

One said, with wisdom in his infant eyes,—
    'The world I never knew;
But love the Holy Child of Bethlehem,
    And He will love you too.'

One said—'The victory is hard to win,
    But love shall conquer death.
The world is sweet, but He is sweeter far,
    The Child of Nazareth.'

One said—'My life was twilight from the first;
    But on my Calvary,
Beside my cross, another Cross was raised
    In utter love for me.'

One said—'The wine-vat it was hard to tread,
    It stained my weary feet;
But one from Bozra trod with me in love,
    And made my vintage sweet.'

One said—'My human loves were pure and fair,
    He would not have them cease;
But knit to His, I bore them in my heart
    Into the land of peace.'

One came, who in the groves of Paradise
    Had latest cut his palm;
He only said—'The floods lift up their voice,
    But love can make them calm.'

I heard a step—I had been long alone,
    I thought they might have missed me—
It was my mother coming o'er the grass;
    I turned—and so she kissed me.

Friends

LIONEL JOHNSON
(1 8 6 7 – 1 9 0 2)

O patron Saints of all my friends!
O guardian Angels of them all!
With them begins, with them still ends,
    My prayer's most passionate call.

You know my voice: you know their names,
That wing so its least selfish tone
Across your white celestial flames,
    And up to the White Throne.

Heaven were not Heaven, and they not there;
Heaven were no Heaven, my friends away:
O Saints and Angels! hear my prayer,
    I pray you every day.

Christmas Carol

MAY PROBYN

Lacking samite and sable,
Lacking silver and gold,
The Prince Jesus in the poor stable
Slept, and was three hours old.

As doves by the fair water,
Mary, not touched of sin,
Sat by Him,—the King's daughter,
All glorious within.

A lily without a stain, a
Star where no spot hath room—
Ave, gratia plena,
Virgo Virginum!

Clad not in pearl-sewn vesture,
Clad not in cramoisie,
She hath hushed, she hath cradled to rest, her
God the first time on her knee.

Where is one to adore Him?
The ox hath dumbly confessed,
With the ass, meek kneeling before Him,
Et homo factus est.

Not throned on ivory or cedar,
Not crowned with a Queen's crown,
At her breast it is Mary shall feed her
Maker, from Heaven come down.

The trees in Paradise blossom
Sudden, and its bells chime—
She giveth Him, held to her bosom,
Her immaculate milk the first time.

The night with wings of angels
Was alight, and its snow-packed ways
Sweet made (say the Evangels)
With the noise of their virelays.

Quem vidistis, pastores?
Why go ye feet unshod?
Wot ye within yon door is
Mary, the Mother of God?

No smoke of spice is ascending
There—no roses are piled—
But, choicer than all balms blending,
There Mary hath kissed her Child.

Dilectus meus mihi
Et ego illi—cold
Small cheek against her cheek, He
Sleepeth, three hours old.

'Is It Nothing to You?'

MAY PROBYN

We were playing on the green together,
    My sweetheart and I—
O! so heedless is the gay June weather
    When the word went forth that we must die.
O! so merrily the balls of amber
    And of ivory tossed we to the sky,
While the word went forth in the King's chamber
    That we both must die.

O! so idly straying thro' the pleasaunce
    Pluck'd we here and there
Fruit and bud, while in the royal presence
    The King's son was casting from his hair
Glory of the wreathen gold that crowned it,
    And, ungirdling all his garments fair,
Flinging by the jewelled clasp that bound it,
    With his feet made bare.

Down the myrtled stairway of the palace,
    Ashes on his head,
Came he, thro' the rose and citron alleys,
    In rough sark of sackcloth habited,
And in the hempen halter—O! we jested
    Lightly, and we laughed as he was led
To the torture, while the bloom we breasted
    Where the grapes grew red.

O! so sweet the birds, when he was dying,
    Piped to her and me—
Is no room this glad June day for sighing—
    He is dead, and she and I go free!
When the sun shall set on all our pleasure
    We will mourn him.—What, so you decree
We are heartless? Nay, but in what measure
    Do you more than we?

The Beloved

MAY PROBYN

When the storm was in the sky,
  And the west was black with showers,
My Beloved came by
  With His Hands full of flowers—
  Red burning flowers,
Like flame that pulsed and throbbed—
  And beyond in the rain-smitten bowers
The turtle-dove sobbed.

(Sweet in the rough weather
  The voice of the turtle-dove—
'Beautiful altogether
  Is my Love.
  His Hands are open spread for love
And full of Jacinth stones—
  As the apple-tree among trees of the grove
Is He among the sons.') . . .

When the night was in the sky,
  And heavily went the hours,
My Beloved drew nigh
  With His Hands full of flowers—
  Burning red flowers,
Like cups of scented wine—
  And He said, 'They are all ours,
Thine and Mine.

'I gathered them from the bitter Tree—
  Why dost thou start?
I gathered the five of them for thee,
  Child of My Heart.
  These are they that have wrung My Heart,
And with fiercest pangs have moved Me—
  I gathered them—why dost thou shrink apart?
In the house of them that loved Me.'

(Sweet through the rain-swept blast
     The moan of the turtle-dove—
'You, that see Him go past,
     Tell Him I languish with love.
     Thou hast wounded my heart, O my Love!
With but one look of Thine eyes,
     While yet the boughs are naked above
And winter is in the skies.

('Honey-laden flowers
     For the children nursed on the knee,
Who sow not bramble among their bowers—
     But what—He said—for Thee?
     Not joys of June for thee,
Not lily, no, nor rose—
     For thee the blossom of the bitter Tree,
More sweet than ought that blows.'

(The voice of the turtle-dove—
     'How shall my heart be fed
With pleasant apples of love,
     When the winter time has fled.
     The rain and the winter fled,
How all His gifts shall grace me,
     When His Left Hand is under my head,
And His Right Hand doth embrace me.')

The Bees of Middleton Manor

MAY PROBYN

Buzzing, buzzing, buzzing, my golden-belted bees:
My little son was seven years old—the mint-flower touched his knees.
     Yellow were his curly locks;
     Yellow were his stocking-clocks;

His plaything of a sword had a diamond in its hilt;
    Where the garden beds lay sunny,
    And the bees were making honey,
'For God and the King—to arms! to arms!' the day long would he lilt.
Smock'd in lace and flowered brocade, my pretty son of seven
Wept sore because the kitten died, and left the charge uneven.
    'I head one battalion, mother—
    Kitty,' sobbed he, 'led the other!
    And when we reach'd the bee-hive bench
    We used to halt and storm the trench:
    If we could plant our standard here,
    With all the bees a-buzzing near,
    And fly the colours safe from sting,
    The town was taken for the King!'

Flitting, flitting over the thyme, my bees with yellow band—
My little son of seven came close, and clipp'd me by the hand;
    A wreath of mourning cloth was wound
    His small left arm and sword-hilt round,
And on the thatch of every hive a wisp of black was bound.
'Sweet mother, we must tell the bees, or they will swarm away:
Ye little bees!' he called, 'draw nigh, and hark to what I say,
And make us golden honey still for our white wheaten bread,
    Though never more
    We rush on war
    With Kitty at our head.
    Who'll give the toast
    When swords are cross'd,
    Now Kitty lieth dead?'

Buzzing, buzzing, buzzing, my bees of yellow girth:
My son of seven changed his mood, and clasp'd me in his mirth.
'Sweet mother, when I grow a man and fall on battle-field,'
He cried, and down in the daisied grass upon one knee he kneel'd,
'I charge thee, come and tell the bees how I for the King lie dead;
And thou shalt never lack fine honey for thy wheaten bread!'
       *   *   *   *   *

Flitting, flitting, flitting, my busy bees, alas!
No footsteps of my soldier son came clinking through the grass.
  Thrice he kiss'd me for farewell;
  And far on the stone his shadow fell;
He buckled spurs and sword-belt on, as the sun began to stoop,
Set foot in stirrup, and sprang to horse, and rode to join his troop.
  To the west he rode, where the winds were at play,
  And Monmouth's army mustering lay;
  Where Bridgewater flew her banner high,
  And gave up her keys, when the Duke came by;
  And the maids of Taunton paid him court
  With colour their own white hands had wrought;
  And red as a field, where blood doth run,
  Sedgemoor blazed in the setting sun.

Broider'd sash and clasp of gold, my soldier son, alas!
The mint was all in flower, and the clover in the grass;
  'With every bed
  In bloom,' I said,
  'What further lack the bees,
  That they buzz so loud,
  Like a restless cloud,
  Among the orchard trees?'
No voice in the air, from Sedgemoor field,
Moan'd out how Grey and the horse had reel'd;
Met me no ghost, with haunting eyes,
That westward pointed 'mid its sighs,
And pull'd apart a bloody vest,
And show'd the sword-gash in his breast.

Empty hives, and flitting bees, and sunny morning hours;
I snipp'd the blossom'd lavender, and the pinks, and the gilly flowers;
  No petal trembled in my hold—
  I saw not the dead stretched stark and cold
  On the trampled turf at the shepherd's door,
  In the cloak and the doublet Monmouth wore,

With Monmouth's scarf and headgear on,
  And the eyes, not clos'd, of my soldier son;
I knew not how, ere the cocks did crow, the fight was fought in the
      dark,
With naught for guide but the enemy's guns, when the flint flash'd
      out a spark,
Till, routed at first sound of fire, the cavalry broke and fled,
And the hoofs struck dumb, where they spurn'd the slain, and the
      meadow stream ran red;
I saw not the handful of horsemen spur through the dusk, and out
      of sight,
My soldier son at the Duke's left hand, and Grey that rode on his right.

Buzzing, buzzing, buzzing, my honey-making bees,
They left the musk, and the marigolds and the scented faint sweet peas;
They gather'd in a darkening cloud, and sway'd, and rose to fly;
A blackness on the summer blue, they swept across the sky.
Gaunt and ghastly with gaping wounds—(my soldier son, alas!)
Footsore and faint, the messenger came halting through the grass.
The wind went by and shook the leaves—the mint-stalk shed its
      flower—
And I miss'd the murmuring round the hives, and my boding heart
      beat slower.
    His soul we cheer'd with meat and wine;
    With woman's craft and balsam fine
    We bathed his hurts, and bound them soft,
    While west the wind played through the croft,
    And the low sun dyed the pinks blood-red,
    And, straying near the mint-flower shed,
    A wild bee wantoned o'er the bed.

He told how my son, at the shepherd's door, kept watch in Monmouth's
      clothes,
While Monmouth donned the shepherd's frock, in hope to cheat his
      foes.
    A couple of troopers spied him stand,
    And bade him yield to the King's command:

223

'Surrender, thou rebel as good as dead,
A price is set on thy traitor head!'
My soldier son, with secret smile,
Held both at bay for a little while,
Dealt them such death-blow as he fell,
Neither was left the tale to tell;
With dying eyes that asked no grace,
They stared on him for a minute's space,
And felt that it was not Monmouth's face.
Crimsoned through was Monmouth's cloak, when the soldier dropped
    at his side—
'Those knaves will carry no word,' he said, and he smiled in his pain,
    and died.
'Two days,' told the messenger, 'did we lie
    Hid in the fields of peas and rye,
    Hid in the ditch of brake and sedge,
    With the enemy's scouts down every hedge,
Till Grey was seized, and Monmouth seized, that under the fern did
    crouch,
Starved and haggard, and all unshaved, with a few raw peas in his
    pouch.'

      *   *   *   *   *

No music soundeth in my ears, but a passing bell that tolls
For gallant lords with head on block—sweet Heaven receive their
    souls!
    And a mound, unnamed, in Sedgemoor grass,
    That laps my soldier son, alas!
        The bloom is shed—
        The bees are fled—
Middleton luck it's done and dead.

Belovèd, It Is Morn

EMILY H. HICKEY
(1 8 4 5 - 1 9 2 4)

Belovèd, it is morn!
    A redder berry on the thorn,
    A deeper yellow on the corn,
For this good day new-born.
        Pray, Sweet, for me
        That I may be
        Faithful to God and thee.

Belovèd, it is day!
    And lovers work, as children play,
    With heart and brain untired alway:
Dear love, look up and pray.
        Pray, Sweet, for me
        That I may be
        Faithful to God and thee.

Belovèd, it is night!
    Thy heart and mine are full of light,
    Thy spirit shineth clear and white,
God keep thee in His sight!
        Pray, Sweet, for me
        That I may be
        Faithful to God and thee.

To Night

JOSEPH BLANCO WHITE
(1 7 7 5 - 1 8 4 1)

Mysterious Night! When our first parent knew
Thee from report divine, and heard thy name,
Did he not tremble for this lovely frame,
This glorious canopy of light and blue?
Yet, 'neath the curtain of translucent dew,
Bathed in the rays of the great setting flame,
Hesperus with the host of heaven came,
And lo! Creation widened on man's view.
Who would have thought such darkness lay concealed
Within thy beams, O sun? or who could find
While fly, and leaf, and insect stood revealed,
That to such countless orbs thou mad'st us blind.
Why do we, then, shun Death with anxious strife?—
If Light can thus deceive, wherefore not Life?

Rosa Mystica

GERARD MANLEY HOPKINS
(1 8 4 4 - 1 8 8 9)

'The rose is a mystery'—where is it found?
Is it anything true? Does it grow upon ground?
It was made of earth's mould, but it went from men's eyes,
And its place is a secret and shut in the skies.
  In the gardens of God, in the daylight divine,
  Find me a place by thee, Mother of mine.

But where was it formerly? Which is the spot
That was blest in it once, though now it is not?

It is Galilee's growth: it grew at God's will
And broke into bloom upon Nazareth hill.
    In the gardens of God, in the daylight divine,
    I shall look on thy loveliness, Mother of mine.

What was its season then? How long ago?
When was the summer that saw the bud blow?
Two thousands of years are near upon past
Since its birth and its bloom and its breathing its last.
    In the gardens of God, in the daylight divine,
    I shall keep time with thee, Mother of mine.

Tell me the name now, tell me its name.
The heart guesses easily: is it the same?
Mary the Virgin, well the heart knows,
She is the Mystery, she is the rose.
    In the gardens of God, in the daylight divine,
    I shall come home to thee, Mother of mine.

Is Mary the rose, then? Mary, the tree?
But the blossom, the blossom there—who can it be?
Who can her rose be? It could but be One
Christ Jesus our Lord, her God and her Son.
    In the gardens of God, in the daylight divine,
    Show me thy Son, Mother, Mother of mine.

What was the colour of that blossom bright?—
White to begin with, immaculate white.
But what a wild flush on the flakes of it stood
When the rose ran in crimsonings down the cross-wood!
    In the gardens of God, in the daylight divine
    I shall worship the wounds with thee, Mother of mine.

How many leaves had it?—Five they were then,
Five like the senses and members of men;

Five is their number by nature, but now
They multiply, multiply—who can tell how?
>In the gardens of God, in the daylight divine
>Make me a leaf in thee, Mother of mine.

Does it smell sweet, too, in that holy place?
Sweet unto God and the sweetness is grace:
The breath of it bathes great heaven above
In grace that is charity, grace that is love.
>To thy breast, to thy rest, to thy glory divine
>Draw me by charity, Mother of mine.

The Starlight Night

GERARD MANLEY HOPKINS

Look at the stars! Look, look up at the skies!
>O look at all the fire-folk sitting in the air!
>The bright boroughs, the circle-citadels there!
Down in dim woods the diamond delves! the elves'-eyes!
The grey lawns cold where gold, where quickgold lies!
>Wind-beat white-beam; airy abeles set on a flare!
>Flake-doves sent floating forth at a farmyard scare!—
Ah well! it is all a purchase, all is a prize.

Buy then! Bid then!—What?—Prayer, patience, alms, vows.—
Look, look! A May-mess, like on orchard boughs;
>Look! March-bloom, like on mealed-with-yellow sallows.—
These are indeed the barn: within-doors house
The shocks. This piece-bright paling shuts the Spouse
>Christ home, Christ and his mother and all his hallows.

Heaven-Haven

[A Nun takes the Veil]

GERARD MANLEY HOPKINS

I have desired to go
  Where springs not fail,
To fields where flies no sharp and sided hail,
  And a few lilies blow.

And I have asked to be
  Where no storms come,
Where the green swell is in the havens dumb,
  And out of the swing of the sea.

Of an Orchard

KATHARINE TYNAN HINKSON
(1 8 6 1 -)

Good is an orchard, the saint saith,
To meditate on life and death,
With a cool well, a hive of bees,
A hermit's grot beneath the trees.

Good is an orchard: very good,
Though one should wear no monkish hood.
Right good when Spring awakes her flute,
And good in yellowing time of fruit.

Very good in the grass to lie
And see the network 'gainst the sky,
A living lace of blue and green,
And boughs that let the gold between.

The bees are types of souls that dwell
With honey in a quiet cell;
The ripe fruit figures goldenly
The soul's perfection in God's eye.

Prayer and praise in a country home,
Honey and fruit; a man might come,
Fed on such meats, to walk abroad,
And in his orchard talk with God.

The Waterlily

JOHN BANISTER TABB

(1 8 4 5 - 1 9 0 9)

Whence, O fragrant form of light,
Hast thou drifted through the night,
Swan-like, to a leafy nest,
On the restless waves, at rest?

Art thou from the snowy zone
Of a mountain-summit blown,
Or the blossom of a dream,
Fashioned in the foamy stream?

Nay, methinks the maiden moon,
When the daylight came too soon,
Fleeting from her bath to hide,
Left her garment in the tide.

The Shepherdess

ALICE MEYNELL
(*1 8 4 9 - 1 9 2 2*)

She walks—the lady of my delight—
    A shepherdess of sheep.
Her flocks are thoughts. She keeps them white;
    She guards them from the steep.
She feeds them on the fragrant height,
    And folds them in for sleep.

She roams maternal hills and bright,
    Dark valleys safe and deep.
Into that tender breast at night
    The chastest stars may peep.
She walks—the lady of my delight—
    A shepherdess of sheep.

She holds her little thoughts in sight,
    Though gay they run and leap.
She is so circumspect and right;
    She has her soul to keep.
She walks—the lady of my delight—
    A shepherdess of sheep.

The Young Neophyte

ALICE MEYNELL

Who knows what days I answer for to-day?
    Giving the bud I give the flower. I bow
    This yet unfaded and a faded brow;
Bending these knees and feeble knees, I pray.

Thoughts yet unripe in me I bend one way,
    Give one repose to pain I know not now,
    One check to joy that comes, I guess not how.
I dedicate my fields when Spring is grey.

O rash! (I smile) to pledge my hidden wheat.
    I fold to-day at altars far apart
Hands trembling with what toils? In their retreat
    I seal my love to-be, my folded art.
I light the tapers at my head and feet,
    And lay the crucifix on this silent heart.

Thoughts in Separation

ALICE MEYNELL

We never meet, yet we meet day by day
    Upon those hills of life, dim and immense—
    The good we love, and sleep, our innocence.
O hills of life, high hills, and, higher than they
Our guardian spirits meet at prayer and play.
    Beyond pain, joy, and hope, and long suspense,
    Above the summits of our souls, far hence,
An angel meets an angel on the way.

Beyond all good I ever believed of thee,
    Or thou of me, these always love and live.
And though I fail of thy ideal of me,
My angel falls not short. They greet each other.
    Who knows, they may exchange the kiss we give.
Thou to thy crucifix, I to my mother.

'I Am the Way'

ALICE MEYNELL

Thou art the Way.
Hadst Thou been nothing but the goal,
    I cannot say
If Thou hadst ever met my soul.

    I cannot see—
I, child of process—if there lies
    An end for me,
Full of repose, full of replies.

    I'll not reproach
The road that winds, my feet that err.
    Access, Approach
Art Thou, Time, Way, and Wayfarer.

Christ in the Universe

ALICE MEYNELL

With this ambiguous earth
His dealings have been told us. These abide:
The signal to a maid, the human birth,
The lesson, and the young Man crucified.

    But not a star of all
The innumerable host of stars has heard
How He administered this terrestrial ball.
Our race have kept their Lord's entrusted Word.

Of His earth-visiting feet
None knows the secret, cherished, perilous,
The terrible, shamefast, frightened, whispered, sweet,
Heart-shattering secret of His way with us.

No planet knows that this
Our wayside planet, carrying land and wave,
Love and life multiplied, and pain and bliss,
Bears, as chief treasure, one forsaken grave.

Nor, in our little day,
May His devices with the heavens be guessed,
His pilgrimage to thread the Milky Way,
Or His bestowals there be manifest.

But in the eternities
Doubtless we shall compare together, hear
A million alien Gospels, in what guise
He trod the Pleiades, the Lyre, the Bear.

O, be prepared, my soul,
To read the inconceivable, to scan
The million forms of God those stars unroll
When, in our turn, we show to them a Man.

To W. M.

[Thoughts at Evening]

ALICE MEYNELL

Home, home from the horizon, far and clear,
        Hither the soft wings sweep,
Flocks of the memories of the day draw near
        The dove-cote doors of sleep.

O, which are they that come through sweetest light
   Of all these homing birds,—
Which with the straightest and the swiftest flight?—
   Your words to me, your words.

The Folded Flock

WILFRID MEYNELL
(1 8 5 2 -   )

I saw the shepherd fold the sheep,
With all the little lambs that leap.

O Shepherd Lord, so I would be
Folded with all my family.

Or go they early, come they late,
Their mother and I must count them eight.

And how, for us, were any heaven
If we, sore-stricken, saw but seven?

Kind Shepherd, as of old Thou'lt run
And fold at need a straggling one.

A Russian Spring Song with Minaiev

THOMAS WALSH
(1 8 7 5 - 1 9 2 8)

She softly droops her maiden eyes
   Behind the casement ledge at home,
And ever and anon she sighs—
   'Ah, if the Spring would only come!'

Another on his bed of pain
 With hope of health and sunshine near,
Warms his faint heart with like refrain,—
 'Ah, if the Spring were only here!'

And soon the Spring with flower and dove
 Brings each a portion on its breath:—
For her, sweet blossomings and love;
 For him, sweet blossomings and death.

Exchange

SISTER M. DOROTHY ANN
(*American Contemporary*)

I am all Thine, Belovèd, for
I come
Unbound and free;
Now I am stripped of everything
I love
To love but Thee;
Of everything, and yet, my Lord,
I have
Fair memory.

The wide world is my home; but once
I knew
A garden close,
And sheltering walls encircled by
The press
Of rambling rose.
In every soul that I may help
My heart
A new home knows.

And once when all my life was young
I dreamt
Of little feet,
And tiny hands and rosy mouth;
Ah! Lord,
Those dreams were sweet!
To-day a thousand little hands
Await
My love to meet.

And in this dream of yesterday,
The whole
Wide world was mine.
I held it close against my heart;
But now
A love divine
Has given more than life can give,
Himself,
The Bread and Wine.

Daisy

FRANCIS THOMPSON
(1 8 5 9 - 1 9 0 7)

Where the thistle lifts a purple crown
    Six foot out of the turf,
And the harebell shakes on the windy hill—
    O breath of the distant surf!—

The hills look over on the South,
    And southward dreams the sea;
And, with the sea-breeze hand in hand
    Came innocence and she.

Where 'mid the gorse the raspberry
 Red for the gatherer springs,
Two children did we stray and talk
 Wise, idle, childish things.

She listened with big-lipped surprise,
 Breast-deep 'mid flower and spine:
Her skin was like a grape whose veins
 Run snow instead of wine.

She knew not those sweet words she spake,
 Nor knew her own sweet way;
But there's never a bird so sweet a song
 Thronged in whose throat that day.

Oh, there were flowers in Storrington
 On the turf and on the spray;
But the sweetest flower on Sussex hills
 Was the Daisy-flower that day!

Her beauty smoothed earth's furrowed face.
 She gave me tokens three:—
A look, a word of her winsome mouth,
 And a wild raspberry.

A berry red, a guileless look,
 A still word,—strings of sand!
And yet they made my wild, wild heart
 Fly down to her little hand.

For standing artless as the air,
 And candid as the skies,
She took the berries with her hand,
 And the love with her sweet eyes.

The fairest things have fleetest end:
    Their scent survives their close,
But the rose's scent is bitterness
    To him that loved the rose!

She looked a little wistfully,
    Then went her sunshine way:—
The sea's eye had a mist on it,
    And the leaves fell from the day.

She went her unremembering way,
    She went and left in me
The pang of all the partings gone,
    And partings yet to be.

She left me marvelling why my soul
    Was sad that she was glad;
At all the sadness in the sweet,
    The sweetness in the sad.

Still, still I seemed to see her, still
    Look up with soft replies,
And take the berries with her hand,
    And the love with her lovely eyes.

Nothing begins, and nothing ends,
    That is not paid with moan,
For we are born in other's pain,
    And perish in our own.

The Kingdom of God

['In No Strange Land']

FRANCIS THOMPSON

O World invisible, we view thee,
O World intangible, we touch thee,
O World unknowable, we know thee,
Inapprehensible, we clutch thee!

Does the fish soar to find the ocean,
The eagle plunge to find the air—
That we ask of the stars in motion
If they have rumour of thee there?

Not where the wheeling systems darken,
And our benumbed conceiving soars!—
The drift of pinions, would we hearken,
Beats at our own clay-shuttered doors.

The angels keep their ancient places;—
Turn but a stone and start a wing!
'Tis ye, 'tis your estrangèd faces,
That miss the many-splendoured thing.

But (when so sad thou canst not sadder)
Cry,—and upon thy so sore loss
Shall shine the traffic of Jacob's ladder
Pitched betwixt Heaven and Charing Cross.

Yea, in the night, my Soul, my daughter,
Cry,—clinging Heaven by the hems;
And lo, Christ walking on the water
Not of Genesareth, but Thames!

Ode to the Setting Sun

FRANCIS THOMPSON

PRELUDE

The wailful sweetness of the violin
    Floats down the hushèd waters of the wind,
The heart-strings of the throbbing harp begin
    To long in aching music. Spirit-pined,

In wafts that poignant sweetness drifts, until
    The wounded soul ooze sadness. The red sun,
A bubble of fire, drops slowly toward the hill,
    While one bird prattles that the day is done.

O setting Sun, that as in reverent days
    Sinkest in music to thy smoothèd sleep,
Discrowned of homage, though yet crowned with rays,
    Hymned not at harvest more, though reapers reap:

For thee this music wakes not. O deceived,
    If thou hear in these thoughtless harmonies
A pious phantom of adorings reaved,
    And echo of fair ancient flatteries!

Yet, in this field where the Cross planted reigns,
    I know not what strange passion bows my head
To thee, whose great command upon my veins
    Proves thee a god for me not dead, not dead!

For worship it is too incredulous,
    For doubt—oh, too believing-passionate!
What wild divinity makes my heart thus
    A fount of most baptismal tears?—Thy straight

Long beam lies steady on the Cross. Ah me!
 What secret would thy radiant finger show?
Of thy bright mastership is this the key?
 Is this thy secret, then? And is it woe?

Fling from thine ear the burning curls, and hark
 A song thou hast not heard in Northern day;
For Rome too daring, and for Greece too dark,
 Sweet with wild wings that pass, that pass away!

ODE

Alpha and Omega, sadness and mirth,
 The springing music, and its wasting breath—
The fairest things in life are Death and Birth,
 And of these two the fairer thing is Death.
Mystical twins of Time inseparable,
 The younger hath the holier array,
  And hath the awfuller sway:
 It is the falling star that trails the light,
 It is the breaking wave that hath the might,
The passing shower that rainbows maniple.
 Is it not so, O thou down-stricken Day,
That draw'st thy splendours round thee in thy fall?
High was thine Eastern pomp inaugural;
But thou dost set in statelier pageantry,
 Lauded with tumults of a firmament:
Thy visible music-blasts make deaf the sky,
 Thy cymbals clang to fire the Occident,
Thou dost thy dying so triumphally:
I see the crimson blaring of thy shawms!
  Why do those lucent palms
Strew thy feet's failing thicklier than their might,
Who dost but hood thy glorious eyes with night,
And vex the heels of all the yesterdays?
  Lo! this loud, lackeying praise
Will stay behind to greet the usurping moon,
 When they have cloud-barred over thee the West.

Oh, shake the bright dust from thy parting shoon!
  The earth not pæans thee, nor serves thy hest;
Be godded not by Heaven! avert thy face,
   And leave to blank disgrace
The oblivious world! unsceptre thee of state and place!

Ha! but bethink thee what thou gazedst on,
  Ere yet the snake Decay had venomed tooth;
The name thou bar'st in those vast seasons gone—
   Candid Hyperion,
  Clad in the light of thine immortal youth!
   Ere Dionysus bled thy vines,
Or Artemis drave her clamours through the wood,
  Thou saw'st how once against Olympus' height
   The brawny Titans stood,
And shook the gods' world 'bout their ears, and how
Enceladus (whom Etna cumbers now)
  Shouldered Mt. Pelion with its swinging pines,
The river unrecked, that did its broken flood
Spurt on his back: before the mountainous shock
   The rankèd gods dislock,
Scared to their skies; wide o'er rout-trampled night
Flew spurned the pebbled stars: those splendours then
  Had tempested on earth, star upon star
  Mounded in ruin, if a longer war
Had quaked Olympus and cold-fearing men.
   Then did the ample marge
   And circuit of thy targe
  Sullenly redden all the vanward fight,
   Above the blusterous clash
   Wheeled thy swung falchion's flash,
  And hewed their forces into splintered flight.

Yet ere Olympus thou wast, and a god!
   Though we deny thy nod,
We cannot spoil thee of thy divinity.
  What know we elder than thee?

When thou didst, bursting from the great void's husk,
Leap like a lion on the throat o' the dusk;
>   When the angels rose-chapleted
>   Sang each to other,
>   The vaulted blaze overhead
>   Of their vast pinions spread,
>   Hailing thee brother;
How chaos rolled back from the wonder,
And the First Morn knelt down to thy visage of thunder!
>   Thou didst draw to thy side
>   Thy young Auroral bride,
>   And lift her veil of night and mystery;
>   Tellus with baby hands
>   Shook off her swaddling-bands,
And from the unswathèd vapours laughed to thee.

Thou twi-form deity, nurse at once and sire!
>   Thou genitor that all things nourishest!
>   The earth was suckled at thy shining breast,
And in her veins is quick thy milky fire.
>   Who scarfed her with the morning? and who set
>   Upon her brow the day-fall's carcanet?
Who queened her front with the enrondured moon?
>   Who dug nights' jewels from their vaulty mine
>   To dower her, past an eastern wizard's dreams,
When, hovering on him through his haschisch-swoon,
>   All the rained gems of the old Tartarian line
Shiver in lustrous throbbings of tinged flame?
>   Whereof a moiety in the Paolis' seams
>   Statelily builded their Venetian name.
>   Thou hast enwoofèd her
>   An empress of the air,
And all her births are propertied by thee:
>   Her teeming centuries
>   Drew being from thine eyes:
Thou fatt'st the marrow of all quality.

Who lit the furnace of the mammoth's heart?
　　Who shagged him like Pilatus' ribbèd flanks?
　　　Who raised the columned ranks
Of that old pre-diluvian forestry,
Which like a continent torn oppressed the sea,
　　When the ancient heavens did in rains depart,
　　　While the high-dancèd whirls
Of the tossed scud made hiss thy drenchèd curls?
　　　Thou rear'dst the enormous brood;
　　　Who hast with life imbued
　　The lion maned in tawny majesty,
　　　The tiger velvet-barred,
　　　The stealthy-stepping pard,
And the lithe panther's flexuous symmetry?

How came the entombèd tree a light-bearer,
　　　Though sunk in lightless lair?
　　　Friend of the forgers of earth,
　　Mate of the earthquake and thunders volcanic,
　　Clasped in the arms of the forces Titanic
　　　Which rock like a cradle the girth
　　　Of the ether-hung world;
Swart son of the swarthy mine,
　　When flame on the breath of his nostrils feeds
How is his countenance half-divine,
　　Like thee in thy sanguine weeds?
　　　Thou gavest him his light,
　　　Though sepultured in night
Beneath the dead bones of a perished world;
　　　Over his prostrate form
　　　Though cold, and heat, and storm,
The mountainous wrack of a creation hurled.

　　　Who made the splendid rose
　　　Saturate with purple glows;
Cupped to the marge with beauty; a perfume-press
　　　Whence the wind vintages

Gushes of warmèd fragrance richer far
    Than all the flavorous ooze of Cyprus' vats?
Lo, in yon gale which waves her green cymar,
      With dusky cheeks burnt red
      She sways her heavy head,
Drunk with the musk of her own odorousness;
    While in a moted trouble the vexed gnats
Maze, and vibrate, and tease the noontide hush.
    Who girt dissolvèd lightnings in the grape?
Summered the opal with an Irised flush?
    Is it not thou that dost the tulip drape,
      And huest the daffodilly,
      Yet who hast snowed the lily,
And her frail sister, whom the waters name,
    Dost vestal-vesture 'mid the blaze of June,
    Cold as the new-sprung girlhood of the moon
Ere Autumn's kiss sultry her cheek with flame?
      Thou sway'st thy sceptred beam
      O'er all delight and dream,
Beauty is beautiful but in thy glance:
      And like a jocund maid
      In garland-flowers arrayed,
Before thy ark Earth keeps her sacred dance.

And now, O shaken from thine antique throne,
    And sunken from thy coerule empery,
Now that the red glare of thy fall is blown
    In smoke and flame about the windy sky,
Where are the wailing voices that should meet
    From hill, stream, grove, and all of mortal shape
Who tread thy gifts, in vineyards as stray feet
    Pulp the globed weight of juiced Iberia's grape?
      Where is the threne o' the sea?
      And why not dirges thee
The wind, that sings to himself as he makes stride
    Lonely and terrible on the Andèan height?

Where is the Naiad 'mid her sworded sedge?
    The Nymph wan-glimmering by her wan fount's verge?
The Dryad at timid gaze by the wood-side?
        The Oread jutting light
On one up-strainèd sole from the rock-ledge?
    The Nereid tip-toe on the scud o' the surge,
With whistling tresses dank athwart her face,
And all her figure poised in lithe Circean grace?
        Why withers their lament?
        Their tresses tear-besprent,
    Have they sighed hence with trailing garment-hem?
      O sweet, O sad, O fair,
      I catch your flying hair,
  Draw your eyes down to me, and dream on them!

A space, and they fleet from me. Must ye fade—
O old, essential candours, ye who made
The earth a living and a radiant thing—
    And leave her corpse in our strained, cheated arms?
    Lo ever thus, when Song with chorded charms
Draws from dull death his lost Eurydice,
    Lo ever thus, even at consummating,
    Even in the swooning minute that claims her his,
    Even as he trembles to the impassioned kiss
    Of reincarnate Beauty, his control
    Clasps the cold body, and forgoes the soul!
      Whatso looks lovelily
Is but the rainbow on life's weeping rain.
Why have we longings of immortal pain,
And all we long for mortal? Woe is me,
And all our chants but chaplet some decay,
As mine this vanishing—nay, vanished Day.
The low sky-line dusks to a leaden hue,
    No rift disturbs the heavy shade and chill,
Save one, where the charred firmament lets through
    The scorching dazzle of Heaven; 'gainst which the hill,
      Out-flattened sombrely,

Stands black as life against eternity.
       Against eternity?
       A rifting light in me
    Burns through the leaden broodings of the mind:
       O blessèd Sun, thy state
       Uprisen or derogate
Dafts me no more with doubt; I seek and find.

    If with exultant tread
       Thou foot the Eastern sea,
       Or like a golden bee
    Sting the West to angry red,
    Thou dost image, thou dost follow
       That King-Maker of Creation,
    Who, ere Hellas hailed Apollo,
       Gave thee, angel-god, thy station;
Thou art of Him a type memorial.
    Like Him thou hang'st in dreadful pomp of blood
       Upon thy Western rood;
    And His stained brow did vail like thine to night,
       Yet lift once more Its light,
And, risen, again departed from our ball,
But when It set on earth arose in Heaven.
Thus hath He unto death His beauty given:
And so of all which form inheriteth
    The fall doth pass the rise in worth;
For birth hath in itself the germ of death,
    But death hath in itself the germ of birth.
It is the falling acorn buds the tree,
The falling rain that bears the greenery,
    The fern-plants moulder when the ferns arise.
    For there is nothing lives but something dies,
And there is nothing dies but something lives.
       Till skies be fugitives,
Till Time, the hidden root of change, updries,
Are Birth and Death inseparable on earth;
For they are twain yet one, and Death is Birth.

The Hound of Heaven

FRANCIS THOMPSON

I fled Him, down the nights and down the days;
    I fled Him, down the arches of the years;
I fled Him, down the labyrinthine ways
    Of my own mind; and in the mist of tears
I hid from Him, and under running laughter.
        Up vistaed hopes I sped;
        And shot, precipitated,
Adown Titanic glooms of chasmèd fears,
    From those strong Feet that followed, followed after.

        But with unhurrying chase,
        And unperturbèd pace
    Deliberate speed, majestic instancy,
        They beat—and a Voice beat
        More instant than the Feet—
    'All things betray thee, who betrayest Me.'

        I pleaded, outlaw-wise,
By many a hearted casement, curtained red,
    Trellised with intertwining charities;
(For, though I knew His love who followèd,
        Yet was I sore adread
Lest, having Him, I must have naught beside);
But, if one little casement parted wide,
    The gust of His approach would clash it to.
    Fear wist not to evade as Love wist to pursue.
Across the margent of the world I fled,
    And troubled the gold gateways of the stars,
    Smiting for shelter on their clangèd bars;
        Fretted to dulcet jars
And silvern chatter the pale ports o' the moon

I said to Dawn: Be sudden; to Eve: Be soon—
    With thy young skyey blossoms heap me over
        From this tremendous Lover!
Float thy vague veil about me, lest He see!
    I tempted all His servitors, but to find
My own betrayal in their constancy,
In faith to Him their fickleness to me,
    Their traitorous trueness, and their loyal deceit.
To all swift things for swiftness did I sue;
   Clung to the whistling mane of every wind.
      But whether they swept, smoothly fleet,
    The long savannahs of the blue;
        Or whether, Thunder-driven,
      They clanged His chariot 'thwart a heaven,
Plashy with flying lightnings round the spurn o' their feet:—
    Fear wist not to evade as Love wist to pursue.

      Still with unhurrying chase,
      And unperturbèd pace,
    Deliberate speed, majestic instancy,
      Came on the following Feet,
      And a Voice above their beat—
    'Naught shelters thee, who wilt not shelter Me.'

I sought no more that after which I strayed
      In face of man or maid;
But still within the little children's eyes
    Seems something, something that replies,
They at least are for me, surely for me!
I turned me to them very wistfully;
But just as their young eyes grew sudden fair
    With dawning answers there,
Their angel plucked them from me by the hair.
'Come then, ye other children, Nature's—share
With me' (said I) 'your delicate fellowship;
    Let me greet you lip to lip,

Let me twine you with caresses,
Wantoning
With our Lady-Mother's vagrant tresses,
Banqueting
With her in her wind-walled palace,
Underneath her azured daïs,
Quaffing, as your taintless way is,
From a chalice
Lucent-weeping out of the dayspring.'
So it was done:
I in their delicate fellowship was one—
Drew the bolt of Nature's secrecies.
I knew all the swift importings
On the willful face of skies;
I knew how the clouds arise
Spumèd of the wild sea-snortings;
All that's born or dies
Rose and drooped with; made them shapers
Of mine own moods, or wailful or divine—
With them joyed and was bereaven.
I was heavy with the even,
When she lit her glimmering tapers
Round the day's dead sanctities.
I laughed in the morning's eyes.
I triumphed and I saddened with all weather,
Heaven and I wept together,
And its sweet tears were salt with mortal mine;
Against the red throb of its sunset heart
I laid my own to beat,
And share commingling heat;
But not by that, by that, was eased my human smart.
In vain my tears were wet on Heaven's grey cheek.
For ah! we know not what each other says,
These things and I; in sound *I* speak—
Their sound is but their stir, they speak by silences.
Nature, poor stepdame, cannot slake my drouth;
Let her, if she would owe me,

251

Drop yon blue bosom-veil of sky, and show me
     The breasts o' her tenderness:
Never did any milk of hers once bless
        My thirsting mouth.
        Nigh and nigh draws the chase,
        With unperturbèd pace,
     Deliberate speed, majestic instancy,
        And past those noisèd Feet
        A voice comes yet more fleet—
     'Lo! naught contents thee, who content'st not Me.'

Naked I wait Thy love's uplifted stroke!
My harness piece by piece Thou hast hewn from me,
        And smitten me to my knee;
     I am defenceless utterly.
     I slept, methinks, and woke,
And, slowly gazing, find me stripped in sleep.
In the rash lustihead of my young powers,
     I shook the pillaring hours
And pulled my life upon me; grimed with smears,
I stand amid the dust o' the moulded years—
My mangled youth lies dead beneath the heap.
My days have crackled and gone up in smoke,
Have puffed and burst as sun-starts on a stream.
     Yea, faileth now even dream
The dreamer, and the lute the lutanist;
Even the linked fantasies, in whose blossomy twist
I swung the earth a trinket at my wrist,
Are yielding; cords of all too weak account
For earth, with heavy griefs so overplussed.
     Ah! is Thy love indeed
A weed, albeit an amaranthine weed,
Suffering no flowers except its own to mount?
     Ah! must—
     Designer infinite!—
Ah! must Thou char the wood ere Thou canst limn with it?
My freshness spent its wavering shower i' the dust;

And now my heart is as a broken fount,
Wherein tear-drippings stagnate, spilt down ever
      From the dank thoughts that shiver
Upon the sightful branches of my mind.
      Such is; what is to be?
The pulp so bitter, how shall taste the rind?
I dimly guess what Time in mists confounds;
Yet ever and anon a trumpet sounds
From the hid battlements of Eternity;
Those shaken mists a space unsettle, then
Round the half-glimpsèd turrets slowly wash again;
      But not ere Him who summoneth
      I first have seen, enwound
With glooming robes purpureal, cypress-crowned;
His name I know, and what His trumpet saith.
Whether man's heart or life it be which yields
      Thee harvest, must Thy harvest fields
      Be dunged with rotten death?

      Now of that long pursuit
      Comes on at hand the bruit;
   That Voice is round me like a bursting sea:
     'And is thy earth so marred,
     Shattered in shard on shard?
Lo, all things fly thee, for thou fliest Me!
Strange, piteous, futile thing!
Wherefore should any set thee love apart?
Seeing none but I makes much of naught' (He said)
'And human love needs human meriting:
     How has thou merited—
Of all man's clotted clay the dingiest clot?
     Alack, thou knowest not
How little worthy of any love thou art!
Whom wilt thou find to love ignoble thee,
     Save Me, save only Me?
All which I took from thee I did but take,
     Not for thy harms,

But just that thou might'st seek it in My arms.
        All which thy child's mistake
Fancies as lost, I have stored for thee at home;
        Rise, clasp My hand, and come!'

      Halts by me that footfall:
      Is my gloom, after all,
Shade of His hand, outstretched caressingly?
      'Ah, fondest, blindest, weakest,
      I am He whom thou seekest!
Thou dravest love from thee, who dravest Me.'

Wine and Water

G. K. CHESTERTON
(1 8 7 4 - 1 9 3 6)

Old Noah he had an ostrich farm and fowls on the largest scale,
He ate his egg with a ladle in an egg-cup big as a pail.
And the soup he took was Elephant Soup and the fish he took was
      Whale.
But they all were small to the cellar he took when he set out to sail;
And Noah he often said to his wife when he sat down to dine,
'I don't care where the water goes if it doesn't get into the wine.'

The cataract of the cliff of heaven fell blinding off the brink
As if it would wash the stars away as suds go down a sink,
The seven heavens came roaring down for the throats of hell to drink,
And Noah he cocked his eye and said, 'It looks like rain, I think,
The water has drowned the Matterhorn as deep as a Mendip mine,
But I don't care where the water goes if it doesn't get into the wine.'

But Noah he sinned, and we have sinned; on tipsy feet we trod,
Till a great big black teetotaller was sent to us for a rod,
And you can't get wine at the P.S.A. or chapel, or Eisteddfod,
But the curse of water has come again because of the wrath of God,
And water is on the Bishop's board and the Higher Thinker's shrine,
But I don't care where the water goes if it doesn't get into the wine.

The Donkey

G. K. CHESTERTON

When fishes flew and forests walked
　　And figs grew upon thorn,
Some moment when the moon was blood
　　Then surely I was born;

With monstrous head and sickening cry
　　And ears like errant wings,
The devil's walking parody
　　On all four-footed things.

The tattered outlaw of the earth,
　　Of ancient crooked will;
Starve, scourge, deride me: I am dumb,
　　I keep my secret still.

Fools! For I also had my hour;
　　One far fierce hour and sweet:
There was a shout about my ears,
　　And palms before my feet.

A Christmas Carol

G. K. CHESTERTON

The Christ-child lay on Mary's lap,
　　His hair was like a light.
(O weary, weary were the world,
　　But here is all aright.)

The Christ-child lay on Mary's breast,
　　His hair was like a star.
(O stern and cunning are the kings,
　　But here the true hearts are.)

The Christ-child lay on Mary's heart,
　　His hair was like a fire.
(O weary, weary is the world,
　　But here the world's desire.)

The Christ-child stood at Mary's knee,
　　His hair was like a crown.
And all the flowers looked up at Him,
　　And all the stars looked down.

Lepanto

G. K. CHESTERTON

White founts falling in the Courts of the sun,
And the Soldan of Byzantium is smiling as they run;
There is laughter like the fountains in that face of all men feared,
It stirs the forest darkness, the darkness of his beard,
It curls the blood-red crescent, the crescent of his lips,
For the inmost sea of all the earth is shaken with his ships.
They have dared the white republics up the capes of Italy,
They have dashed the Adriatic round the Lion of the Sea,
And the Pope has cast his arms abroad for agony and loss,
And called the kings of Christendom for swords about the Cross.
The cold queen of England is looking in the glass;
The shadow of the Valois is yawning at the Mass;
From evening isles fantastical rings faint the Spanish gun,
And the Lord upon the Golden Horn is laughing in the sun.

Dim drums throbbing, in the hills half heard,
Where only on a nameless throne a crownless prince has stirred,
Where, risen from a doubtful seat and half-attainted stall,
The last knight of Europe takes weapons from the wall,
The last and lingering troubadour to whom the bird has sung,
That once went singing southward when all the world was young.
In that enormous silence, tiny and unafraid,

Comes up along a winding road the noise of the Crusade.
Strong gongs groaning as the guns boom far,
Don John of Austria is going to the war,
Stiff flags straining in the night-blasts cold,
In the gloom black-purple, in the glint old-gold,
Torchlight crimson on the copper kettle-drums,
Then the tuckets, then the trumpets, then the cannon, and he comes.
Don John laughing in the brave beard curled,
Spurning of his stirrups like the thrones of all the world,
Holding his head up for a flag of all the free.
Love-light of Spain—hurrah!
Death-light of Africa!
Don John of Austria
Is riding to the sea.

Mahound is in his paradise above the evening star,
(*Don John of Austria is going to the war.*)
He moves a mighty turban on the timeless houri's knees,
His turban that is woven of the sunsets and the seas.
He shakes the peacock gardens as he rises from his ease,
And he strides among the tree-tops and is taller than the trees;
And his voice through all the garden is a thunder sent to bring
Black Azrael and Ariel and Ammon on the wing.
Giants and the Genii,
Multiplex of wing and eye,
Whose strong obedience broke the sky
When Solomon was king.

They rush in red and purple from the red clouds of the morn,
From the temples where the yellow gods shut up their eyes in scorn;
They rise in green robes roaring from the green hells of the sea
Where fallen skies and evil hues and eyeless creatures be;
On them the sea-valves cluster and the grey sea-forests curl,
Splashed with a splendid sickness, the sickness of the pearl;
They swell in sapphire smoke out of the blue cracks of the ground,—
They gather and they wonder and give worship to Mahound.

257

And he saith, 'Break up the mountains where the hermit-folk can hide,
And sift the red and silver sands lest bone of saint abide,
And chase the Giaours flying night and day, not giving rest,
For that which was our trouble comes again out of the West.
We have set the seal of Solomon on all things under sun,
Of knowledge and of sorrow and endurance of things done.
But a noise is in the mountains, in the mountains, and I know
The voice that shook our palaces—four hundred years ago:
It is he that saith not "Kismet"; it is he that knows not Fate;
It is Richard, it is Raymond, it is Godfrey in the gate!
It is he whose loss is laughter when he counts the wager worth,
Put down your feet upon him, that our peace be on the earth.'
For he heard drums groaning and he heard guns jar,
(*Don John of Austria is going to the war*).
Sudden and still—hurrah!
Bolt from Iberia!
Don John of Austria
Is gone by Alcalar.

St. Michael's on his Mountain in the sea-roads of the North
(*Don John of Austria is girt and going forth.*)
Where the grey seas glitter and the sharp tides shift
And the sea-folk labour and the red sails lift.
He shakes his lance of iron and he claps his wings of stone;
The noise is gone through Normandy; the noise is gone alone;
The North is full of tangled things and texts and aching eyes,
And dead is all the innocence of anger and surprise,
And Christian killeth Christian in a narrow dusty room.
And Christian dreadeth Christ that hath a newer face of doom,
And Christian hateth Mary that God kissed in Galilee,—
But Don John of Austria is riding to the sea.
Don John calling through the blast and the eclipse
Crying with the trumpet, with the trumpet of his lips,
Trumpet that sayeth *ha!*
Domino Gloria!
Don John of Austria
Is shouting to the ships.

King Philip's in his closet with the Fleece about his neck,
(*Don John of Austria is armed upon the deck.*)
The walls are hung with velvet that is black and soft as sin,
And little dwarfs creep out of it and little dwarfs creep in.
He holds a crystal phial that has colours like the moon,
He touches, and it tingles, and he trembles very soon,
And his face is as a fungus of a leprous white and grey
Like plants in the high houses that are shuttered from the day,
And death is in the phial and the end of noble work,
But Don John of Austria has fired upon the Turk.
Don John's hunting, and his hounds have bayed—
Booms away past Italy the rumour of his raid.
Gun upon gun, ha! ha!
Gun upon gun, hurrah!
Don John of Austria
Has loosed the cannonade.

The Pope was in his chapel before day or battle broke,
(*Don John of Austria is hidden in the smoke.*)
The hidden room in man's house where God sits all the year,
The secret window whence the world looks small and very dear.
He sees as in a mirror on the monstrous twilight sea
The crescent of his cruel ships whose name is mystery;
They fling great shadows foe-wards, making Cross and Castle dark,
They veil the plumèd lions on the galleys of St. Mark;
And above the ships are palaces of brown, black-bearded chiefs,
And below the ships are prisons where with multitudinous griefs,
Christian captives sick and sunless, all a labouring race repines
Like a race in sunken cities, like a nation in the mines.
They are lost like slaves that swat, and in the skies of morning hung
The stairways of the tallest gods when tyranny was young.
They are countless, voiceless, hopeless as those fallen or fleeing on
Before the high Kings' horses in the granite of Babylon.
And many a one grows witless in his quiet room in hell
Where a yellow face looks inward through the lattice of his cell,
And he finds his God forgotten, and he seeks no more a sign—
(*But Don John of Austria has burst the battle line!*)

259

Don John pounding from the slaughter-painted poop,
Purpling all the ocean like a bloody pirate's sloop,
Scarlet running over on the silvers and the golds,
Breaking of the hatches up and bursting of the holds,
Thronging of the thousands up that labour under sea
White for bliss and blind for sun and stunned for liberty.
Vivat Hispania!
Domino Gloria!
Don John of Austria
Has set his people free!

Cervantes on his galley sets the sword back in the sheath
(*Don John of Austria rides homeward with a wreath.*)
And he sees across a weary land a straggling road in Spain,
Up which a lean and foolish knight forever rides in vain,
And he smiles, but not as Sultans smile, and settles back the blade. . . .
(*But Don John of Austria rides home from the Crusade.*)

The House of Christmas

G. K. CHESTERTON

There fared a mother driven forth
Out of an inn to roam;
In the place where she was homeless
All men are at home.
The crazy stable close at hand,
With shaking timber and shifting sand,
Grew a stronger thing to abide and stand
Than the square stones of Rome.

For men are homesick in their homes,
And strangers under the sun,
And they lay their heads in a foreign land
Whenever the day is done.
Here we have battle and blazing eyes,

And chance and honour and high surprise,
But our homes are under miraculous skies
Where the yule tale was begun.

A Child in a foul stable,
Where the beasts feed and foam,
Only where He was homeless
Are you and I at home;
We have hands that fashion and heads that know,
But our hearts we lost—how long ago!—
In a place no chart nor ship can show
Under the sky's dome.

This world is wild as an old wives' tale,
And strange the plain things are.
The earth is enough and the air is enough
For our wonder and our war;
But our rest is as far as the fire-drake swings
And our peace is put in impossible things
Where clashed and thundered unthinkable wings
Round an incredible star.

To an open house in the evening
Home shall men come,
To an older place than Eden
And a taller town than Rome.
To the end of the way of the wandering star,
To the things that cannot be and that are,
To the place where God was homeless
And all men are at home.

The Convert

G. K. CHESTERTON

After one moment when I bowed my head
And the whole world turned over and came upright,
And I came out where the old road shone white,
I walked the ways and heard what all men said,
Forests of tongues, like autumn leaves unshed,
Being not unlovable but strange and light;
Old riddles and new creeds, not in despite
But softly, as men smile about the dead.

The sages have a hundred maps to give
That trace their crawling cosmos like a tree.
They rattle reason out through many a sieve
That stores the sand and lets the gold go free:
And all these things are less than dust to me
Because my name is Lazarus and I live.

Tarantella

HILAIRE BELLOC
(1870–   )

Do you remember an Inn,
Miranda?
Do you remember an Inn?
And the tedding and the spreading
Of the straw for a bedding,
And the fleas that tease in the High Pyrenees,
And the wine that tasted of the tar?
And the cheers and the jeers of the young muleteers,
(Under the vine of the dark veranda)?

Do you remember an Inn,
Miranda?
Do you remember an Inn?
And the cheers and the jeers of the young muleteers
Who hadn't got a penny,
And who weren't paying any,
And the hammer at the doors and the din?
And the *hip! hop! hap!*
Of the clap
Of the hands to the twirl and the swirl
Of the girl gone chancing,
Glancing,
Dancing,
Backing and advancing,
Snapping of the clapper to the spin
Out and in—
And the *ting, tong, tang* of the guitar!
Do you remember an Inn,
Miranda,
Do you remember an Inn?

Never more,
Miranda,
Never more,
Only the high peaks hoar:
And Aragon a torrent at the door.
No sound
In the walls of the halls where falls
The tread
Of the feet of the dead on the ground.
No sound:
But the boom
Of the far waterfall like doom.

The South Country

HILAIRE BELLOC

When I am living in the Midlands
    That are sodden and unkind,
I light my lamp in the evening:
    My work is left behind;
And the great hills of the South Country
    Come back into my mind.

The great hills of the South Country
    They stand along the sea;
And it's there walking in the high woods
    That I could wish to be,
And the men that were boys when I was a boy
    Walking along with me.

The men that live in North England
    I saw them for a day:
Their hearts are set upon the waste fells,
    Their skies are fast and grey;
From their castle-walls a man may see
    The mountains far away.

The men that live in West England
    They see the Severn strong,
A-rolling on rough water brown
    Light aspen leaves along.
They have the secret of the Rocks,
    And the oldest kind of song.

But the men that live in the South Country
    Are the kindest and most wise,
They get their laughter from the loud surf,
    And the faith in their happy eyes

Comes surely from our Sister the Spring
    When over the sea she flies;
The violets suddenly bloom at her feet,
    She blesses us with surprise.

I never get between the pines
    But I smell the Sussex air;
Nor I never come on a belt of sand
    But my home is there.
And along the sky the line of the Downs
    So noble and so bare.

A lost thing could I never find,
    Nor a broken thing mend:
And I fear I shall be all alone
    When I get towards the end.
Who will there be to comfort me
    Or who will be my friend?

I will gather and carefully make my friends
    Of the men of the Sussex Weald;
They watch the stars from silent folds,
    They stiffly plough the field.
By them and the God of the South Country
    My poor soul shall be healed.

If I ever become a rich man,
    Or if ever I grow to be old,
I will build a house with deep thatch
    To shelter me from the cold,
And there shall the Sussex songs be sung
    And the story of Sussex told.

I will hold my house in the high wood
    Within a walk of the sea,
And the men that were boys when I was a boy
    Shall sit and drink with me.

Stanzas Written on Battersea Bridge
During a Southwesterly Gale

HILAIRE BELLOC

The woods and downs have caught the mid-December,
    The noisy woods and high sea-downs of home;
The wind has found me and I do remember
    The strong scent of the foam.

Woods, darling of my wandering feet, another
    Possesses you, another treads the Down;
The South West Wind that was my elder brother
    Has come to me in town.

The wind is shouting from the hills of morning,
    I do remember and I will not stay.
I'll take the Hampton road without a warning
    And get me clean away.

The Channel is up, the little seas are leaping,
    The tide is making over Arun Bar;
And there's my boat, where all the rest are sleeping
    And my companions are.

I'll board her, and apparel her, and I'll mount her,
    My boat, that was the strongest friend to me—
That brought my boyhood to its first encounter
    And taught me the wide sea.

Now shall I drive her, roaring hard a' weather,
    Right for the salt and leave them all behind;
We'll quite forget the treacherous streets together
    And find—or shall we find?

There is no Pilotry my soul relies on
    Whereby to catch beneath my bended hand,

Faint and beloved along the extreme horizon
　　That unforgotten land.

We shall not round the granite piers and paven
　　To lie to wharves we know with canvas furled,
My little Boat, we shall not make the haven—
　　It is not of the world.

Somewhere of English forelands grandly guarded
　　It stands, but not for exiles, marked and clean;
Oh! not for us. A mist has risen and marred it:—
　　My youth lies in between.

So in this snare that holds me and appals me,
　　Where Honour hardly lives nor loves remain,
The Sea compels me and my Country calls me,
　　But stronger things restrain.

England, to me that never have malingered,
　　Nor spoken falsely, nor your flattery used,
Nor even in my rightful garden lingered:—
　　What have you not refused?

Crusade

HILAIRE BELLOC

The kings come riding home from the Crusade,
　　The purple kings with all their mounted men.
They fill the street with clamorous cavalcade.
　　The kings have broken down the Saracen.
Singing a great song of the Eastern wars,
　　In crimson ships across the sea they came,
With crimson sails and diamonded dark oars
　　That made the Mediterranean flash like flame.

And, reading how in that dark month the ranks
    Formed on the edge of the desert, armoured all,
        I wished to God that I had been with them,
When Godfrey led the foremost of the Franks,
    And the first Norman leaped upon the wall,
        And young Lord Raymond stormed Jerusalem.

Her Faith

HILAIRE BELLOC

Because my faltering feet may fail to dare
    The first descendant of the steps of hell,
Give me the Word in time that triumphs there,
    I too must pass into the misty hollow
Where all our living laughter stops; and hark
The tiny stuffless voices of the dark
        Have called me, called me till I needs must follow.
        Give me the Word and I'll attempt it well.

Say it's the little winking of an eye
    Which in that issue is uncurtained quite,
A little sleep to help a moment by,
    Between the thin dawn and the large daylight.
Oh tell me more than e'er was hoped of men!
Say that's true now, and I'll believe it then.

Our Lord and Our Lady

HILAIRE BELLOC

They warned Our Lady for the Child
    That was Our blessed Lord,
And She took Him into the desert wild,
    Over the camel's ford.
And a long song She sang to Him
    And a short story told:
And She wrapped Him in a woolen cloak
    To keep Him from the cold.

But when Our Lord was grown a man,
    The Rich they dragged Him down,
And they crucified Him in Golgotha,
    Out and beyond the Town.

They crucified Him on Calvary,
    Upon an April day;
And because He had been Her little Son,
    She followed Him all the way.

Our Lady stood beside the Cross,
    A little space apart,
And when She heard Our Lord cry out,
    A sword went through Her heart.

They laid Our Lord in a marble tomb,
    Dead, in a winding sheet,
But Our Lady stands above the world
    With the white Moon at Her feet.

Duncton Hill

HILAIRE BELLOC

He does not die that can bequeathe
Some influence to the land he knows,
Or dares, persistent, interwreathe
Love permanent with the wild hedgerows;
    He does not die, but still remains
    Substantiate with his darling plains.

The spring's superb adventure calls
His dust athwart the woods to flame;
His boundary river's secret falls
Perpetuate and repeat his name.
    He rides his loud October sky:
    He does not die.   He does not die.

The beeches know the accustomed head
Which loved them, and a peopled air
Beneath their benediction spread
Comforts the silence everywhere;
    For native ghosts return and these
    Perfect the mystery in the trees.

So, therefore, though myself be crosst
The shuddering of that dreadful day
When friend and fire and home are lost,
And even children drawn away—
    The passer-by shall hear me still
    A boy that sings on Duncton Hill.

I See His Blood Upon the Rose

JOSEPH MARY PLUNKETT
(1 8 8 7 – 1 9 1 6)

I see His blood upon the rose
And in the stars the glory of His eyes,
His body gleams amid eternal snows,
His tears fall from the skies.

I see His face in every flower;
The thunder and the singing of the birds
Are but His voice—and carven by His power,
Rocks are His written words.

All pathways by His feet are worn,
His strong heart stirs the ever-beating sea,
His crown of thorns is twined with every thorn,
His cross is every tree.

Ode for a Master Mariner Ashore

LOUISE IMOGEN GUINEY
(1 8 6 1 – 1 9 2 0)

There in his room, whene'er the moon looks in,
And silvers now a shell, and now a fin,
And o'er his chart glides like an argosy,
Quiet and old sits he.
Danger! he hath grown homesick for thy smile.
Where hidest thou the while, heart's boast,
Strange face of beauty sought and lost,
Star-face that lured him out from boyhood's isle?
Blown clear from dull indoors, his dreams behold
Night-water smoke and sparkle as of old,

271

The taffrail lurch, the sheets triumphant toss
Their phosphor-flowers across.
Towards ocean's either rim the long-exiled
Wears on, till stunted cedars throw
A lace-like shadow over snow,
Or tropic fountains wash their agates wild.

Awhile, play up and down the briny spar
Odours of Surinam and Zanzibar,
Till blithely thence he ploughs, in visions new,
The Labradorian blue;
All homeless hurricanes about him break;
The purples of spent day he sees
From Samos to the Hebrides,
And drowned men dancing darkly in his wake.

Where the small deadly foam-caps, well descried,
Top, tier on tier, the hundred-mountained tide,
Away, and far away, his pride is borne,
Riding the noisy morn,
Plunges, and preens her wings, and laughs to know
The helm and tightening halyards still
Follow the urging of his will,
And scoff at sullen earth a league below.

Mischance hath barred him from his heirdom high,
And shackled him with many an inland tie,
And of his only wisdom made a jibe
Amid an alien tribe:
No wave abroad but moans his fallen state,
The trade-wind ranges now, the trade-wind roars!
Why is it on a yellowing page he pores?
Ah, why this hawser fast to a garden gate?

Thou friend so long withdrawn, so deaf, so dim,
Familiar Danger, O forget not him!
Repeat of thine evangel yet the whole
Unto his subject soul,

Who suffers no such palsy of her drouth,
Nor hath so tamely worn her chain,
But she may know that voice again,
And shake the reefs with answer of her mouth.

O give him back, before his passion fail,
The singing cordage and the hollow sail,
And level with those agèd eyes let be
The bright unsteady sea;
And move like any film from off his brain
The pasture wall, the boughs that run
Their evening arches to the sun,
The hamlet spire across the sown champaign;

And on the shut space and the trivial hour,
Turn the great floods! and to thy spousal bower,
With rapt arrest and solemn loitering,
Him whom thou lovedst bring:
That he, thy faithful one, with praising lip,
Not having, at the last, less grace
Of thee than had his roving race,
Sum up his strength to perish with a ship.

The Kings

LOUISE IMOGEN GUINEY

A man said unto his Angel:
'My spirits are fallen low,
And I cannot carry this battle:
O brother! Where might I go?

'The terrible Kings are on me
With spears that are deadly bright;
Against me so from the cradle
Do fate and my fathers fight.'

Then said to the man his Angel:
'Thou wavering witless soul,
Back to the ranks! What matter
To win or to lose the whole,

'As judged by the little judges
Who hearken not well, nor see?
Not thus, by the outer issue,
The Wise shall interpret thee.

'Thy will is the sovereign measure
And only event of things:
The puniest heart defying,
Were stronger than all these Kings.

'Though out of the past they gather,
Mind's Doubt, and Bodily Pain,
And pallid Thirst of the Spirit
That is kin to the other twain,

'And Grief, in a cloud of banners,
And ringletted Vain Desires,
And Vice, with spoils upon him
Of thee and thy beaten sires,—

'While Kings of Eternal evil
Yet darken the hills about,
Thy part is with broken sabre
To rise on the last redoubt;

'To fear not sensible failure,
Nor covet the game at all,
But fighting, fighting, fighting,
Die, driven against the wall.'

Song

[In Leinster]

LOUISE IMOGEN GUINEY

I try to knead and spin, but my life is low the while.
Oh, I long to be alone, and walk abroad a mile;
Yet if I walk alone, and think of naught at all,
Why from me that's young should the wild tears fall?

The shower-sodden earth, the earth-colored streams,
They breathe on me awake, and moan to me in dreams
And yonder ivy fondling the broke castle-wall,
It pulls upon my heart till the wild tears fall.

The cabin-door looks down a furze-lighted hill,
And far as Leighlin Cross the fields are green and still;
But once I hear the blackbird in Leighlin hedges call,
The foolishness is on me, and the wild tears fall!

The Last Communion

[In Memory of My Father, Wilfrid Ward]

LEO WARD

(1 8 9 6 - 1 9 4 2)

There is a time wherein eternity
Takes rest upon the world; King Charity
Bowed to our fallen state, the God of Grace
Made visible upon a human face;—
When the deep Harmony, the eternal Word,
The unfallen Wisdom, only love has heard,
Touches the troubled body, bruised and hard
With the long fight, yet now set heavenward,—
When the deep argument of souls must cease,
Dying, to meet the victory of peace!

Four Friends

LEO WARD

Full life, sweet rest, great love that cannot cease—
  Surely Bach saw the beatific host!
  As the deep waters of the Holy Ghost
On young Mozart rained purity and ease—
'Twas a full heart, God-centered and at peace;
   While, from that awful gloom where souls are lost,
   Or raised to the height of hope, confessed and crossed,
The vision of Beethoven sought release,

Taking each beam of grace that pierced his world
  To light the fearsome steps from hell to Heaven
   And paint the hard-won victory over death! . . .
And now upon life's battle Franck has hurled
  The mystery of Christ: yea, death is riven,
   And nature one with God, at Nazareth!

Assisi

ALFRED NOYES
(1 8 8 0 –   )

I know a city on a hill, a mountain's castled crown,
Where, like the stairs the angels tread, the streets go up and down,
A city very small and kind and full of strange renown.

It stands upon an eastern height and looks towards the West.
Far off, it sees Perugia, its ancient foe, at rest;
And all the birds of Italy are gathered to its breast.

So small, so kind, but smaller far in the dim gulf below,
The world of men and all the tides that toss them to and fro,
While on its crag that city stands, crowned with the sunset glow.

Still, like a leen dark cypress there, against the clouds on high,
Brother of sun and moon and star, he towers into the sky,
As long ago, with arms up-stretched, while all things else went by.

Stone of his own immortal hill has made those ramparts bright,
The warm white stone that glows at dusk with a soft unearthly light,
And delicate tones of heaven's own rose while the plains are lost in
        night.

They told me of the lamp-lit tomb where dust in dust was laid,
Of painted wings from Paradise that on their walls decayed;
But not of this, this flower of light, that fades, and cannot fade.

They did not tell me how it chanced that the small bright streets were
        bare,
And hushed for love, as love went up, by cloister and winding stair,
Till a little lamp-lit window shone like an altar lit for prayer.

Oh bravely, bravely flash the swords beneath St. Peter's dome.
Proudly the silver trumpets ring across the world from Rome;
But this was on a higher hill, and a little nearer home.

A little nearer home that night, when skies had ceased to glow;
And the great plain of Umbria was dark as death below,
Assisi grew into the light, as flowers and children grow.

Creation

ALFRED NOYES

In the beginning, there was nought
    But Heaven, one Majesty of Light
Beyond all speech, beyond all thought,
    Beyond all depth, beyond all height,

Consummate Heaven, the first and last,
    Enfolding in its perfect prime
No future rushing to the past,
    But one rapt Now, that knew not Space or Time.

Formless it was, being gold on gold,
    And void—but with that complete Life
Where music could no wings unfold
    Till lo, God smote the strings of strife!
'Myself unto Myself am Throne,
    Myself unto Myself am Thrall
I that am All, am all alone,'
    He said, 'Yea, I have nothing, having all.'

And, gathering round His mount of bliss
    The angel-squadrons of His will,
He said, 'One battle yet there is
    To win, one vision to fulfil!
Since Heaven where'er I gaze expands,
    And power that knows no strife or cry,
Weakness shall bind and pierce My hands
    And make a world for Me wherein to die.

'All might, all vastness and all glory
    Being Mine, I must descend and make
Out of My heart, a song, a story
    Of little hearts that burn and break;
Out of My passion without end
    I will make little azure seas,
And into small sad fields descend
    And make green grass, white daisies, rustling trees.'

Then shrank His angels, knowing He thrust
    His arms out East and West and gave
For every little dream of dust
    Part of His life as to a grave!

'*Enough, O Father, for Thy words*
   Have pierced Thy hands!' But, low and sweet,
He said, 'Sunsets and streams and birds,
   And drifting clouds!'—The purple stained His feet.—

'*Enough!*' His angels moaned in fear,
   '*Father, Thy words have pierced Thy side!*'
He whispered, 'Roses shall grow there,
   And there must be a hawthorn tide,
And ferns dewy at dawn,' and still
   They moaned—'*Enough, the red drops bleed!*'
'And,' sweet and low, 'on every hill,'
   He said, 'I will have flocks and lambs to lead.'

His angels bowed their heads beneath
   Their wings till that great pang was gone:
'*Pour not Thy soul—out unto death!*'
   They moaned; and still His Love flowed on,
'There shall be small white wings to stray
   From bliss to bliss, from bloom to bloom,
And blue flowers in the wheat; and—' '*Stay!*
   Speak not!' they cried, '*the word that seals Thy tomb!*'

He spake—'I have thought of a little child
   That I will have there to embark
On small adventures in the wild,
   And front slight perils in the dark;
And I will hide from him and lure
   His laughing eyes, with suns and moons,
And rainbows that shall not endure;
   And—when he is weary, sing him drowsy tunes.'

His angels fell before Him weeping
   '*Enough! Tempt not the gates of Hell!*'
He said, 'His soul is in his keeping
   That we may love each other well,

And lest the dark too much affright him,
    I will strow countless little stars
Across his childish skies to light him
    That he may wage in peace his mimic wars;

'And oft forget Me as he plays
    With swords and childish merchandize,
Or with his elfin balance weighs,
    Or with his foot-rule metes the skies;
Or builds his castles by the deep,
    Or tunnels through the rocks, and then—
Turns to Me as he falls asleep,
    And in his dreams, feel for My hand again.

'And when he is older he shall be
    My friend and walk here by My side;
Or—when he wills—grow young with Me,
    And, to that happy world where once we died
Descending through the calm blue weather,
    Buy life once more with our immortal breath,
And wander through the little fields together,
    And taste of Love and Death.'

The Messenger

ALFRED NOYES

And, in the night, the Spirit came
    And softly smiled, and said—
I am the messenger of God.
    I am the happy dead.

I cannot tell you what I see
    Or whisper what I know;
But through and through your three-walled sleep
    Our shining legions go.

From worlds outside your Time and Space
  (You cannot know how near)
You cannot see the happy face
  That bends above you, dear.

I cannot grieve to see your grief
  More than a mother may
Who stoops above her child to soothe
  Its midnight fears away.

I have been near you all the while,
  I watched you, while you slept—
Then morning broke, then morning broke,
  And I forgot, and wept.

The Double Fortress

ALFRED NOYES

Time, wouldst thou hurt us? Never shall we grow old.
  Break as thou wilt these bodies of blind clay,
Thou canst not touch us here, in our stronghold,
  Where two, made one, laugh all thy powers away.

Though ramparts crumble and rusty gates grow thin,
  And our brave fortress dwine to a hollow shell,
Thou shalt hear heavenly laughter, far within,
  Where, young as Love, two hidden lovers dwell.

We shall go clambering up our twisted stairs
  To watch the moon through rifts in our grey towers.
Thou shalt hear whispers, kisses, and sweet prayers
  Creeping through all our creviced walls like flowers.

Wouldst wreck us, Time? When thy dull leaguer brings
The last wall down, look heavenward. We have wings.

281

You That Sing in the Blackthorn

ALFRED NOYES

Tell me you
 That sing in the black-thorn
Out of what Mind
 Your melody springs.
Is it the World-soul
 Throbs like a fountain
Up through the throat
 Of an elf with wings?

Five sweet notes
 In a golden order,
Out of that deep realm
 Quivering through,
Flashed like a phrase
 Of light through darkness.
But *Who* so ordered them?
 Tell me, *Who?*

You whose throats
 In the rain-drenched orchard
Peal your joys
 In a cadenced throng;
You whose wild notes,
 Fettered by Beauty,
Move like the stars
 In a rounded song;

Yours is the breath
 But *Whose* is the measure,
Shaped in an ecstasy
 Past all art?
Yours is the spending;
 Whose is the treasure?

Yours is the blood-beat;
  Whose is the heart?

Minstrels all
    That have woven your houses
Of withies and twigs
    With a Mind in-wrought,
Ye are the shuttles;
    But, out of what Darkness
Gather your thoughtless
    Patterns of thought?

Bright eyes glance
    Through your elfin doorways,
Roofed with rushes,
    And lined with moss.
Whose are the voiceless
    Pangs of creation?
Yours is the wild bough:
    Whose is the *Cross*?

Carols of light
    From a lovelier kingdom,
Gleams of a music
    On earth unheard,
Scattered like dew
    By the careless wayside,
Pour through the lifted
    Throat of a bird.

Old Man Mountain

ALFRED NOYES

Old Man Mountain had a one-mule track,
And a lump of quartz in the hump on his back—

Quartz that glinted with a hint of gold;
His bones were granite. He was æons old.

But he slept like a child, with a squirrel on his breast,
And his wild-hawk's feather and his eagle's nest,

While the chipmunks nibbled at their nuts in his bed,
And the mountain deer walked over his head.

Old Man Mountain had honey for the bear.
He had sage at his feet and snow on his hair.

His beard was a pine-wood. His knuckles and his knees
Were hard and gnarled as his live-oak trees.

He was kin to the Rockies, those bleak-souled kings,
But his heart was fixed on kindlier things.
And he liked the song that a chickadee sings.

So he looked at the ranch on the slopes below,
Where the peach-bloom shone like a rosier snow,

Where the ghost of an Angelus tolled again
From an old white tower that remembered Spain.

For the purple canyons grew dark and deep,
And the sea and the palm-trees whispered sleep,

Where softly a-glow on her cypressed hill,
Santa Barbara, hushed and still,

Shone like a pearl in that rosary strung
By the Brothers in grey when the West was young,

And their worn feet straightened the King's Highway
From San Diego to Monterey.

Then the ghost of a bell at Capistrano
Called to a ghost at lost Solano.

The rose-light died from the soft white walls,
And, alone with his crags, where the wild-hawk calls,

Old Man Mountain felt the sky growing cold . . .
But he knew that the tale was not yet told.

He looked at the stars, as a mountain dares,
And the clouds drew round him, while he said his prayers.

Messages

[From The Last Voyage]

ALFRED NOYES

Messages,—from the dead?
Thou hast not heard them? No;
Nor shalt thou ever hear
What whisperings come and go.
But, when thou hast bowed thy head
In the quietude of despair,
When thou hast ceased to listen,
A meaning shall draw near
And startle thee like a light,
From valleys of surprise,
Opening out of sight
Behind thee; for 'tis written
They must not meet thine eyes.
Between effect and cause
They dare not intervene.
From the unseen to the seen
Their roads are Nature's laws;
But, through them, they can breathe

What none could speak aloud;
And quietly inter-wreathe
Through sea-wave and white cloud
Strange gleams of loveliness
Whose deep unearthly drift
Thou couldst not even guess;
Light that no eyes can see;
Music no ear hath heard;
Till they strike home to thee
Through star and sunset rift
Or the cry of a wandering bird;
And where the rainbow shone
Across unshadowing skies,
Clear as through tear-lashed eyes
Thy love smiles, and is gone.

Rememberest thou that hour,
Under the naked boughs,
When, desolate and alone,
Returning to thy house,
Thou stoodst amazed to find
Dropt on the lintel-stone
Which thou hadst left so bare,
A radiant dew-drenched flower—
And thou couldst never know
Whose hand had dropt it there,
Fragrant and white as snow,
To save thy soul from hell?
Yet, in thy deepest mind,
Thou didst know, and know well.

Not thine to understand
How the two worlds accord,—
The will of Love, our Lord,
With this dark wheel of Time.
Yet thou didst hear them chime
Like one deep Sanctus bell

For the pure host revealed
In the exquisite miracle
Of that white chance-dropt flower;
A flower from a known field,
And dropt by a mortal hand;
But, breathing its wild dew,
O, simply as tears flow,
Thou didst most surely know
The hand from which it fell
Was thy lost angel's, too.

Under the Pyrenees

ALFRED NOYES

Under the Pyrenees,
    Where the warm sea-wind drifts thro' tamarisk boughs,
There is a lonely house upon a hill-top
    That I shall never forget or see again.

I shall not see that garden, filled with roses,
    On the high sun-burnt plateau, girdled round
With that low parapet, on the lonely hill-top,
    By sunlight, or by moonlight, ever again.

In that lost garden stands a little chapel,
    And the strange ship wherein we made our voyage,
Our little mortal ship of thoughts and visions,
Hangs there, in chains, before the twilit altar.
    The doors are locked. The lamp is quenched for ever;
Though, at one corner of the house, Our Lady
    Looks out, across the valley, to the sea.

And, on the landward side, across a valley
    Purple as grapes in autumn, the dark mountains,
With peaks like broken swords, and splintered helmets,
    Remembering Roland's death, are listening still.

Look down, look down, upon the sunlit valley,
    Over the low white parapet of that garden;
And you shall see the long white road go winding
    Through the Basque vineyards. . . .
           But you shall not see
One face, nor shall you hear one voice that whispered
    Love, as it died. . . .
           Only one wooden Image
Knows where she knelt, among the lonely mountains
    At Roncesvalles, in one last prayer for me. . . .

The Strong City

[From *The Last Voyage*]

ALFRED NOYES

And, when it was darkest, I came to a strong City.
    No earthly tongue can tell how I journeyed there,
Deaf to this world's compassion,
    Blind to its pity,
With a heart wrung empty, even of its last dumb prayer.

I had left the clattering throngs in the night behind me,
    And stumbled into a desert that had no name.
Torn, bleeding of foot,
    Through cactus and thorn I stumbled,
And, when it was darkest, to that strong City I came.

Gate there was none, nor window. It towered above me
    Like a vast fortress into the midnight sky.
And I beat on the granite walls,
    But I found no entry;
And the blood ran over my wrists, but I heard no reply.

288

Yet, I knew well—no tongue can tell how I knew it—
　　Though the walls were harder than adamant, blacker than night,
Within that City
　　　Was glory beyond all glory
Of wisdom and power enthroned in absolute light.

Could I have entered there, all doubts were over.
　　　Stones would be bread at last, and water wine;
All questioning closed
　　　In absolute vision;
The long sad riddle solved, and the answer mine.

But oh, on those cloud-wreathed walls there stood no sentry.
Naked as cliffs they towered, abrupt as doom.
　　　No shining gate,
　　　　　No shadowy postern,
No least small spark of a window broke their gloom.

Hour after hopeless hour I groped around them.
　　　League after league, I followed that girdling wall.
Burning with thirst,
　　　I dragged through the drifted sand-heaps
Round its great coigns, and found them adamant all.

Once, every league, a shadowy buttress,
　　　Like a vast Sphinx outstretched in the moon's pale sheen,
Loomed through the night,
　　　With flanks worn sleek by the sand-storms,
And calm strange face that gazed as at worlds unseen.

I groped around them; I groped around them;
　　　Stared up at their cold eyes and found them stone;
And crawled on, on,
　　　Till I overtook strange footprints
Going my way, and knew them for my own;

Strange footprints, clotted with blood, in the sand before me,
　　Trailing the hopeless way I had trailed before;
For, in that night,
　　I had girdled the whole dark City,
Feeling each adamant inch, and found no door.

I fell on my face in the rank salt of the desert.
　　Slow, hot, like blood, out of my hopeless eyes,
The salt tears bled.
　　The salt of the desert drank them,
And I cried, once, to God, as a child cries.

Then, then, I cannot tell
　　What strange thing happened,
Only, as at a breath of the midnight air,
　　These eyes, like two staunched wounds, had ceased their bleeding
And my despair had ended my despair.

Far over the desert, like shadows trailed by a moon-cloud,
　　I saw a train of mourners, two by two,
Following an open coffin.
　　They halted near me.
And I beheld, once more, the face I knew.

Blissful the up-turned face—the cold hands folded;
　　Blissful the up-turned face, cold as cold stone,
Cold as a midnight flower.
　　I bent above it—
Strange sweet cold kiss, the saddest earth had known.

Quietly they moved on, in slow procession.
　　They breathed no prayer. They sang no funeral song.
Up to the adamant walls
　　Of that strong City,
Slowly they moved, a strange inscrutable throng.

Behind their shining burden they stole like shadows
    Up to the shadowy City, two by two.
And like two ponderous doors of a tomb revolving
    Two stones in the wall swung back,
        And they passed through.

I followed after. I followed after.
    Theirs was the secret key and the sure goal:
And the adamant doors
    Revolved again like midnight,
And closed, like a silent thunder, behind my soul.

Dark! It was dark; but through that strange new darkness
    Great aisles of beauty rapturously burned;
And I stole on,
    Like a remembering pilgrim
From a long exile, now at last returned.

All round me burned strange lights and banners.
    Above, great arches grasped and spanned the sky.
Then, like a bell,
    In the armoured hands of Michael,
I heard Time ring its æons out and die.

I saw that strange procession winding
    On through a veil that shielded my dazed sight
From the absolute Dark that would have drowned me
    At the first dreadful touch of absolute Light.

Yet I saw glory on glory on glory
    Burning through those ethereal folds
Dusked by a myriad dawns, a myriad sunsets
    With smouldering mercies, merciful blood-red golds.

Before it smoked the Eternal Altar
    Branched with great trembling lights that shone
As though at last all stars, all constellations,
    Had swung to their true place before God's throne.

There, there, at last, they burned in order,
    Round that high Altar, under that rich East.
All clouds, all snows, on that pure Table
    Were spread like one white cloth for God's own feast.

And I heard *Sanctus, Sanctus, Sanctus,*
    Dominus Deus, echoing everywhere,
In tongues of earth, in tongues of ocean,
    In tongues of fire, in tongues of air.

Far off, I heard once more, the centuries pealing
    Like one brief sacring bell. I heard Time die.
I saw Space fading, forms dissolving,
    I saw the Host uplifted high.

Spirit and Substance, Victim-Victor,
    One life in all, all lives in One,
Fast-bound to feed man's bounded vision
    Shone through that strict concentering Sun.

Anima Mundi, World-Sustainer
    Sower to whom all seeds returned,
Through earth's dissolving mist of atoms
    The Body of God in splendour burned.

And I heard *Agnus, Agnus Dei,*
    Pleading for man with Love's own breath;
And Love drew near me,
    And Love drew near me
And I drank Life through God's own death.

Prayer of a Soldier in France

JOYCE KILMER
(1 8 8 6 – 1 9 1 8)

My shoulders ache beneath the pack
(Lie easier, Cross, upon His back).

I march with feet that burn and smart
(Tread, Holy Feet, upon my heart).

Men shout at me who may not speak
(They scourged Thy back and smote Thy cheek).

I may not lift a hand to clear
My eyes of salty drops that sear.

(Then shall my fickle soul forget
Thy Agony of Bloody Sweat?)

My rifle hand is stiff and numb
(From Thy pierced palm red rivers come).

Lord, Thou didst suffer more for me
Than all the hosts of land and sea.

So, let me render back again
This millionth of Thy gift.   Amen.

The Plougher

PADRAIC COLUM
(*1 8 8 1 –*)

Sunset and silence! A man: around him earth savage, earth broken;
Beside him two horses—a plough!

Earth savage, earth broken, the brutes, the dawn-man there in the sunset,
And the Plough that is twin to the Sword, that is founder of cities!

'Brute-tamer, plough-maker, earth-breaker! Canst hear? There are ages
between us.
Is it praying you are as you stand there alone in the sunset?

'Surely our sky-born gods can be naught to you, earth child and earth
master?
Surely your thoughts are of Pan, or of Wotan, or Dana?

'Yet, why give thought to the gods? Has Pan led your brutes where
they stumble?
Has Dana numbed pain of the child-bed, or Wotan put hands to your
plough?

'What matter your foolish reply! O man, standing lone and bowed
earthward,
Your task is a day near its close. Give thanks to the night-giving God.'

Slowly the darkness falls, the broken lands blend with the savage;
The brute-tamer stands by the brutes, a head's breadth only above them.

A head's breadth? Ay, but therein is hell's depth, and the height up to
heaven,
And the thrones of the gods and their halls, their chariots, purples, and
splendours.

An Old Woman of the Roads

PADRAIC COLUM

Oh, to have a little house!
To own the hearth and stool and all!
The heaped-up sods upon the fire,
The pile of turf against the wall!

To have a clock with weights and chains
And pendulum swinging up and down!
A dresser filled with shining delph
Speckled and white and blue and brown!

I could be busy all the day
Clearing and sweeping hearth and floor,
And fixing on their shelf again
My white and blue and speckled store!

I could be quiet there at night
Beside the fire and by myself,
Sure of a bed, and loath to leave
The ticking clock and the shining delph!

Och! but I'm weary of mist and dark,
And roads where there's never a house nor bush,
And tired I am of bog and road,
And the crying wind and the lonesome hush!

And I am praying to God on high,
And I am praying Him night and day,
For a little house—a house of my own—
Out of the wind's and the rain's way.

A Cradle Song

PADRAIC COLUM

O men from the fields,
　　Come gently within.
Tread softly, softly,
　　O men coming in!

Mavourneen is going
　　From me and from you,
Where Mary will fold him
　　With mantle of blue!

From reek of the smoke
　　And cold of the floor
And the peering of things
　　Across the half-door.

O men of the fields,
　　Soft, softly come thro'.
Mary puts round him
　　Her mantle of blue.

Fuchsia Hedges in Connacht

PADRAIC COLUM

I think some saint of Eirinn wandering far
Found you and brought you here—
Demoiselles!
For so I greet you in this alien air!

And like those maidens who were only known
In their own land as daughters of the King,

Children of Charlemagne—
You have, by following that pilgrim-saint,
Become high vot'resses—
You have made your palace—beauty dedicate,
And your pomp serviceable:
You stand beside our folds!

I think you came from some old Roman land—
Most alien, but most Catholic you are:
Your purple is the purple that enfolds,
In Passion Week, the Shrine,
Your scarlet is the scarlet of the wounds:
You bring before our walls, before our doors,
Lamps of the Sanctuary;
And in this stony place
The time the robin sings,
Through your bells rings the Angelus!

The Stations of the Cross

PADRAIC COLUM

I

Here Pilate's Court is:
None may clatter nor call
Where the Wolf giving suck
To the Twins glares on all.
'Strip Him and scourge Him
Till flesh shows the blood,
And afterwards nail Him
On cross of wood.'

O Lord,
Silence in us the condemning word!

II

Heaven witnesseth, but only in the heart
Is any aid:
'They know not what they do,' and then on Him
The Cross is laid—
The Cross that's wide and long enough to bear
His flesh and bone:
A spectacle unto the crowded way,
The Man goes on.

The Father's will
May we know also, and may we fulfill!

III

Beneath the load
The knees quail;
The heart pants,
The joints fail;
Almost the bones break;
He faints, his breath being loss;
He sinks beneath the Cross!

May we
Be mindful of this road to Calvary!

IV

Jesus His Mother meets:
She looks on Him and sees
The Saviour in Her Son:
The Angel's word comes back:
Within her heart she says,
'Unto me let this be done!'
Still is she full of grace.

By us, too, be it won,
The grace that brings us revelation!

V

'If He should die upon the road
That were a turn of ill:
'Tis fixed the Crucifixion be
Upon that skull-shaped hill.
Ho, man who looks with pity on
The Man we take to death—
Bear you the Cross—I order it—
Until He wins back breath.'

We take,
Our hearts being moved, the Cross up for Thy sake!

VI

Down to her face His face He bends:
The helper she, the heartner:
His image in her cloth He leaves;
He leaves it, too, to all like her
Who serve within a little room,
But run to help outside the door,
Who mend and brighten needed things:
He leaves it to good hearts, the Poor!

May we, too, wait,
Like her, and help, and be compassionate!

VII

The Spirit is willing—aye,
But weak the flesh put on;
Deadly the Cross's weight;
He stumbles on a stone,
And lies upon the road,
Seeing His body's blood.

May we
Forget not in these times that agony!

VIII

Heavy the Cross is:
He drags beneath its beam,
Yet, women of Jerusalem,
Weep not for Him:
Weep for your children, rather,
For that they cannot see
The true Son of David,
The Saviour, shown ye.

O Lord,
Also to us say the revealing word!

IX

The skull-shaped hill is near:
The earth and heaven are bare
Of light, and sight, and sound;
He falls upon the ground,
Knowing that journey's end
Without one to befriend.

O Lord,
Bring us to Life according to Thy word!

X

'Wouldst have me share this cloth,
Dividing it with sword?—
Nay, fellow, we will keep it whole,
But hearken to my word:
Behind the Cross the dice
We'll throw; who wins will get
What's high enough in price
To pay a tavern debt.'

The vesture that makes one with Thee our soul,
May we keep whole!

XI

'This thong, I know, will last;
Draw out the arm and make it fast;
Through hand and board with strength
Drive the nail of mickle length.
Now, King of the Jews, in the sun,
Gape, for our work is done.'

God send
That our labors have no evil end!

XII

The birds are flying home,
Now darkened is the sky,
And He hath given up
With that great bitter cry
The ghost, and on the Cross
(His Mother stays by it),
The title rightly His,
KING—is writ.

May we draw near
Considering in our hearts what Man is here!

XIII

Though pitiful it is to see
The wounds, the broken Body,
(The body of Him that was
As fair as lily of the grass!)
Though the brow with thorns is riven,
And a spear through the side is driven,
It was all for our healing done,
Mother, by thy Son!

May we
This Body in its glory come to see!

XIV

Now in the tomb is laid
One who had neither house nor hall,
Who in the wide world walked,
Who talked with one and all;
Who told the sparrow's worth,
The lily's praises said,
Who kept wakeful in the garden,
Now in the tomb is laid.

His Spirit still doth move
On a new way of love!

L'ENVOI

Prince, by thine own darkened hour,
Live with me, heart and brain;
Let my hands not slip the rein!

Ah, how long ago the hour
Since a comrade rode with me:
Now, a moment, let me see

Thyself, lonely in the dark,
Perfect, without wound nor mark!

Wishes for My Son

[Born on St. Cecilia's Day, 1912]

THOMAS MacDONAGH
(*1 8 7 8 - 1 9 1 6*)

Now, my son, is life for you,
And I wish you joy of it,—
Joy of power in all you do,
Deeper passion, better wit

Than I had who had enough,
Quicker life and length thereof,
More of every gift but love.

Love I have beyond all men,
Love that now you share with me—
What have I to wish you then
But that you be good and free,
And that God to you may give
Grace in stronger days to live?

For I wish you more than I
Ever knew of glorious deed,
Though no rapture passed me by
That an eager heart could heed,
Though I followed heights and sought
Things the sequel never brought:

Wild and perilous holy things
Flaming with a martyr's blood,
And the joy that laughs and sings
Where a foe must be withstood,
Joy of headlong happy chance
Leading on the battle dance.

But I found no enemy,
No man in a world of wrong,
That Christ's word of Charity
Did not render clean and strong—
Who was I to judge my kind,
Blindest groper of the blind?

God to you may give the sight
And the clear undoubting strength
Wars to knit for single right,

Freedom's war to knit at length,
And to win, through wrath and strife,
To the sequel of my life,

But for you, so small and young,
Born on Saint Cecilia's Day,
I in more harmonious song
Now for nearer joys should pray—

Simple joys: the natural growth
Of your childhood and your youth.
Courage, innocence, and truth:

These for you, so small and young,
In your hand and heart and tongue.

The Maid

KATHERINE BRÉGY
(1 8 8 8 –   )

The whiteness of the lily once was thine,
O little maid, who watched Domremy's sheep—
Thy converse with the saints, whose words occult
Thou, like Another, in thy heart didst keep.

And thine the whiteness of the cleaving sword,
So blinding pure from out earth's blood-shedding,
When, in the gloom of Rheims' imperial shrine,
Thy lord of France was hallowed into King.

But now, more ardent whiteness wraps thee round,
O martyr-saint, rejected and betrayed. . . .
The sacrificial whiteness of the flame
Is thine—swift-soaring, unafraid!

The smoke is ours; its shame, its blindness, too,
The tears of the way thou valiantly hast trod;
But thou, white warrior maid, on high art raised,
A votive taper between us and God!

The Housewife's Prayer

BLANCHE MARY KELLY
(*1 8 8 1* –   )

Lady, who with tender word
Didst keep the house of Christ the Lord,
Who didst set forth the bread and wine
Before the Living Wheat and Vine,
Reverently didst make the bed
Whereon was laid the holy Head
That such a cruel pillow prest
For our behoof, on Calvary's crest;
Be beside me while I go
About my labors to and fro.
Speed the wheel and speed the loom,
Guide the needle and the broom,
Make my bread rise sweet and light,
Make my cheese come foamy white,
Yellow may my butter be
As cowslips blowing on the lea.
Homely though my tasks and small,
Be beside me at them all.
Then when I shall stand to face
Jesu in the judgment place,
To me thy gracious help afford,
Who art the Handmaid of the Lord.

The Mirror

BLANCHE MARY KELLY

Lord, make my soul
To mirror Thee,
Thyself alone
To shine in me,
That men may see
Thy love, Thy grace,
Nor note the glass
That shows Thy Face.

The Kingfisher

BLANCHE MARY KELLY

A lone kingfisher skims the river's crest,
Breast against crystal breast,
Winging his steady flight between two skies.
He needs not, like the lark, aloft to rise
To have his heaven in the firmament.
So, by Divine intent,
A mirrored heaven lies about their feet
Whose wings with steadfast beat
Bear them along the way of God's behest,
Breast on His breast.

Brother Juniper

BLANCHE MARY KELLY

As unto Francis Poverty,
So Folly was a bride to thee.
Not the jade that fashions quips
For the smiles of mocking lips,

And in the face of stony Death
Capers till she's out of breath,
But the maid that moves and sings
About divinely foolish things,
She that gives her substance all
For love, and laughs to find it small,
She that drew God's Son to be
A butt, a jest on Calvary,
And 'neath the leper's guise doth know
The King in his incognito.

The world is grown too wise, and we
Go our sad ways sensibly.
O would that our lean souls might win
Some grace of thine, God's harlequin,
Whose days were lavished like fool's gold
Upon his pleasures manifold.
'Would God,' cried Francis, on his knees,
'I had a forest of such trees!'

'Peace Is the Tranquillity of Order'
—St. Augustine

ROBERT WILBERFORCE
(*English Contemporary*)

The splendours of this passing world
    Reflected in the mind
Offer a more imperial prize
    To those who seek and find.

When I have found the way of peace
    No king surpasses me.
My rule extends beyond the land,
    Beyond the distant sea.

My palaces are numberless;
        A throne in every town;
A scepter can be mine at will
        While memories form my crown.

But if above this kingdom
        I abdicate my sway,
Fierce warfare suddenly breaks out.
        My realm's in disarray.

To govern all these imaged things,
        The subjects of our thought,
The secret of an ordered peace
        Is in the rule Christ taught.

Quarrel

JEAN MCDOUGALL
(*American Contemporary*)

I might have touched you where you lay
        Counting the long night hours away
In silence, pillowed hot and deep,
        Lying too quietly for sleep.

My tongue that struggles and is slow
        Was swift before to deal the blow,
But sudden pain could not disguise
        The sober judgment of your eyes.

I might have reached to take your hand—
        The gesture you would understand—
And failing utterance, to seek
        Your lips, the shelter of your cheek.

But dawn came up while the only talk
    In the room was made by a noisy clock
Stabbing, accusing, chattering, loud:
    Too proud, too proud, too proud, too proud.

Prodigal

ELLEN GILBERT
(*American Contemporary*)

Like a bird that trails a broken wing,
    I have come home to Thee;
Home from a flight and freedom
    That was never meant for me.

And I, who have known far spaces,
    And the fierce heat of the sun,
Ask only the shelter of Thy wings,
    Now that the day is done.

Like a bird that trails a broken wing,
    I have come home, at last. . . .
O hold me to Thy Heart once more,
    And hide me from the past.

The Spinner

CHARLES L. O'DONNELL
(1 8 8 4 - 1 9 3 4)

Mary the Mother of Jesus,
    A lady of high degree,
Sat by her cottage spinning
    In Nazareth of Galilee.

A light fell over her shoulder
    As she sat in the plane-tree's shade,
While a delicate lace of shadows
    The sun and the green leaves made.

Busy her foot on the treadle,
    And her wheel busily whirled
As a Child looked out from the doorway,
    A Child who had made the world.

Deftly she handled the distaff,
    And happily whirred her wheel
As the Child came down from the doorway
    And ran at her side to kneel.

'Mother,' He said as He watched her
    There while she sat and spun,
'Some things are more fair than I dreamed them
    The day that I made the sun.

'And you are My heart of all beauty,
    My star of all seas, of all lands—'
'Hush, Child,' whispered Mary His Mother,
    Her tears falling down on His hands.

Address to the Crown

CHARLES L. O'DONNELL

He made them and He called them good
As they had grown in the bramble wood,
Long and glistening, green and brown
Thorns that now in a woven crown
Approached to clasp His stricken head,
As gently chiding them He said:
'Children, My Thorns, on the wild thorn tree
That were your proper place to be.
Along your woods young April goes
And sweet in the brake is the wind that blows,
Here indeed you have lost your skies;
Why are you twisted circle-wise,
What do you here in the hands of men?'
And it seems the thorns gave answer then:
'You know, my Lord, it is not we
Have left our place on the bramble tree,
But evil hearts that cry for Blood
Have torn us away from the April wood.
There is a thing which men call sin,
We think it is this that drives us in:
With Blood above, and Blood below,
You know we would not have it so,
With Blood below, and Blood above,
Believe it is a clasp of love
We take upon Your holy head,
Forgive us living, and love us dead.'
And He who had made them and called them good,
The long sharp thorns of the young spring wood,
He bowed His holy head to them
And went to His death in their diadem.

Resolution

CHARLES L. O'DONNELL

Love, You have struck me straight, my Lord!
　　Past innocence, past guilt,
I carry in my soul the sword
　　You buried to the hilt.

And though to eyes in terrible pain
　　Heaven and earth may reel,
For fear You may not strike again
　　I will not draw the steel.

A Rime of the Rood

CHARLES L. O'DONNELL

A Word of mystery is told
　　Whose secret shall remain,
That the heart of happiness should ache
　　With hungering for pain.

That God in those years of silent
　　And sole eternity
Should know Himself a homeless Man
　　Dead on a wayside tree.

For in the mirror of His mind
　　All things that come to pass
Are, from the mystery of man
　　To the miracle of grass.

Himself is the enigma
　　That from His triune tower

Moves barefoot down those timeless coasts
  To make and meet His hour.

Before the fallen princes
  Set the balefires of their doom,
God from His central stillness
  Moves to a Maiden's womb.

He sees when we can not foresee,
  He does what we shall do,
And Rome is there, and its iron rule
  And the unborn race of the Jew.

All in His everlastingness,
  Before His time began,
Something there was that shook His world
  And made Him man.

Not yet had swung the planets
  No one was yet to name,
There was not king or country,
  Honor was not or shame.

Before a foot was on the earth
  Or any earth to tread,
God chose Himself a deathbed
  And God was dead.

Then worlds were turned where woods might grow
  With sap tides running free,
Unnumbered cycles making
  A tree for Him, a tree.

God, in His day that had no dawn,
  Visioned a fallen sky
Against whose storm-stirred edges
  Himself should hang and die.

And time came down to a little span
  When men contrived these bars
Known as a cross, esteemed a curse,
  An insult to the stars.

The Roman, when he broke the back
  Of Jewry and its pride,
Came with his legioned banners
  And this thing at his side.

Straight as a Roman spear and strong
  As a pine in the Norse wood,
The Roman brought the cross from Rome
  And its omen was not good.

High on a hill or by the road
  Where all might see who pass,
'This is the way,' the Roman said,
  'We deal with Barrabas.'

'And I, if I be lifted up,'—
  What infinite jest is this
On lips that had eternally
  A foretaste of that bliss?

Before the star of Lucifer
  Fell, or Eden's loss,
God in those years of wonder
  Was in love with the Cross.

They can be trusted, wood and iron,
  To do their hapless part,
Under the brawn of the Roman arms
  And the hate in the high priest's heart.

They fixed it firm in the blasted hill,
  He looked and called it good,

As the hour that He had hurried to
    Struck in His Blood.

A turn of pain and darkness,
    A space of tortured breath,
And every fibre of the wood
    Grows alive with His death.

An afternoon of April
    Fulfils the eternal plan
That evermore His men might say,
    'Behold the Man!'

That evermore while sight shall be,
    Cross-bar and upright rod
Shall bear to the eyes of all the world
    The broken body of God.

This is that terrible garment
    He could alone conceive—
A stiff red cloak of wood and iron
    His hand nailed to His sleeve.

Who walked His worlds of wonder,
    God of very God,—
He will not move in the shoes of iron
    Wherewith He now is shod.

Men shall not say a hidden Heart
    Is His and doubt thereat—
A Roman spear and a Roman arm
    Have seen to that.

Fixed in an iron certainty
    No power shall undo
God hangs, His own love story,
    And this tale is true.

There He shall be till the worlds are gone,
 In Manhood and Godhead,
He who so loved one little world,
 Love's and life's Giver, dead.

For Him men plough the desert,
 Furrow the foam for Him,
Because for them He trained His eyes
 Beyond the Seraphim.

Because before there was any thing
 Or any one but He,
God for His own Name's glory
 Put His Name on the tree.

And when the trump of doom shall blow
 To strike the living dumb,
The King in His beauty shall appear
 And His Kingdom come.

Then shall the top of heaven
 And the last deep be spanned
By the bridge the Roman soldiers built
 With its sign in Pilate's hand.

A bridge, a throne, a doorway,
 A banner, a reward,
Adorable as no other thing:
 The Cross of the Lord.

Ecce nunc in tenebris,
 Crux est lumen lucis,
Semper in coelestibus,
 Ecce lignum crucis!

Sequel to Finality

PATRICK F. KIRBY
(1 8 9 1 -   )

They drove the hammered nails into His hands,
His hands that shaped the hot sun overhead;
Then all prepared to return to their own lands,
Glad in the knowledge God at last was dead.

"Now Babel can be built, and none deny!
In its cool gardens shall we take our ease;
Nor need we fear the everseeing eye,—
Our gods shall be whatever gods we please.

"Ishtar shall guard us, mother of all men,
And Bel rejoice us when the winds blow spiced
From Indus. Wine and song shall glad us then,—
We never loved this wistful, pallid Christ!"

So each rode homeward. And by each one's side
Unseen One rode, Who had been crucified.

Rain

PATRICK F. KIRBY

Bright eyes and laughing lips,
    See, I will hold you here,
Close pressed against my heart,
    Away from fear.

Dark clouds are in the sky,
    And on the window-pane
Incessantly I hear
    The beat of rain.

And high above the wind
    The ceaseless tread of feet
That go from morn to night
    Along the street.

They weary of the rain,
    I think, and of the cold,—
It is so hard to bear
    When one is old.

And all the day they pass,
    Each one with drooping head,—
There are none walk the earth
    Except these dead!

Press closer, heart, and lift
    Lips to my lips, and smile,—
We, too, shall be in the rain
    A long, long while.

Song for These Days

PATRICK F. KIRBY

V.—Only from Chaos
    Is Creation;
    Only from the formless void
    Light struck a fiat
    And the emergent firmament
    Divided;

Only out of Chaos
Order
And all living things
And the great whales that inhabit the seas.

R.—We who were formed from earth's clods
Had purposed to become as gods,
Until the taste of brother's blood
Blinded us to brotherhood,
Until with eager joy we sold
Our rightful heritage for gold,
Until for satiated lust
We were content to be but dust.

V.—Moves any spirit
Now upon these black, shoreless waters?
Is there any voice to cry unto this darkness
"Let there be light,"
That light be again made,
That day divided from night?
That from this Chaos come
Order, and all fruitful things,—
Bearers of seed that renew the earth?
Is there any among us—?
Can any of this bloodless, bewildering generation
Breathe back into this calced, sterile clay
The breath of life?

R.—Now is the full circle run
And Chaos once again begun;
Now is neither day nor night,
Now is darkness one with light;
Now the ruined crumbling earth
Waits the word to give it birth,
And we who find our worlds destroyed
Ourselves are without form and void.

V.—Only from Chaos
    Is Creation;
    Only out of disorder
    Order;
    Only in the darkness
    Light;
    And in the deep unsounding silences
    The stars, singing.

R.—Let others raise the mighty song
    Of right triumphant over wrong,
    And bring to this despairing night
    The deep exultant joy of light;
    Let others with their breath restore
    To earth a living soul once more;
    Our treasures have fed moth and rust
    And we ourselves are only dust.

V.—Only out of Chaos
    Creation;
    Only out of confusion
    Order;
    Only from our decay
    The new shoots of a New Earth;
    Only out of our darkness
    Light unquenchable,
    And a new Heaven
    Filled with new stars!

ALL.—O Brave New World
    That shall come after us,—
    That shall be created from our chaos!

Consecration

PATRICK F. KIRBY

Silence,—and a muted bell rings;
Old words are spoken in an ancient tongue;
And music ceases; before these Holy things
    Be song unsung.

Within this Holy place none trod
Until the High Priest opened wide the door;
Now God and man are mingled in one God!
    Kneel and adore!

Across the wine-cup trembling hands
Move cruciform,—"these things—remembering Me";
Lifting a deathless Christ, the cross stands
    At Calvary!

Riddles

PATRICK F. KIRBY

Afterwards, let us make riddles,—
When the mind quickens, and the freed urge
Goes probing into dusty corridors,—
Afterward, we may speak
Of such things, and make riddles:
Not now would we let down the mind's gates!

Rather let us eschew profundities; explain
No ultimates; let us cogitate simplicities
In simple words suiting the dulled brain.

Let us talk now of equinoxes in procession,
And the red-shift in the spectrum, and mull datum
Indicative of uncertainties in light's speed.
Let us concern ourselves with nebular recession
With Relativity, and the structure of the atom.

Only take no heed
Of ultimates; have no speech
With ghosts; and avoid music! Dangerous
Are crickets and Beethoven
And all Poetry! speak not of summer nights
Fragrant with moonlight; nor of winds
Heavy with honeysuckle; nor of lovers
That walk softly among the cypresses,
Having achieved wisdom!
These things are riddles:
It is best to avert the eyes.
Come, let us discuss the parallaxes of stars,
("The eyes see stars,—
Or something behind eyes—")

Or consider the curvature of Space.
("No bound to Omicron, and in Omicron
Neither Alpha nor Omega!")

Lie still, Lazarus!
Not now would we let down the mind's gates.

Compline

PATRICK F. KIRBY

The day is over, Mother, see
How all are gathered at your knee;
If we forgot you all the day
And spent the time in idle play,

Forgive us now. At least you knew
That night would bring us back to you,
And when the last brief prayer was said
Your arms would fold us safe in bed.

Some of us danced the hours away
Or sat at table all the day,
And others, playing in the sand
Built towns and temples,—there they stand!
What matter if we built beside
The sea's relentless, reckless tide;
We found it pleasant sport to play,—
How else could we have spent the day?

And many played a soldier's game
For crowns and victories and fame;
A few were presidents and kings,
Perplexed about a thousand things.
Some of us (Was the wisdom ours?)
Looked on as others spent the hours,
And laughed. Now our brief day is past,
And, Mother, here we are at last.

Ordination

SISTER MARY IMMACULATE

You have no mortal lineaments this day.
   In eyes where once I saw my own, I find
   The soul of God. My son, I cannot bind
Your strength; no sinews that I gave can stay
Nor compass it. My fetters must give way
   Before all might, and flesh my love designed
   To love's infinity: a sign is signed
Indelibly with spirit on this clay.

323

Yet you are mine, my son! I walked a far,
　　Deep valley, seeking you, and showed your wild
　　　　Young feet this pilgrimage. What shall I dread
When you lead home, whence all our questings are?
　　　Your eyes my light, your strength my staff, O child!
　　　　　And for my hunger, you will give me Bread.

Identity

SISTER MARY HELEN

Should you meet a little saint
　　Abroad in heaven town,
Shy and sweet and gentle,
　　In a modest gown;

Should you find her worrying
　　About such things
As broken harp cords
　　Or bruised wings;

Should you see her glancing
　　Down toward earth,
Then she is the mother
　　Who gave me birth.

Should she step cautiously
　　Out among the stars,
When Peter isn't looking
　　And let down the bars,

So that all the sinners
　　May quietly slip in
That God may forgive them
　　And wash away their sin;

Should she seem uneasy
    When Michael wields his sword,
Then she is my mother,
    The handmaid of the Lord.

Should you see her watching
    With an anxious air
As every newcomer
    Mounts the golden stair,

Eager and expectant,
    She's hoping to see
A ragged little sinner
    Looking like me.

Should you see her wandering
    Far out of sight,
Pray do not blame her,
    Heaven is so bright,

And she, little grey bird,
    Seeks a quiet nest
Among the birds and flowers
    Where she may rest,

Until all her children
    Are safely home at last,
And the days of waiting
    And sorrow are past.

Should you chance to meet her,
    Tell her, my friend,
That we love and need her
    World without end.

November Afternoons

SISTER M. MADELEVA

(1 8 8 7 -   )

Now they have come, those afternoons in November,
    When all the air is still and branches are bare,
And the long, lovely light that I remember
    Invades with luminous peace the untroubled air.

Off to the west a dozen trees together
    Stand in grey loveliness, bemused with light;
Slender and silver they stand in the autumn weather,
    Waiting the inevitable winter, the inevitable night.

Blossoming light they bear as a single flower,
    And silence more singing sweet than a lone bird's call.
Off to the west I stand, sharing their hour,
    At peace with beauty and needing no song at all.

Gates

SISTER M. MADELEVA

The oranges at Jaffa gate
Are heaped in hills; men sell and buy
Or sit and watch the twisted road
Or David's tower against the sky.

The Golden Gate is walled with stone.
No king can pass nor prophet see
The valley of Jehoshaphat,
The olives of Gethsemane.

St. Stephen's is a quiet gate,
A simple door that lets in dawn.

Its hill, its walls, its ancient stones,
What strange things they have looked upon!

Asses, belabored, stumble past;
Traffickers clamor; priests debate;
A child begs alms; a blind man gropes
To sunshine at Damascus gate.

The world has narrow gates and wide;
Men seek their loves through all of them,
And I have come here, seeking mine,
Jerusalem, Jerusalem!

Peace by Night

SISTER M. MADELEVA

A velvet beautiful and dark
    With hunched horizon lines of trees,
A silence boundaried by stars:
    I will remember these;

And all our speech resolved into
    An utter impotence of words,
Helplessly mute with living song
    Like dream-bewildered birds.

Beyond this time of breathing peace,
    This moth-still mystery of night,
I shall not need the dawn's elate
    Apocalypse of light.

Leave me this hour of deep content
    With darkness upon darkness spread,
Your face against its velvet set,
    And blue stars overhead.

327

New Things and Old

[Christmas, 1941]

SISTER M. MADELEVA

The dark is shattered
With wild, new fear;
An ass's feet stumbling
Is the sound that I hear.

The night is brighter
Than day should be;
A strange star's splendor
Is the light that I see.

And above the terror
Of earth and sky
I can hear, if I listen,
A young Child's cry;

I can see, if I look,
Legions of wings,
And a woman who ponders
On all these things.

Design for a Stream-lined Sunrise

SISTER M. MADELEVA

If you must draw mere beauty,
Subtend one third of the whole arc of heaven
With a grey chord of cloud
Stretched from the quick south east to the still dubious west.
Edge all the chord with white, bright, mutable silver.

Draw it on cloudlessness at daybreak,
If you would draw mere beauty.
But you cannot do this
Because the artless air achieved this brief design for sunrise,
Once and forever,
Today, at dawn.
And then this long line, cutting with sheer simplicity of silver
The breathless, deep blue arc of the south
Became, because of my beholding,
Beyond potential beauty, beautiful.

Snow Storm

SISTER M. MADELEVA

The air is white and winds are crying,
I think of swans in Galway flying.

Winds are wings; snow is a rover;
Swans of Galway are flying over.

Winds are birds; snow is a feather;
Wild white swans are wind and weather.

Wings drift downward; snow is falling;
Swans are wild winds crying, calling.

Winds are white with snow but alway
Mine are white with swans from Galway.

Wardrobe

SISTER M. MADELEVA

My love gave me a king's robe,
Mock purple and red;
My love gave me a white coat,
A fool's coat, He said;
My love gave me a weft crown
Of thorns for my head.
Because He is my true love
He wore them instead.

Archers of the King

SISTER M. GENOVEVA

Time was, no archer with impunity
Pierced my proud armor. Never arrow flew
But passed its mate midway. Whose livery
The bowman wore I took no heed, nor knew
What master artisan with faultless craft
Had forged the arrows, till one hour of stress
When stricken sore I drew the splintered shaft
And found engraven on it, I.H.S.

O Arrow-Maker with the wounded hands,
My bitterness is shattered into tears,
And now at length my dull heart understands
The need of pain. I wait the coming years
With empty quiver and a slackening string,
Disarmed before the archers of the King.

Poet's Bread

SISTER M. PHILIP

Hunger is a
Poet's bread,
So never a poet but
Goes well fed.

If poet's bread were
Poet's pay,
Many a one would
Starve on the way.

But poets sing,
While thin-lipped years
Make hunger-bread of
Beauty and tears.

To-day

SISTER M. PHILIP

To-day my thoughts
Are swift and cool
As goldfish in
A lily pool.

To-morrow, like as not,
They'll be
Brown turtles blinking
Hard at me.

And I shall be
As dull as they
And blink back, too.
But oh, to-day!

I Am the Mountainy Singer

JOSEPH CAMPBELL
(1 8 8 1 – 1 9 4 4)

I am the mountainy singer—
The voice of the peasant's dream,
The cry of the wind on the wooded hill,
The leap of the fish in the stream.

Quiet and love I sing—
The carn on the mountain crest
The *cailin* in her lover's arms,
The child at its mother's breast.

Beauty and peace I sing—
The fire on the open hearth,
The *cailleach* spinning at her wheel,
The plough in the broken earth.

Travail and pain I sing—
The bride on the childing bed,
The dark man laboring at his rhymes,
The eye in the lambing shed.

Sorrow and death I sing—
The canker come on the corn,
The fisher lost in the mountain loch,
The cry at the mouth of morn.

No other life I sing,
For I am sprung of the stock
That broke the hilly land for bread,
And built the nest in the rock!

I Will Go with My Father A-ploughing

JOSEPH CAMPBELL

I will go with my father a-ploughing
To the green field by the sea,
And the rooks and the crows and the seagulls
Will come flocking after me.
I will sing to the patient horses
With the lark in the white of the air,
And my father will sing the plough-song
That blesses the cleaving share.

I will go with my father a-sowing
To the red field by the sea,
And the rooks and the gulls and the starlings
Will come flocking after me.
I will sing to the striding sowers
With the finch on the greening sloe,
And my father will sing the seed-song
That only the wise men know.

I will go with my father a-reaping
To the brown field by the sea,
And the geese and the crows and the children
Will come flocking after me.
I will sing to the tan-faced reapers
With the wren in the heat of the sun,
And my father will sing the scythe-song
That joys for the harvest done.

The Old Woman

JOSEPH CAMPBELL

As a white candle
    In a holy place,
So is the beauty
    Of an agèd face.

As the spent radiance
    Of the winter sun,
So is a woman
    With her travail done,

Her brood gone from her,
    And her thoughts as still
As the waters
    Under a ruined mill.

Esther

FRAY ANGELICO CHAVEZ
(1 9 1 0 -   )

My Lady Esther, beautiful
With beauty indescribable,
Of guileless grace and modest mien,
With much of handmaid and of queen,
Nor less of mother than of maid,
Dared stand in awe, yet unafraid
Of all the pains that death might bring,
Before the presence of her King.

Where no man dared approach, alone
She came and pleaded for her own,

Sure that her beauty would be heard
For me, whose life lay on his word.
Oh, never beamed a star so fair
As did my Lady Esther there;
For Heaven's eyes, if lightning clear,
Still lack the sparkle of a tear.

And that great King of mind unknown
By love was fixed fast to his throne,
Transformed by joy to know that here
Was one whose love surpassed her fear.
Well might have Sheba's queen foregone
Not only all of Solomon,
But the whole world and everything
For just one smile from such a King.

How much that smile did mean to me
My Lady Esther knows, for she
Of guileless grace and modest mien,
As much a handmaid as a queen,
Nor less a mother than a maid,
Dared stand alone and unafraid
Before her King, who smiled upon
Her tears and said: "Behold, thy son."

Joculator Domini

SISTER M. JOHN FREDERICK

"God give you peace!" Your happy lay
Won all to your pacific sway;
    Cathari, Guelf and Ghibelline
    Forswore the wonted battle scene
To learn a simple roundelay.

Your friends, the birds, were apt, they say,
In singing it the proper way.
    How glad their chorus must have been:
    "God give you peace!"

God's troubadour, on earth to-day
The ways of men would quite gainsay
    Such songs of yours. No more is seen
    The peace of poverty, your queen.
Teach us who had forgot to pray:
    "God give you peace!"

All Souls' Eve

MARY E. MANNIX
(*1 9 0 3 –*)

Wild the sea clamors from its echoing caves,
But other voices rise above the waves:
"As now you are, O friends, so once were we;
As now we are, so one day you shall be!"
And still they rise and plead and hurry by,
Sobbing and breaking in that long, sad cry—
    "Orate pro nobis!"

Father of all, be merciful to all!
Hold not these faithful servants long in thrall;
Open to them Thy blessed dwelling-place,
Hide not too long the glory of Thy face.
Mother of pity, harken to that cry,
Cleaving the clouds, and quivering to the sky—
    "Orate pro nobis!"

Chant of Departure

A Missionary's Prayer

ALFRED BARRETT, S.J.

(1 9 0 6 -   )

Woman who walked home on the arm of John
Another way from that your Son had gone,
Woman who walked
And talked,
Unwavering, of what must yet be done—
Woman, behold your son!

Behold
Him who in boyhood haunts will not grow old;
Who goes predestined to an alien grave
In clay or sand or wave—
Yet sails enamored of one hope: to see,
As John from his dawn-lit faces on the shore
At Shantung or the coast of Travancore.

Woman who walked home on the arm of John,
When on
Some night of tears I hear the palm trees toss,
Stand by my side beneath the Southern Cross.

Unearth

ALFRED BARRETT, S.J.

Gardener of Eden and Gethsemane,
Gently unearth this rosebush that has grown
In the sunken garden of my heart, and be
Gentle to her who yields it yet unblown.
Gardener of Eden, where this tender stem

Henceforth will know the strength of other fingers,
And these leaves brush another's garment hem—
You will not care if round the root there lingers
Something of native soil to swell the bud
Till that root sinks in You as once in me. . . .
Unearth the rosebush of my flesh and blood,
Gardener of Eden—and Gethsemane!

The Rosebush and the Trinity

ALFRED BARRETT, S.J.

Saint John Damascene
Thought a man might see
The semblance of the Trinity,
The how and why of One and Three
(Father, Son and Holy Ghost)
In a rosebush most.
> To-night I mean to walk
> From book
> To bower—
> Intently look
> At the paternal stalk
> Lifting the filial flower—
> Be aware
> Of both of them,
> Bloom and stem,
> Before I see the bush or yet draw near it—
> The rose's triune beauty finally share,
> Led by its essence loosed upon the air,
> As on our world is breathed the Holy Spirit!
I thank John Damascene
For pages that disclose
To me
(If not the Trinity)
More about the rose.

A Martyr's Mass

[Father Miguel Pro, S.J., Executed at Mexico City,
November 23, 1927]

ALFRED BARRETT, S.J.

Kneeling he spoke the Names he loved the most
    As the air was fanned by the whir of invisible wings;
He seemed like a priest about to breathe on the Host
    After the Sanctus rings.

"This is My Body," he said on his First-Mass Day,
    When the rose of priesthood slipped its snowy bud,
Lifting his chaliced heart now could he say
    At death, "This is My Blood."

Swift as an altar chime the rifles rang. . . .
    The stole of crimson flowing over his breast,
How bright it burned, and how his sealed lips sang
    The *Ite, Missa Est!*

Requiem

THEODORE MAYNARD
(*1 8 9 0 -*   )

When my last song is sung and I am dead
    And laid away beneath the kindly clay,
Set a square stone above my dreamless head,
    And sign me with the cross and signing say:
"Here lieth one who loved the steadfast things
    Of his own land, its gladness and its grace,
The stubbled fields, the linnets' gleaming wings,
    The long low gables of his native place,

Its gravelled paths, and the strong wind that rends
   The boughs about the house, the hearth's red glow,
The surly, slow good fellowship of friends,
   The humour of the men he used to know,
And all their swinging choruses and mirth"—
Then turn aside and leave my dust in earth.

Dwell with Me, Lovely Images

THEODORE MAYNARD

Dwell with me, lovely images,
And let all lowing thoughts depart;
Shine like bright moonlight on the seas,
And in my heart.

Send in their tender innocence
Hedgeroses blushing mile on mile,
The thrush that drives the darkness hence,
The dawn's slow smile.

All forms of beauty and of joy,
Hasten to warm and nourish me;
Now strives the Phantom to destroy
Life's ecstasy.

Come, though but glinting is a weed,
To hint at glories hid afar—
A candle in my darkest need,
Twin to a star.

Signum Cui Contradicetur

SISTER MARY ANGELITA, B.V.M.
(1 8 7 8 -   )

Long months He lay within the womb,
    Prisoned from every lovely sight,
Wrapped round in darkness and in gloom,
    Who was the Light.

In a rude stable cold and dim,
    Maid Mary our Redeemer bore;
All doors were harshly closed on Him,
    Who was the Door.

Long time by silence did He teach,
    A helpless Infant, ere was heard
His first quaint, stammering baby speech,
    Who was the Word.

Three anguished days they strove to trace
    His childish footsteps gone astray.
Lost, in the crowded, alien place!
    Who was the Way.

Meekly He did His parents' will;
    They gave commands, with secret awe,
And He was subject to them still,
    Who was the Law.

With wounded hands and feet and side,
    All mangled from the cruel strife,
He bowed His head and, shuddering died,
    Who was the Life.

To a Poet

[Grace After Reading]

SISTER MARY ANGELITA

This is no book.
It is a cloistered garden wherein grows
The proud and perfect rose,
And all the lovely children of the year
Bloom in this sheltered close,
While every little singing wind
Bears fragrant cargoes, of that sweetness wrought,
And everywhere I find
Celestial honey for my bees of thought.

This is no book. It is a pleasure place
Of ordered beauty, tranquil grace—
The loveliness of shaded paths,
Smooth lawns on which the slanting sunlight lies;
And sudden vistas opening wide
To far horizons, peaks austere and pure,
The wide blue glory of the steadfast skies,
Still pools that hold all heaven in their span.

This is no book. It is an armory
Where I may gird my spirit for the strife,
The difficult battle that we men call life,
Choosing what weapons most are to my mind:
High truth, supreme resolve,
And poverty and pain—
Cold, sharp, and beautiful,
Two-edged, for blessings or for bane—
And prayer, that slender blade so swift and sure,
And simple tenderness, quiet and kind.

No book, I say. There is a window here
That looks on earth and heaven, and through its glass
I see heroic figures pass
Of olden days or of the newer time:
Shakespeare and Keats, who, seeking laurels, found
A bed of amaranth and asphodel;
Jerome and Benedict, a brotherhood more dear,
Martin, whom chivalrous hearts have loved so well,
And Francis, dweller of the Umbrian clime;
A queen—the lowly Maid of Nazareth,
Whose beauty lays a hush upon the heart;
And ah! a Child's white feet,
Small, and very sweet,
Pass and repass,
Their footfalls making music in my soul
As swift they move to their appointed goal,
The awful Mount of Love and Death.

This is no book. Rather a vial, say,
Wherein are precious essences distilled
Of blissful solitude;
A jar with fragrant petals filled
That keep the memory of summer suns
And summer skies,
To breathe them forth
Into the bleakness of our wintry North.
Beauty is here, wearing in thoughtful mood
A cloak of quiet hues, most dear disguise!
This is no book,
No thing of paper and of printer's ink,
No tinkling rosary of rhyme on rhyme.
How can I think
Of books, when every page is like a chime
Of golden bells at twilight, and the words
Are flocks of singing birds?

343

Late Autumn

A. M. SULLIVAN
(1896–   )

The falling leaf betrays the fawn
Standing rigid by the oak;

The wind that rises in the dawn
Blows away the meadow smoke

And frames against a greening sky
The mallard in the fowler's sight;

New tracks on hoarfrost publish why
The beagles yelp with young delight,

And early snow abets the treason
No words of pity may atone,

For Nature has a bitter season
When she informs upon her own.

The Sextant

A. M. SULLIVAN

Euclid devised the trap
    By which the sailor's eye
Captures the angle of light
    To mark his compass by,
And he follows the dancing sun
    Over an arc of sky.

Though waters be dark and strange,
    Heaven's a familiar place
As the stars their map unroll
    To the man who measures space
With the light of a thousand suns
    Burning upon his face.

Lost with the churn of the wheel
    And the glow of the phosphor wick
Is the ship that fades in the mist;
    But the sailor has learned the trick
Of steering home with a star
    At the end of a golden stick.

Repeated Pilgrimage

JOHN GILLAND BRUNINI
(1 8 9 9 –   )

Return and go again and yet return!
    No stealthy steps will startle these sad trees
To whisper love, no ambush set will snare
    Her tender words lost on a jealous breeze.

Regard the violet, the green, the stone!
    This scene suffices memory, this glade
Repeats the stage that knew my ecstasy
    Which neither time nor reason has betrayed.

Here, here was happiness; the seasons' rains
    Have sunk into the moss and wrought no change,
Nor has my love despaired of years that show
    My dearest wish impoverished and strange.

Such constancy, whose hope took root in stone,
    At last is disciplined in pain, nor past,

Nor measured now in wild protests of years
    Sore levied for old debts too few hours massed.

Were then this denser bush to part and pass
    The woman she became—or should now be—
Something distilled in immortality
    Would rise to parch my throat—and I would flee.

Boy Playing an Organ

FRANCIS SWEENEY
(A m e r i c a n   C o n t e m p o r a r y)

Francis, my brother, in the clear, wide morning,
Alone in the chapel, with young, tentative hands
Builds his soaring fugues. The melody drifts
Beyond the garden wall; the pasture lands

Are dearer for the far whisper of song.
The old house listens rapt and keeps the scent
Of music in its rooms like incense after
Benediction. And all innocent

Of artifice and pride of work, my brother
Weaves his thronging tapestries of sound,
His long, brown fingers quick upon the loom,
The bright web gay with falcon, lance and hound,

And vigils watched, and maids with golden hair,
Beseeching succor from the beardless knight;
The dragon's rage, the goodly sword unsheathed,
And all the bloody fortune of the fight.

Francis, my brother, youngest of my brothers,
With all his secret pennons still unfurled,
Builds his battlements of music up
Amid a falling world.

Venite Adoremus

MARGERY CANNON
(*American Contemporary*)

She was the human chalice
Delicate and fine.
He was the Infinite Substance,
He was the Wine.

She was the voice that angels
Very often heard.
He was the sound unspoken,
He was the Word.

She was the slender taper
Enclosing Him that night.
He was the Flame eternal,
He was the Light.

It Is the Reed

SISTER MARIS STELLA
(*1 8 9 9 –*)

I did not cut myself this hollow reed,
I did not seek it in the shallows growing.
In all my life I paid but little heed
To burnished reeds in the bright shallows blowing.
And this that now is thrust into my hand
Mysteriously cut and tuned for singing
Was gathered in a strange and distant land
And has immortal airs about it clinging.
An unseen piper tuned its ghostly note.
O who would dare to touch it—who would dare?
From out the fearful hollow of its throat
Such music pours as I am unaware
How to devise. I did not think these things.
It is the reed, it is the reed that sings.

San Marco Museum, Florence

SISTER MARIS STELLA

San Marco was as quiet on that day
In the deep shadow of its cedar tree
As an old shrine. Pale yellow sunlight lay
Across the cloister garth, and one could see
Faintly within the shadow the dark stone
Where sandaled feet had worn with noiseless tread
A thousand paths and into silence gone.
Now strangers wandered through the convent, led
Like men in dreams to where on dimlit wall,
One sees at last from out that dimness grow
The Annunciation with the Virgin all
Mildness and grace, and Gabriel bowing low.
No prayers were chanted or no tapers here
Were lit but for the spirit's eye and ear.

Oxford Bells

SISTER MARIS STELLA

Always the ghost of these will wake again,
When other bells have clamored and are still.
Nowhere are bells that half so sweetly fill
The shaken tower, the drifting flaws of rain;
Of myriad sounds these only will remain.
Even the waters pouring all night under the mill
May be forgot, but on some distant hill,
When carillons die out across the plain,
There will come back some morning's purity
Of bells, peal after peal of silver song,
Magdalen's sweet tune, or the tumultuous chimes
Of all the bells on some high noon in glee
Reverberant; or, echoing deep and long,
The bell of Christ's, tolling its hundred times.

This One Heart-shaken

SISTER MARIS STELLA

It was only my own voice that I had heard,
But at first I did not know it for my own.
Although my lips had formed no single word,
And the voice seemed one that I had never known,
Still it was mine. I knew that it must be:
This secret voice that I had not surmised,
This cry flung from the unsuspected sea
Of loneliness by which I was surprised.
It was as though my other selves came thronging
To see this wonder washed up on the shore,
This one, heart-shaken with immortal longing,
That must possess its life forever more.
And over and over again one cry she made:
"I am afraid of silence. I am afraid."

The Voice

SISTER MARIS STELLA

I am afraid of silence. I am afraid
Of my own soul. I am afraid of hearing
A voice—one voice above all voices—made
Clear in the silence. I shall grow old fearing
This silence that goes with me wherever I go.
I cannot keep it in or bar it out.
Always within, around, above, below,
It beats upon me. I am hedged about
Most utterly. Surrounded. Yet I raise
Even now a futile barrier of sound
Against the voice in silence I dispraise,
Against the voice I dread that hems me round;
To which, did I but listen, I should be
Afraid of nothing. Nothing could frighten me.

349

I Who Had Been Afraid

SISTER MARIS STELLA

I who had been afraid of the dark at night
As a child here in this room, even when I lay
Safe by my mother's bed, now without fright
Watched here alone until the break of day
My mother lying in the last sleep of all.
Never would she wake into the night again.
Here was the beautiful end. No child would call,
No grief disturb, no terrible, torturing pain
Constrain her from the quiet. Here was at last
Catharsis—all pity and terror spent.
Sorrow, splendor, living, dying—past.
All things fulfilled and nothing to lament.
I who had been afraid of the darkness, here
Alone with the beloved dead found nothing to fear.

Now That Can Never Be Done

SISTER MARIS STELLA

I shall never forget my mother's voice singing.
It was a true voice that no one could forget
Who had heard it once. It came like water springing
From a deep spring that must be running yet
Somewhere for someone else to sing from. I
Could wish that spring were mine, for like no other
Singing was my mother's singing. Why,
I never knew for sure. Always my mother
Had her songs by heart and sang them so—
Old songs that everyone knew and dozens more—
But though I loved them it is only the tunes I know.
The words are half forgot. I thought before,
While she still sang her songs, that one by one
I should write them down. Now that can never be done.

Love Is Not Solace

SISTER MARIS STELLA

Love is not solace else it is not love
That binds me here against the body's cry
Within such bonds as I am mistress of
Yet will not ever loose until I die.
Love is not warmth and brightness since I know
Darkness and cold as well as day and night.
Forewarned of mutability I go
With frugal comfort through the shifting light.
Love is not love that for love will not lack
The bread of sweetness and the wine of tears,
Nor dare to relish hunger and the rack,
Nor weigh it overmuch nor count the years,
But will endure through bounty and through dearth,
A deep-heard river in the heart's deep earth.

Afternoon in a Tree

SISTER MARIS STELLA

If you have climbed a laden apple tree
And worked your way through branches intertwined,
You will excuse the prodigality
Of flickers, grackles, and all much maligned
Orchard thieves who tipple where they will,
Leaving three-cornered holes in the red sun-dapples
Where they have pecked with epicurean bill,
And sucked warm cider sweetening in new apples.
You will excuse, and you will envy, too,
From your secure bough, every flying thing
That drops down with a furtive eye on you,
To apples beyond your reach . . . tastes them . . . takes wing. . . .

You are an alien in this air where go
The tribe of those who neither reap nor sow.

Bay Violets

SISTER MARIS STELLA

Then, like a miracle, the violets came out
All around the bay. Up to the very door
The lovely, heart-shaped leaves had spread, without
The children's notice, at least not before
The violets had begun to open their eyes
Back in the woods, by the shore, at the spring, everywhere.
One day they took the children by surprise:
Bright clumps of yellow violets, and rare
White violets growing, damp and cool as dew;
Deep purple violets, crowding thick and sweet,
Covering the ground with purple, and great blue
Meadow violets with leaves like meadowlark's feet.
The whole bay was scented with violets. Even yet
The children never forget them. They can never forget.

Grapes

SISTER MARIS STELLA

Then there were the grapes turned purple in the sun
Hanging in heavy bunches close and low.
These were great purple garden grapes. Not one
Of the children had ever seen any but wild grapes grow.
Wild-running grapes are tart and spare and small.
You find the vines on big trees, clinging high
To withered branches, or on the sun-facing wall
Of an old farmhouse. Invariably they lie
Well out of reach, and tempting, and you find
Gooseberry patches near them, and you gather
Berries in buckets. Here you had no mind
To gather berries in buckets. Here you had rather
Suck the sweet grapes out of their juicy blue
Pockets and let the sun pour down on you.

The Pelicans My Father Sees

SISTER MARIS STELLA

Early one morning the bay will be full of pelicans.
(I have never seen pelicans except through his eyes.)
Over on the sandbar beneath the pearly hills
Dozens of great white pelicans will settle and rise
With long wings powerfully pushing the air aside,
Slashing and cutting the sunlight, circling wide. . . .

Early one morning he will look out over the water.
(O, hello, there are the pelicans. More than last year.)
Over on the sandbar below the pearly hills
He will find big birds moving, flapping wings—here
A long beak dipping into the water. He
Will bring his binoculars out the better to see.

Early one morning he will wake up to the pelicans
(On a cold bright morning after the ice is out)
On the sandbar and the rocks beneath the pearly hills
Stretching their necks and wings and milling about.
He will wake up to the pelicans resting from flight.
After the long dark winter. After the night.

Whatsoever I Do

MARY LOUISE HECTOR
(1 9 2 4 -)

I break my smooth, full loaf of warm white bread,
And give the half away. The beggar's eyes
On mine, I hear the lark say in her song
Who goes in the stranger's guise.

As I ride richly by, a poor man weeps
With cold—I divide my warmth in one glad stroke.
You move my heart and hand who are the one
I cover with my cloak.

When I am called from western windows in
The spring's gold evening, by a tear-burned face,
I ask to share the alien sorrow, watch
One hour in the lonely place.

I give away these dear, small things—for wealth
A hundredfold. Oh, I have learned from you,
To do with eagerly, utterly offering heart
All things whatsoever I do.

For a Girl in Love

FLORENCE HYNES WILLETTE
(*American Contemporary*)

Ruthlessly 'twixt palm and thumb
Break the prickly
Branches quickly
Of the wild, the white-starred plum.

But be wary as you go;
There are nettles thick below.

How the plum blooms scent the air!
Shake them lightly,
Rich and whitely
They will nestle in your hair.
They will kiss your mouth and eyes
Shyly, sweetly,
Less completely
Than your lover and more wise.

Thick below the nettles spring—
Now you know how nettles sting!

Years hence almost any tree
Wild and twisted,
White star-misted,
Will remind you poignantly

Of an hour in a wood
Where white petals
And gray nettles
Kissed and stung you as you stood;
Waspishly the nettles pressed. . . .
Can you bear them,
Break them, wear them,
With the blossoms on your breast?

The Latin Tongue

JAMES J. DALY, S.J.

(1 8 7 2 –   )

Like a loud-booming bell shaking its tower
Of granite blocks, the antique Latin tongue
Shook the whole earth; over all seas it flung
Triremes of war, and bade grim legions scour
The world's far verges. Its imperial dower
Made Tullius a god; and Flaccus strung
Its phrases into garlands; while among
The high enchanters it gave Maro power.

Then Latin lost its purple pomp of war,
Its wine-veined laughter and patrician tears;
It cast its fleshly grossness, won a soul,
And trafficked far beyond the farthest star
With angel-cohorts, echoing through the years
In sacred Embassies from pole to pole.

355

Do What You Will

DOROTHY HOBSON

(*American Contemporary*)

Wait! It would be insane to call—
She would be startled and would fall;
She would plunge past you, if she fell,
Into the emptiness of Hell;

She had not dared to climb so high
Had you not seemed to be close by;
She had not ventured far above
The ledge of human warmth and love,
If she had felt you lose the zest
Of sharing in her own mad quest—
If she had seen you weary soon
Of rare blue cold and the chill white moon
And wander down away from her
To the warm fire where the others were. . . .

She does not know, she still climbs on
Not realizing you are gone,
Nor that the hand to which she clings
Was born of her imaginings—
Till on a lofty edge of rock
She turns, and with a sudden shock
Discovers that you are not there;
Alone, she leans on dizzy air
Who always was afraid, despite
Their lure, of loneliness and height. . . .

Do what you will to save her—shout
That you are coming, and call out
Brave words to still her tottering;
But whether love for you can bring

Her safely downward to the ledge
Or whether you renew your pledge,
Daring the alien quest again—
Something of her is freed by pain:
Something of her that slipped and fell
Past you and the others into Hell—
And something else that, ether-shod,
Ran straight for comfort up to God.

The Case of Thomas More

SISTER MARY ST. VIRGINIA, B.V.M.
(1 9 0 7 –   )

Slowly, my lords, go slowly. In this man:
Still stand your sires, stubborn, at Runnymede;
Blood speaks at Canterbury; across a span
Of a thousand years brothers of Alcuin and Bede
Wield wisdom's words; and England signs the sky
At Salisbury in a Norman syllable meant—
By sons of Saxons—still to ratify
The contract Saint Augustine brought to Kent.
Not that this man is good, friend to the poor,
Defender of the freedoms of the City,
Consider now. But do not now abjure
England. Do not lightly silence the witty
And noble word England speaks. You are sure
This profits you? Use prudence, my lords; not pity.

Convent Cemetery: Mount Carmel

SISTER MARY ST. VIRGINIA

Twilight: and pine trees keep the blessed enclosure,
Transpose the secular breeze to Compline, hush
The garden to the ultimate composure,
Bar out the alien day, cloister the thrush,
Guard the Great Silence's unyielding grating
While maiden bodies—each within a cell
Whose solitude is a native land—are waiting
Through the long vigil for the rising bell.

An interlude composed for nuns the night
Immuring, in the shadows above the river,
The brow that crumbles—granting time's last fetter—
Beneath familiar crucifix and white
And maiden mother close to Christ forever. . . .
Night will be good; and Morning will be better.

TRIBUTARY POEMS
BY
NON-CATHOLICS

The Red-Cross Knight

[From *The Faerie Queene*]

EDMUND SPENSER

(1 5 5 2 – 1 5 9 9)

A gentle knight was pricking on the plain,
Yclad in mighty arms and silver shield,
Wherein old dints of deep wounds did remain,
The cruel marks of many a bloody field;
Yet arms till that time did he never wield.
His angry steed did chide his foaming bit,
As much disdaining to the curb to yield:
Full jolly knight he seemed, and fair did sit
As one for knightly jousts and fierce encounters fit.

But on his breast a bloody cross he bore,
The dear remembrance of his dying Lord,
For whose sweet sake that glorious badge he wore,
And dead as living ever him adored:
Upon his shield the like was also scored,
For sovereign hope, which in his help he had:
Right faithful true he was in deed and word;
But of his cheer did seem too solemn sad,
Yet nothing did he dread, but ever was ydrad.

The Bright Squadrons

[From *The Faerie Queene*]

EDMUND SPENSER

And is there care in heaven? And is there love
In heavenly spirits to these creatures base,
That may compassion of their evils move?
There is; else much more wretched were the case

Of men than beasts; but O! th' exceeding grace
Of highest God that loves His creatures so,
That all His works with mercy doth embrace,
That blessèd angels He sends to and fro,
To serve to wicked man, to serve His wicked foe!

How oft do they their silver bowers leave
To come to succour us that succour want!
How oft do they with golden pinions cleave
The flitting skies, like flying pursuivant,
Against foul fiends to aid us militant!
They for us fight, they watch and duly ward,
And their bright squadrons round about us plant;
And all for love and nothing for reward;
O, why should Heavenly God to men have such regard!

Soul Is Form

[From *An Hymne in Honour of Beautee*]

EDMUND SPENSER

What time this world's great Workmaster did cast
To make all things such as we now behold,
It seems that he before his eye has plast
A goodly paterne, to whose perfect mould
He fashioned them as comely as he could,
That now so faire and seemely they appeare,
As nought may be amended any wheare.

*   *   *   *   *

So every spirit, as it is most pure,
And hath in it the more of heavenly light,
So it the fairer bodie doth procure
To habit in, and it more fairely dight
With chearfull grace and amiable sight;
For of the soule the bodie form doth take;
For soule is forme, and doth the bodie make.

The Divine Harmony

[From *The Merchant of Venice* .V.1]

WILLIAM SHAKESPEARE
(1 5 6 4 – 1 6 1 6)

Enter LORENZO *and* JESSICA.

LORENZO: The moon shines bright: in such a night as this,
When the sweet wind did gently kiss the trees
And they did make no noise, in such a night
Troilus methinks mounted the Troyan walls,
And sigh'd his soul toward the Grecian tents,
Where Cressid lay that night.

JESSICA: In such a night
Did Thisbe fearfully o'ertrip the dew,
And saw the lion's shadow ere himself,
And ran dismay'd away.

LORENZO: In such a night
Stood Dido with a willow in her hand
Upon the wild sea banks, and waft her love
To come again to Carthage.

JESSICA: In such a night
Medea gather'd enchanted herbs
That did renew old Æson.

LORENZO: In such a night
Did Jessica steal from the wealthy Jew,
And with an unthrift love did run from Venice
As far as Belmont.

JESSICA: In such a night
Did young Lorenzo swear he loved her well,
Stealing her soul with many vows of faith
And ne'er a true one.

LORENZO: In such a night
Did pretty Jessica, like a little shrew,
Slander her love, and he forgave it her.

JESSICA:	I would out-night you, did no body come;
	But, hark, I hear the footing of a man.

Enter STEPHANO.

LORENZO:	Who comes so fast in silence of the night?
STEPHANO:	A friend.
LORENZO:	A friend! what friends? your name, I pray you, friend?
STEPHANO:	Stephano is my name; and I bring word
	My mistress will before the break of day
	Be here at Belmont: she doth stray about
	By holy crosses, where she kneels and prays
	For happy wedlock hours.
LORENZO:	Who comes with her?
STEPHANO:	None but a holy hermit and her maid.
	I pray you, is my master yet return'd?
LORENZO:	He is not, nor we have not heard from him.

* * * * *

Sweet soul, let's in, and there expect their coming.
And yet no matter: why should we go in?
My friend Stephano, signify, I pray you,
Within the house, your mistress is at hand;
And bring your music forth into the air.

Exit STEPHANO.

How sweet the moonlight sleeps upon this bank!
Here will we sit, and let the sounds of music
Creep in our ears: soft stillness and the night
Become the touches of sweet harmony.
Sit, Jessica. Look how the floor of heaven
Is thick inlaid with patines of bright gold:
There's not the smallest orb which thou beholds't
But in his motion like an angel sings,
Still quiring to the young-eyed cherubins;
Such harmony is in immortal souls;
But whilst this muddy vesture of decay
Doth grossly close it in, we cannot hear it.

Friar Laurence's Cell

[From *Romeo and Juliet*. III.6]

WILLIAM SHAKESPEARE

Enter FRIAR LAURENCE *and* ROMEO.

FRIAR: So smile the heavens upon this holy act,
That after hours with sorrow chide us not!
ROMEO: Amen, amen! but come what sorrow can,
It cannot countervail the exchange of joy
That one short minute gives me in her sight:
Do thou but close our hands with holy words,
Then love-devouring death do what he dare;
It is enough I may but call her mine.
FRIAR: These violent delights have violent ends,
And in their triumph die, like fire and powder,
Which, as they kiss, consume: the sweetest honey
Is loathesome in its own deliciousness
And in the taste confounds the appetite:
Therefore love moderately; long love doth so;
Too swift arrives as tardy as too slow.

Enter JULIET.

Here comes the lady: O! so light a foot
Will ne'er wear out the everlasting flint:
A lover may bestride the gossamer
That idles in the wanton summer air,
And yet not fall; so light is vanity.
JULIET: Good even to my ghostly confessor.
FRIAR: Romeo shall thank thee, daughter, for us both.
JULIET: As much as him, else are his thanks too much.
ROMEO: Ah! Juliet, if the measure of thy joy
Be heaped like mine, and that thy skill be more
To blazon it, then sweeten with thy breath
This neighbour air, and let rich music's tongue

Unfold the imagined happiness that both
Receive in either by this dear encounter.

FRIAR: Conceit, more rich in matter than in words,
Brags of his substance, not of ornament:
They are but beggars that can count their worth;
But my true love is grown to such excess
I cannot sum up half my sum of wealth.

FRIAR: Come, come with me, and we will make short work;
For, by your leaves, you shall not stay alone
Till holy church incorporate two in one.

Man New Made

[From *Measure for Measure*. II.2]

WILLIAM SHAKESPEARE

ANGELO: He's sentenced, 'tis too late.

* * * * *

ISABEL: Too late? Why, no; I, that do speak a word,
May call it back again. Well, believe this,
No ceremony that to great ones 'longs,
Not the king's crown, nor the deputed sword,
The marshals' truncheon, not the judge's robe,
Become them with one half so good a grace
As mercy does. . . .

ANGELO: Your brother is a forfeit of the law
And you but waste your words.

ISABEL: Alas, alas!
Why, all the souls that were forfeit once;
And He that might the vantage best have took
Found out the remedy. How would you be,
If He, which is the top of judgement, should
But judge you as you are? O, think on that;
And mercy then will breathe within your lips
Like man new made.

True Love

WILLIAM SHAKESPEARE

Let me not to the marriage of true minds
Admit impediments. Love is not love
Which alters when it alteration finds,
Or bends with the remover to remove:
O, no! it is an ever-fixèd mark,
That looks on tempests and is never shaken;
It is the star to every wandering bark,
Whose worth's unknown, although his height be taken.
Love's not Time's fool, though rosy lips and cheeks
Within his bending sickle's compass come;
Love alters not with his brief hours and weeks,
But bears it out even to the edge of doom.
  If this be error, and upon me proved,
  I never writ, nor no man ever loved.

Soul and Body

WILLIAM SHAKESPEARE

Poor soul, the centre of my sinful earth,
[Thrall to] [1] these rebel powers that thee array,
Why dost thou pine within and suffer dearth,
Painting thy outward walls so costly gay?
Why so large cost, having so short a lease,
Dost thou upon thy fading mansion spend?
Shall worms, inheritors of this excess,
Eat up thy charge? Is this thy body's end?
Then, soul, live thou upon thy servant's loss,
And let that pine to aggravate thy store;
Buy terms divine in selling hours of dross;

[1] These two words are lacking.

Within be fed, without be rich no more:
    So shalt thou feed on Death, that feeds on men,
    And Death once dead, there's no more dying then.

Never Weather-beaten Sail

THOMAS CAMPION
(1 5 6 7 - 1 6 2 0)

Never weather-beaten sail more willing bent to shore,
Never tired Pilgrim's limbs affected slumber more,
Than my wearied sprite now longs to fly out of my troubled breast.
O come quickly, sweetest Lord, and take my soul to rest.

Ever-blooming are the joys of Heav'n's high paradise,
Cold age deafs not there our ears, nor vapour dims our eyes:
Glory there the sun outshines, whose beams the blessèd only see;
O come quickly, glorious Lord, and raise my sprite to thee.

A Hymn to God the Father

JOHN DONNE
(1 5 7 3 - 1 6 3 1)

Wilt Thou forgive that sin where I begun;
    Which was my sin, though it were done before?
Wilt Thou forgive that sin through which I run,
    And do run still, though still I do deplore?
When Thou hast done, Thou hast not done;
    For I have more.

Wilt Thou forgive that sin which I have won
    Others to sin, and made my sins their door?
Wilt Thou forgive that sin which I did shun
    A year or two, but wallowed in a score?
When Thou hast done, Thou hast not done;
    For I have more.

I have a sin of fear, that when I've spun
    My last thread, I shall perish on the shore;
But swear by Thyself that at my death Thy Son
    Shall shine as He shines now, and heretofore;
And having done that, Thou hast done;
    I fear no more.

Batter My Heart

JOHN DONNE

Batter my heart, three-personed God: for you
As yet but knock; breathe, shine, and seek to mend;
That I may rise and stand, o'erthrow me, and bend
Your force, to break, blow, burn, and make me new.
I, like an usurped town, to another due,
Labour to admit you, but oh, to no end;
Reason, your viceroy in me, me should defend,
But is captived, and proves weak or untrue.
Yet dearly I love you, and would be lovèd fain,
But am betrothed unto your enemy;
Divorce me, untie, or break that knot again,
Take me to you, imprison me, for I,
Except you enthrall me, never shall be free;
Nor ever chaste, except you ravish me.

Death, Be Not Proud

JOHN DONNE

Death, be not proud, though some have called thee
Mighty and dreadful, for thou art not so;
For those whom thou think'st thou dost overthrow
Die not, poor Death; nor yet canst thou kill me.
From rest and sleep, which but thy pictures be,
Much pleasure; then from thee much more must flow;
And soonest our best men with thee do go—
Rest of their bones, and souls' delivery!
Thou'rt slave to fate, chance, kings, and desperate men,
And dost with poison, war, and sickness dwell;
And poppy or charms can make us sleep as well
And better than thy stroke. Why swell'st thou then?
    One short sleep past, we wake eternally,
      And Death shall be no more: Death, thou shalt die.

Hymn to God, My God, in My Sickness

JOHN DONNE

Since I am coming to that holy room,
Where, with thy choir of saints for evermore,
I shall be made thy music; as I come
I tune the instrument here at the door,
And what I must do then, think here before.

Whilst my physicians by their love are grown
Cosmographers, and I their map, who lie
Flat on this bed, that by them may be shown
That this is my south-west discovery
Per fretum febris, by these straits to die,

I joy, that in these straits, I see my west;
For, though their currents yield return to none,
What shall my west hurt me? As west and east
In all flat maps (and I am one) are one,
So death doth touch the resurrection.

Is the pacific sea my home? Or are
The eastern riches? Is Jerusalem?
Anyan, and Magellan, and Gibraltar,
All straits, and none but straits, are ways to them,
Whether where Japhet dwelt, or Cham, or Sem.

We think that Paradise and Calvary,
Christ's Cross, and Adam's tree, stood in one place;
Look, Lord, and find both Adams met in me;
As the first Adam's sweat surrounds my face,
May the last Adam's blood my soul embrace.

So, in his purple wrapp'd receive me, Lord,
By these his thorns give me his other crown;
And as to others' souls I preach'd thy word,
Be this my text, my sermon to mine own,
Therefore that he may raise the Lord throws down.

On the Death of Crashaw

ABRAHAM COWLEY
(1 6 1 8 – 1 6 6 7)

Poet and Saint! to thee alone are given
The two most sacred names of earth and heaven:
The hard and rarest union which can be,
Next that of Godhead with humanity.
Long did the Muses banished slaves abide,
And build vain pyramids to mortal pride;

Like Moses thou (though spells and charms withstand)
Hast brought them nobly home back to their holy land.

Ah, wretched we, poets of earth! but thou
Wert, living, the same poet which thou'rt now;
Whilst angels sing to thee their airs divine,
And join in an applause as great as thine,
Equal society with them to hold,
Thou need'st not make new songs, but say the old;
And they, kind spirits! shall all rejoice, to see
How little less than they exalted man may be.

The Catholic Amen

[From *The Song of David*]

CHRISTOPHER SMART

(1 7 2 2 - 1 7 7 1)

He sang of God—the mighty source
Of all things—the stupendous force
　　On which all strength depends;
From whose right arm, beneath whose eyes,
All period, power, and enterprise
　　Commences, reigns, and ends.

Tell them, I AM, Jehovah said
To Moses; while earth heard in dread,
　　And, smitten to the heart,
At once above, beneath, around,
All Nature, without voice or sound,
　　Replied, O Lord, Thou Art.

The world, the clustering spheres, He made;
The glorious light, the soothing shade,
　　Dale, champaign, grove, and hill;

The multitudinous abyss,
Where Secrecy remains in bliss,
    And Wisdom hides her skill.

The pillars of the Lord are seven,
Which stand from earth to topmost heaven;
    His Wisdom drew the plan;
His Word accomplished the design,
From brightest gem to deepest mine;
    From Christ enthroned, to Man.

For Adoration, David's Psalms
Lift up the heart to deeds of alms;
    And he, who kneels and chants,
Prevails his passions to control,
Finds meat and medicine to the soul,
    Which for translation pants.

For Adoration, in the dome
Of Christ, the sparrows find a home,
    And on His olives perch:
The swallow also dwells with thee,
O man of God's humility,
    Within his Saviour's church.

Sweet is the dew that falls betimes,
And drops upon the leafy limes;
    Sweet, Hermon's fragrant air:
Sweet is the lily's silver bell,
And sweet the wakeful tapers' smell
    That watch for early prayer.

Sweet the young nurse, with love intense,
Which smiles o'er sleeping innocence;
    Sweet, when the lost arrive:
Sweet the musician's ardor beats,
While his vague mind's in quest of sweets,
    The choicest flowers to hive.

Strong is the horse upon his speed;
Strong in pursuit the rapid glede,
 Which makes at once his game:
Strong the tall ostrich on the ground;
Strong through the turbulent profound
 Shoots Xiphias to his aim.

Strong is the lion—like a coal
His eyeball,—like a bastion's mole
 His chest against the foes:
Strong the gier-eagle on his sail;
Strong against tide the enormous whale
 Emerges as he goes.

But stronger still, in earth and air,
And in the sea, the man of prayer,
 And far beneath the tide:
And in the seat to fate assigned,
Where ask is have, where seek is find,
 Where knock is open wide.

Precious the penitential tear;
And precious is the sigh sincere,
 Acceptable to God:
And precious are the winning flowers.
In gladsome Israel's feast of bowers
 Bound on the hallowed sod.

Glorious the sun in mid-career;
Glorious the assembled fires appear;
 Glorious the comet's train:
Glorious the trumpet and alarm:
Glorious the Almighty's stretched-out arm;
 Glorious the enraptured main;

Glorious the northern lights astream;
Glorious the song, when God's the theme;
 Glorious the thunder's roar;

Glorious Hosanna from the den;
Glorious the catholic Amen;
 Glorious the martyr's gore:

Glorious—more glorious—is the crown
Of Him that brought salvation down,
 By meekness called thy Son:
Thou that stupendous truth believed;—
And now the matchless deed's achieved,
 Determined, dared, and done!

Christmas in the Olden Time

[From *Marmion*]

SIR WALTER SCOTT
(1771 – 1832)

Heap on more wood!—the wind is chill;
But let it whistle as it will,
We'll keep our Christmas merry still.
Each age has deemed the newborn year
The fittest time for festal cheer.
Even, heathen yet, the savage Dane
At Iol more deep the mead did drain;
High on the beach his galleys drew,
And feasted all his pirate crew;
Then in his low and pine-built hall,
Where shields and axes decked the wall,
They gorged upon the half-dressed steer;
Caroused in seas of sable beer;
While round, in brutal jest, were thrown
The half-gnawed rib and marrow-bone;
Or listened all, in grim delight,
While Scalds yelled out the joys of fight.

Then forth in frenzy would they hie,
While wildly-loose their red locks fly;
And, dancing round the blazing pile,
They make such barbarous mirth the while,
As best might to the mind recall
The boisterous joys of Odin's hall.

And well our Christian sires of old
Loved when the year its course had rolled
And brought blithe Christmas back again
With all its hospitable train.
Domestic and religious rite
Gave honor to the holy night:
On Christmas eve the bells were rung;
On Christmas eve the mass was sung;
That only night, in all the year,
Saw the stoled priest the chalice rear.
The damsel donned her kirtle sheen;
The hall was dressed with holly green;
Forth to the wood did merrymen go,
To gather in the mistletoe.
Then opened wide the baron's hall
To vassal, tenant, serf, and all;
Power laid his rod of rule aside;
And Ceremony doffed her pride.
The heir, with roses in his shoes,
That night might village partner choose;
The lord, underogating, share
The vulgar game of "post and pair,"
All hailed with uncontrolled delight,
And general voice, the happy night
That to the cottage, as the crown,
Brought tidings of salvation down.

The fire, with well-dried logs supplied,
Went roaring up the chimney wide;
The huge hall-table's oaken face,
Scrubbed till it shone, the day to grace,

Bore then upon its massive board
No mark to part the squire and lord.
Then was brought in the lusty brawn,
By old blue-coated serving-man;
Then the grim boar's-head frowned on high
Crested with bays and rosemary.
Well can the green-garbed ranger tell
How, when, and where the monster fell;
What dogs before his death he tore,
And all the baiting of the boar.
The wassail round, in good brown bowls,
Garnished with ribbons, blithely trowls.
There the huge sirloin reeked; hard by
Plum-porridge stood, and Christmas pie;
Nor failed old Scotland to produce,
At such high-tide, her savory goose.
Then came the merry maskers in,
And carols roared with blithesome din;
If unmelodious was the song,
It was a hearty note, and strong.
Who lists may in their mumming see
Traces of ancient mystery;
White skirts supplied the masquerade,
And smutted cheeks the visors made:
But, oh! what maskers richly dight
Can boast of bosoms half so light!
England was merry England when
Old Christmas brought his sports again.
'Twas Christmas broached the mightiest ale;
'Twas Christmas told the merriest tale;
A Christmas gambol oft could cheer
The poor man's heart through half the year.

The Abbess

[From *Marmion*]

SIR WALTER SCOTT

The Abbess was of noble blood,
But early took the veil and hood,
Ere upon life she cast a look,
Or knew the world that she forsook.
Fair too she was, and kind had been
As she was fair, but ne'er had seen
For her a timid lover sigh,
Nor knew the influence of her eye.
Love, to her ear, was but a name
Combined with vanity and shame;
Her hopes, her fears, her joys, were all
Bounded within the cloister wall:
The deadliest sin her mind could reach
Was of monastic rule the breach;
And her ambition's highest aim
To emulate Saint Hilda's fame.
For this she gave her ample dower
To raise the convent's eastern tower;
For this, with carving, rare and quaint,
She decked the chapel of the saint,
And gave the relic-shrine of cost,
With ivory and gems embossed.
The poor her convent's bounty blest,
The pilgrim in its hall found rest.

Black was her garb, her rigid rule
Reformed on Benedictine school;
Her cheek was pale, her form was spare;
Vigils, and penances austere
Had early quenched the light of youth.
But gentle was the dame, in sooth:

Though vain of her religious sway,
She loved to see her maids obey,
Yet nothing stern was she in cell,
And the nuns loved their Abbess well.

Hymn to the Virgin

SIR WALTER SCOTT

Ave Maria! Maiden mild!
Listen to a maiden's prayer:
Thou canst hear though from the wild,
Thou canst save amid despair.
Safe may we sleep beneath thy care,
Though banished, outcast, and reviled.
Maiden! hear a maiden's prayer;
Mother, hear a suppliant child!
Ave Maria!

Ave Maria! undefiled!
The flinty couch we now must share,
Shall seem with down of eider piled,
If thy protection hover there.
The murky cavern's heavy air
Shall breathe of balm if thou hast smiled;
Then, Maiden, hear a maiden's prayer,
Mother, list a suppliant child!
Ave Maria!

Ave Maria! stainless styled!
Foul demons of the earth and air,
From this their wonted haunt exiled,
Shall flee before thy presence fair.

379

We bow us to our lot of care,
　Beneath thy guidance reconciled;
Hear for a maid a maiden's prayer!
　And for a father hear his child!
　　Ave Maria!

Dies Iræ

SIR WALTER SCOTT

The mass was sung, and prayers were said,
And solemn requiem for the dead;
The bells tolled out their mighty peal,
For the departed spirit's weal;
And ever in the office close
The hymn of intercession rose;
And far the echoing aisles prolong
The awful burthen of the song,—

　　Dies iræ, dies illa,
　　Solvet sæclum in favilla,

While the pealing organ rung;
　Meet it were with solemn strain
　To close my lay, so light and vain,
Thus the holy Fathers sung:—

HYMN FOR THE DEAD

That day of wrath, that dreadful day,
When heaven and earth shall pass away,
What power shall be the sinner's stay?
How shall he meet that dreadful day?

When, shriveling like a parchèd scroll,
The flaming heavens together roll;

When louder yet, and yet more dread,
Swells the high trump that wakes the dead!

O! on that day, that wrathful day,
When man to judgment wakes from clay,
Be *Thou* the trembling sinner's stay,
Though heaven and earth shall pass away!

Lumen de Lumine

PERCY BYSSHE SHELLEY
(1792 - 1822)

These concluding lines of *Adonaïs,* which so strangely fore-
shadow the author's death at sea, are perhaps his finest. They
embody a version of the opening lines of Dante's *Paradiso,* together with the central thought of the first canto, which sup-
plies the answer to the Pantheism of the Romantic school:

La gloria di colui che tutto muove
per l'universo penetra, e risplende
in una parte più, e meno altrove.

The One remains, the many change and pass;
Heaven's light forever shines, Earth's shadows fly;
Life, like a dome of many-colored glass,
Stains the white radiance of Eternity,
Until Death tramples it to fragments. Die,
If thou wouldst be with that which thou dost seek!
Follow where all is fled! Rome's azure sky,
Flowers, ruins, statues, music, words, are weak
The glory they transfuse with fitting truth to speak.

* * * * *

That Light whose smile kindles the Universe,
That Beauty in which all things work and move,
That Benediction which the eclipsing Curse
Of birth can quench not, that sustaining Love
Which through the web of being blindly wove

381

By man and beast and earth and air and sea,
Burns bright or dim, as each are mirrors of
The fire for which all thirst, now beams on me,
Consuming the last clouds of cold mortality.

The breath whose might I have invoked in song
Descends on me; my spirit's bark is driven
Far from the shore, far from the trembling throng
Whose sails were never to the tempest given;
The massy earth and sphered skies are riven!
I am borne darkly, fearfully, afar;
Whilst burning through the inmost veil of Heaven,
The soul of Adonaïs, like a star,
Beacons from the abode where the Eternal are.

The Virgin

WILLIAM WORDSWORTH
(1 7 7 0 - 1 8 5 0)

Mother! Whose virgin bosom was uncrossed
With the least shade of thought to sin allied;
Woman! Above all women glorified,
Our tainted nature's solitary boast;
Purer than foam on central ocean tost;
Brighter than eastern skies at daybreak strewn
With fancied roses, than the unblemished moon
Before her wane begins on heaven's blue coast;

Thy Image falls to earth. Yet some, I ween,
Not unforgiven, the suppliant knee might bend,
As to a visible power, in which did blend
All that was mixed and reconciled in thee
Of mother's love with maiden purity,
Of high with low, celestial with terrene.

Inside of King's College Chapel, Cambridge

WILLIAM WORDSWORTH

Tax not the royal saint with vain expense,
With ill-matched aims the Architect who planned,
Albeit labouring for a scanty band
Of white-robed scholars only, this immense
And glorious Work of fine intelligence!
Give all thou canst; high Heaven rejects the lore
Of nicely-calculated less or more;
So deemed the man who fashioned for the sense
These lofty pillars, spread that branching roof
Self-poised, and scooped into ten thousand cells,
Where light and shade repose, where music dwells
Lingering—and wandering on as loath to die;
Like thoughts whose very sweetness yieldeth proof
That they were born for immortality.

Divina Commedia

HENRY WADSWORTH LONGFELLOW
(1 8 0 7 – 1 8 8 2)

I

Oft have I seen at some cathedral door
A laborer, pausing in the dust and heat,
Lay down his burden and with reverent feet
Enter, and cross himself, and on the floor
Kneel to repeat his paternoster o'er;
Far off the noises of the world retreat;
The loud vociferations of the street
Become an undistinguishable roar.
So, as I enter here from day to day,

And leave my burden at this minster gate,
Kneeling in prayer, and not ashamed to pray,
The tumult of the time disconsolate
To inarticulate murmurs dies away,
While the eternal ages watch and wait.

II

How strange the sculptures that adorn these towers!
This crowd of statues, in whose folded sleeves
Birds build their nests; while canopied with leaves
Parvis and portal bloom like trellised bowers,
And the vast minster seems a cross of flowers!
But fiends and dragons on the gargoyled eaves
Watch the dead Christ between the living thieves,
And, underneath, the traitor Judas lowers!
Ah! from what agonies of heart and brain,
What exultations trampling on despair,
What tenderness, what tears, what hate of wrong,
What passionate outcry of a soul in pain,
Uprose this poem of the earth and air,
This mediaeval miracle of song!

III

I enter, and I see thee in tne gloom
Of the long aisles, O poet saturnine!
And strive to make my steps keep pace with thine.
The air is filled with some unknown perfume;
The congregation of the dead make room
For thee to pass; the votive tapers shine;
Like rooks that haunt Ravenna's groves of pine
The hovering echoes fly from tomb to tomb.
From the confessionals I hear arise
Rehearsals of forgotten tragedies,
And lamentations from the crypts below;
And then a voice celestial that begins
With the pathetic words, "Although your sins
As scarlet be," and ends with "as the snow."

IV

I lift mine eyes, and all the windows blaze
With forms of Saints and holy men who died,
Here martyred and hereafter glorified;
And the great Rose upon its leaves displays
Christ's Triumph, and the angelic roundelays,
With splendor upon splendor multiplied;
And Beatrice again at Dante's side
No more rebukes, but smiles her words of praise.
And then the organ sounds, and unseen choirs
Sing the old Latin hymns of peace and love
And benedictions of the Holy Ghost;
And the melodious bells among the spires
O'er all the house-tops and through heaven above
Proclaim the elevation of the Host!

V

O star of morning and of liberty!
O bringer of the light, whose splendor shines
Above the darkness of the Apennines,
Forerunner of the day that is to be!
The voices of the city and the sea,
The voices of the mountains and the pines,
Repeat thy song, till the familiar lines
Are footpaths for the thought of Italy!
Thy flame is blown abroad from all the heights,
Through all the nations, and a sound is heard,
As of a mighty wind, and men devout,
Strangers of Rome, and the new proselytes,
In their own language hear the wondrous word,
And many are amazed and many doubt.

Midnight Mass for the Dying Year

HENRY WADSWORTH LONGFELLOW

Yes, the Year is growing old,
    And his eye is pale and bleared!
Death, with frosty hand and cold,
    Plucks the old man by the beard,
        Sorely, sorely!

The leaves are falling, falling,
    Solemnly and slow;
Caw! caw! the rooks are calling,
    It is a sound of woe,
        A sound of woe!

Through woods and mountain passes
    The winds, like anthems, roll;
They are chanting solemn masses,
    Singing, "Pray for this poor soul,
        Pray, pray!"

And the hooded clouds, like friars,
    Tell their beads in drops of rain,
And patter their doleful prayers;
    But their prayers are all in vain,
        All in vain!

There he stands in the foul weather,
    The foolish, fond Old Year,
Crowned with wild flowers and with heather,
    Like weak, despisèd Lear,
        A king, a king!

Then comes the summer-like day,
    Bids the old man rejoice!

His joy! his last! Oh, the old man gray
    Loveth that ever-soft voice,
      Gentle and low.

To the crimson woods he saith,
    To the voice gentle and low
Of the soft air, like a daughter's breath,
    "Pray do not mock me so!
      Do not laugh at me!"

And now the sweet day is dead;
    Cold in his arms it lies;
No stain from its breath is spread
    Over the glassy skies,
      No mist or stain!

Then, too, the Old Year dieth,
    And the forests utter a moan,
Like the voice of one who crieth
    In the wilderness alone,
      "Vex not his ghost!"

Then comes, with an awful roar,
    Gathering and sounding on,
The storm-wind from Labrador,
    The wind Euroclydon,
      The storm-wind!

Howl! howl! and from the forest
    Sweep the red leaves away!
Would, the sins that thou abhorrest,
    O Soul! could thus decay,
      And be swept away!

For there shall come a mightier blast,
    There shall be a darker day;

And the stars, from heaven down-cast
Like red leaves be swept away!
Kyrie, eleyson!
Christe, eleyson!

Valedictory

ALFRED, LORD TENNYSON
(1809 - 1892)

The two following poems were written by Tennyson in
memory of two leading Catholics in the Isle of Wight—his
friends and neighbors, W. G. Ward and Sir John Simeon. The
former was a prominent figure in the Oxford Movement.
The great cedar described in *Maud* grew in the garden at
Swainston.

I

In Memoriam—W. G. Ward

Farewell, whose like on earth I shall not find,
    Whose Faith and Work were bells of full accord,
My friend, the most unworldly of mankind,
    Most generous of all Ultramontanes, Ward,
How subtle at tierce and quart of mind with mind,
    How loyal in the following of thy Lord!

II

In the Garden at Swainston

Nightingales warbled without,
        Within was weeping for thee;
Shadows of three dead men
        Walk'd in the walks with me,
Shadows of three dead men, and thou
        Wast one of the three.

Nightingales sang in his woods,
    The Master was far away;
Nightingales warbled and sang
    Of a passion that lives but a day;
Still in the house in his coffin
    The Prince of courtesy lay.

Two dead men have I known
    Of a courtesy like to thee;
Two dead men have I loved
    With a love that will ever be;
Three dead men have I loved,
    And thou art last of the three.

Prayer for the Dead

[From *Morte D'Arthur*]

ALFRED, LORD TENNYSON

"The old order changeth, yielding place to new,
And God fulfils Himself in many ways,
Lest one good custom should corrupt the world.
Comfort thyself: what comfort is in me?
I have lived my life, and that which I have done
May He within Himself make pure! but thou,
If thou shouldst never see my face again,
Pray for my soul. More things are wrought by prayer
Than this world dreams of. Wherefore, let thy voice
Rise like a fountain for me night and day.
For what are men better than sheep or goats
That nourish a blind life within the brain,
If, knowing God, they lift not hands of prayer
Both for themselves and those who call them friend?
For so the whole round earth is every way
Bound by gold chains about the feet of God. . . ."

Lancelot and the Grail

[From *Idylls of the King*]

ALFRED, LORD TENNYSON

"Thou, too, my Lancelot," ask'd the King, "my friend,
Our mightiest, hath this Quest avail'd for thee?"

"Our mightiest!" answer'd Lancelot, with a groan;
"O King!"—and when he paused, methought I spied
A dying flame of madness in his eyes—
"O King, my friend, if friend of thine I be,
Happier are those that welter in their sin,
Swine in the mud, that cannot see for slime,
Slime of the ditch; but in me lived a sin,
So strange, of such a kind, that all of pure,
Noble, and knightly in me twined and clung
Round that one sin, until the wholesome flower
And poisonous grew together, each as each,
Not to be pluck'd asunder; and when thy knights
Sware, I sware with them only in the hope
That could I touch or see the Holy Grail
They might be pluck'd asunder. Then I spake
To one most holy saint, who wept and said
That save they could be pluck'd asunder, all
My quest were but in vain; to whom I vow'd
That I would work according as he will'd.
And forth I went, and while I yearn'd and strove
To tear the twain asunder in my heart,
My madness came upon me as of old,
And whipt me into waste fields far away;
There was I beaten down by little men,
Mean knights, to whom the moving of my sword
And shadow of my spear had been enow
To scare them from me once; and then I came
All in my folly to the naked shore,

Wide flats, where nothing but coarse grasses grew;
But such a blast, my King, began to blow,
So loud a blast along the shore and sea,
Ye could not hear the waters for the blast,
Tho' heapt in mounds and ridges all the sea
Drove like a cataract, and all the sand
Swept like a river, and the clouded heavens
Were shaken with the motion and the sound.
And blackening in the sea-foam sway'd a boat,
Half-swallow'd in it, anchor'd with a chain;
And in my madness to myself I said,
'I will embark and I will lose myself,
And in the great sea wash away my sin.'
I burst the chain, I sprang into the boat.
Seven days I drove along the dreary deep,
And with me drove the moon and all the stars;
And the wind fell, and on the seventh night
I heard the shingle grinding in the surge,
And felt the boat shock earth, and looking up,
Behold, the enchanted towers of Carbonek,
A castle like a rock upon a rock,
With chasm-like portals open to the sea,
And steps that met the breaker! There was none
Stood near it but a lion on each side
That kept the entry, and the moon was full.
Then from the boat I leapt, and up the stairs,
There drew my sword. With sudden-flaring manes
Those two great beasts rose upright like a man,
Each gript a shoulder, and I stood between;
And, when I would have smitten them, heard a voice,
'Doubt not, go forward; if thou doubt, the beasts
Will tear thee piecemeal.' Then with violence
The sword was dash'd from out my hand, and fell.
And up into the sounding hall I past;
But nothing in the sounding hall I saw,
No bench nor table, painting on the wall
Or shield of knight; only the rounded moon

Thro' the tall oriel on the rolling sea.
But always in the quiet house I heard,
Clear as a lark, high o'er me as a lark,
A sweet voice singing in the topmost tower
To the eastward. Up I climbed a thousand steps
With pain: as in a dream I seem'd to climb
For ever: at the last I reach'd a door,
A light was in the crannies, and I heard,
'Glory and joy and honour to the Lord
And to the Holy Vessel of the Grail!'
Then in my madness I essay'd the door;
It gave, and thro' a stormy glare, a heat
As from a seven-times-heated furnace, I,
Blasted and burnt, and blinded as I was,
With such a fierceness that I swoon'd away—
O, yet methought I saw the Holy Grail,
All pall'd in crimson samite, and around
Great angels, awful shapes, and wings and eyes!
And but for all my madness and my sin,
And then my swooning, I had sworn I saw
That which I saw; but what I saw was veil'd
And cover'd; and this Quest was not for me."

The Word

[From *In Memoriam*]

ALFRED, LORD TENNYSON

Tho' truths in manhood darkly join,
    Deep-seated in our mystic frame,
    We yield all blessing to the name
Of Him that made them current coin;

For Wisdom dealt with mortal powers
    Where truth in closest words shall fail,
    When truth embodied in a tale
Shall enter in at lowly doors.

And so the Word had breath, and wrought
    With human hands the creed of creeds
    In loveliness of perfect deeds,
More strong than all poetic thought;

Which he may read that binds the sheaf,
    Or builds the house, or digs the grave,
    And those wild eyes that watch the wave ·
In roarings round the coral reef.

St. Agnes' Eve

ALFRED, LORD TENNYSON

Deep on the convent-roof the snows
    Are sparkling to the moon;
My breath to heaven like vapor goes;
    May my soul follow soon!
The shadows of the convent-towers
    Slant down the snowy sward,
Still creeping with the creeping hours
    That lead me to my Lord:
Make Thou my spirit pure and clear
    As are the frosty skies,
Or this first snowdrop of the year
    That in my bosom lies.

As these white robes are soiled and dark,
    To yonder shining ground;
As this pale taper's earthly spark,
    To yonder argent round;

So shows my soul before the Lamb,
    My spirit before Thee;
So in mine earthly house I am,
    To that I hope to be.
Break up the heavens, O Lord! and far,
    Thro' all yon starlight keen,
Draw me, Thy bride, a glittering star,
    In raiment white and clean.

He lifts me to the golden doors;
    The flashes come and go;
All heaven bursts her starry floors,
    And strews her lights below,
And deepens on and up! the gates
    Roll back, and far within
For me the Heavenly Bridegroom waits,
    To make me pure of sin.
The sabbaths of Eternity,
    One sabbath deep and wide—
A light upon the shining sea—
    The Bridegroom with his bride!

Iona

FREDERICK TENNYSON
(1 8 0 7 – 1 8 9 8)

I landed on Iona's holy isle,
    And wandered through its ancient ruins bare,
    And felt the great Columba's self was there.
Thirteen long centuries seemed "a little while"
Before the unchanging sea and sky, whose smile
    He knew. He trod these paths; he breathed this air;
    These waves once rolled responsive to his prayer,
Whose murmuring ripples now my ear beguile.

Nor to the Saint alone closer I stand,
    Nearer the Lord I seem, upon this shore;
The solid rock of this historic strand
    Helps me to bridge Time's waste of waters o'er,
And grasp His feet, and feel His loving hand
    In whom all saints are one for evermore!

An Incident

FREDERICK TENNYSON

At the Lord's Table waiting, robed and stoled,
    Till all had knelt around, I saw a sign!
    In the full chalice sudden splendours shine,
Azure and crimson, emerald and gold.
I stooped to see the wonder, when, behold!
    Within the cup a Countenance divine
    Looked upward at me through the trembling wine,
Suffused with tenderest love and grief untold.

The comfort of that sacramental token
    From Memory's page Time never can erase;
The glass of that rich window may be broken,
    But not the mirrored image of His grace,
Through which my dying Lord to me has spoken,
    At His own Holy Table, face to face!

The Guardian Angel

[A Picture at Fano]

ROBERT BROWNING
(1 8 1 2 - 1 8 8 9)

Dear and great Angel, wouldst thou only leave
    That child, when thou hast done with him, for me!
Let me sit all the day here, that when eve
    Shall find performed thy special ministry,
And time come for departure, thou, suspending
Thy flight, may'st see another child for tending,
    Another still, to quiet and retrieve.

Then I shall feel thee step one step, no more,
    From where thou standest now, to where I gaze,
—And suddenly my head is covered o'er
    With those wings, white above the child who prays
Now on that tomb—and I shall feel thee guarding
Me, out of all the world; for me, discarding
    Yon heaven thy home, that waits and opes its door.

I would not look up thither past thy head
    Because the door opes, like that child, I know,
For I should have thy gracious face instead,
    Thou bird of God! And wilt thou bend me low
Like him, and lay, like his, my hands together,
And lift them up to pray, and gently tether
    Me, as thy lamb there, with thy garment's spread?

If this was ever granted, I would rest
    My head beneath thine, while thy healing hands
Close-covered both my eyes beside thy breast,
    Pressing the brain, which too much thought expands,
Back to its proper size again, and smoothing

Distortion down till every nerve had soothing,
    And all lay quiet, happy and suppressed.

How soon all worldly wrong would be repaired!
    I think how I should view the earth and skies
And sea, when once again my brow was bared
    After thy healing, with such different eyes.
O world, as God has made it! All is beauty:
And knowing this, is love, and love is duty.
    What further may be sought for or declared?

Guercino drew this angel I saw teach
    (Alfred, dear friend!)—that little child to pray,
Holding the little hands up, each to each
    Pressed gently,—with his own head turned away
Over the earth where so much lay before him
Of work to do, though heaven was opening o'er him,
    And he was left at Fano by the beach.

We were at Fano, and three times we went
    To sit and see him in his chapel there,
And drink his beauty to our souls' content
    —My angel with me too: and since I care
For dear Guercino's fame (to which in power
And glory comes this picture for a dower,
    Fraught with a pathos so magnificent)—

And since he did not work thus earnestly
    At all times, and has else endured some wrong—
I took one thought his picture struck from me,
    And spread it out, translating it to song.
My love is here. Where are you, dear old friend?
How rolls the Wairoa at your world's far end?
    This is Ancona, yonder is the sea.

Karshish and Lazarus

[From *Karshish, the Arab Physician*]

ROBERT BROWNING

The Man had something in the look of him—
His case has struck me far more than 'tis worth.

* * * * *

'Tis but a case of mania—subinduced
By epilepsy, at the turning-point
Of trance prolonged unduly some three days.

* * * * *

And first—the man's own firm conviction rests
That he was dead (in fact, they buried him),
That he was dead and then restored to life
By a Nazarene physician of his tribe.

* * * * *

Thou wilt object—why have I not ere this
Sought out the sage himself, the Nazarene
Who wrought this cure, inquiring at the source.

* * * * *

Alas! it grieveth me, the learnèd leech
Perished in a tumult many years ago,
Accused—our learning's fate—of wizardry.

* * * * *

His death which happened when the earthquake fell

* * * * *

Was wrought by the mad people—that's their wont!

On vain recourse, as I conjecture it,
To his tried virtue, for miraculous help—
How could he stop the earthquake? That's their way!
The other imputations must be lies:
But take one, though I loathe to give it thee,
In mere respect for any good man's fame!
(And after all, our patient Lazarus
Is stark mad—should we count on what he says?
Perhaps not—though in writing to a leech
'Tis well to keep back nothing of a case.)
This man so cured regards the curer then
As—God forgive me—who but God Himself,
Creator and Sustainer of the world,
That came and dwelt in flesh on it awhile!
—'Sayeth that such an One was born and lived,
Taught, healed the sick, broke bread at his own house,
Then died, with Lazarus by, for aught I know,
And yet was . . . what I said nor choose repeat.

* * * * *

Why write of trivial matters, things of price
Calling at every moment for remark?
I noticed on the margin of a pool
Blue-flowering borage, the Aleppo sort,
Aboundeth, very nitrous. It is strange!

* * * * *

The very God! think, Abib; dost thou think?
So, the All-Great were the All-Loving too—
So, through the thunder comes a human voice
Saying, "O heart I made, a heart beats here!
Face, my hands fashioned, see it in myself.
Thou hast no power nor mayst conceive of mine,
But love I gave thee, with myself to love,
And thou must love me who have died for thee!"
The madman saith He said so: it is strange.

Last Lines

EMILY BRONTË
(1 8 1 8 – 1 8 4 8)

No coward soul is mine,
No trembler in the world's storm-troubled sphere;
I see Heaven's glories shine,
And faith shines equal, arming me from fear.

O God within my breast,
Almighty, ever-present Deity!
Life—that in me has rest,
As I—undying life—have power in Thee!

Vain are the thousand creeds
That move men's hearts: unutterably vain;
Worthless as withered weeds,
Or idlest froth amid the boundless main.

To waken doubt in one
Holding so fast by Thine infinity;
So surely anchored on
The steadfast rock of immortality.

With wide-embracing love
Thy Spirit animates eternal years,
Pervades and broods above,
Changes, sustains, dissolves, creates and rears.

Though earth and man were gone,
And suns and universes ceased to be,
And Thou were left alone,
Every existence would exist in Thee.

There is not room for Death
Nor atom that his might could render void:
Thou—THOU art Being and Breath,
And what THOU art may never be destroyed.

Jacopone da Todi

MATTHEW ARNOLD

(*1 8 2 2 - 1 8 8 8*)

That son of Italy who tried to blow,
    Ere Dante came, the trump of sacred song,
    In his bright youth amid a festal throng
Sate with his bride, to see a public show.
Fair was his bride, and on her front did glow
    Youth like a star; and what to youth belong—
    Gay raiment, sparkling gauds, elation strong.
A prop gave 'way! Crash fell a platform! lo,

Mid struggling sufferers, hurt to death, she lay!
    Shuddering they drew her garments off—and found
        A robe of sackcloth next her smooth white skin.
Such, poets, is your bride, the Muse! young, gay,
    Radiant, adorned outside, a hidden ground
        Of thought and of austerity within.

Passing Away

CHRISTINA G. ROSSETTI

(*1 8 3 0 - 1 8 9 4*)

Passing away, saith the World, passing away;
Chances, beauty and youth sapped day by day:
Thy life never continueth in one stay.
Is the eye waxen dim, is the dark hair changing to gray
That hath won neither laurel nor bay?
I shall clothe myself in Spring and bud in May:
Thou, root-stricken, shalt not rebuild thy decay
On my bosom for aye.
Then I answered: Yea.

Passing away, saith my Soul, passing away:
With its burden of fear and hope, of labor and play,
Harken what the past doth witness and say:
Rust in thy gold, a moth is in thine array,
A canker is in thy bud, thy leaf must decay.
At midnight, at cockrow, at morning, one certain day,
Lo, the Bridegroom shall come and shall not delay:
Watch thou and pray.
Then I answered: Yea.

Passing away, saith my God, passing away:
Winter passeth after the long delay:
New grapes on the vine, new figs on the tender spray,
Turtle calleth turtle in Heaven's May.
Though I tarry, wait for me, trust me, watch and pray,
Arise, come away; night is past, and lo, it is day;
My love, my sister, my spouse, thou shalt hear me say—
Then I answered: Yea.

Mary's Girlhood

[For a Picture]

DANTE GABRIEL ROSSETTI
(1 8 2 8 - 1 8 8 2)

This is that blessèd Mary, pre-elect
    God's Virgin. Gone is a great while, and she
    Dwelt young in Nazareth of Galilee.
Unto God's will she brought devout respect,
Profound simplicity of intellect,
    And supreme patience. From her mother's knee
    Faithful and hopeful; wise in charity;
Strong in grave peace; in pity circumspect.

So held she through her girlhood; as it were
    An angel-watered lily, that near God
        Grows and is quiet. Till, one day at home,
She woke in her white bed, and had no fear
    At all,—yet wept till sunshine, and felt awed:
        Because the fulness of the time was come.

Ave

DANTE GABRIEL ROSSETTI

    Mother of the Fair Delight,
Thou handmaid perfect in God's sight,
Now sitting fourth beside the Three,
Thyself a woman-Trinity,—
Being a daughter borne to God,
Mother of Christ from stall to rood,
And wife unto the Holy Ghost:—
Oh when our need is uttermost,
Think that to such as death may strike
Thou once wert sister sisterlike!
Thou headstone of humanity,
Groundstone of the great Mystery,
Fashioned like us, yet more than we!

    Mind'st thou not (when June's heavy breath
Warmed the long days in Nazareth,)
That eve thou didst go forth to give
Thy flowers some drink that they might live
One faint night more amid the sands?
Far off the trees were as pale wands
Against the fervid sky: the sea
Sighed farther off eternally
As human sorrow sighs in sleep.
Then suddenly the awe grew deep,

As of a day to which all days
Were footsteps in God's secret ways:
Until a folding sense, like prayer,
Which is, as God is, everywhere,
Gathered about thee; and a voice
Spake to thee without any noise,
Being of the silence:—"Hail," it said,
"Thou that art highly favorèd;
The Lord is with thee here and now;
Blessed among all women thou."

    Ah! knew'st thou of the end, when first
That Babe was on thy bosom nurs'd?—
Or when He tottered round thy knee
Did thy great sorrow dawn on thee?—
And through His boyhood, year by year
Eating with Him the Passover,
Didst thou discern confusedly
That holier sacrament, when He
The bitter cup about to quaff,
Should break the bread and eat thereof?—
Or came not yet the knowledge, even
Till on some day forecast in Heaven
His feet passed through thy door to press
Upon His Father's business?—
Or still was God's high secret kept?

    Nay, but I think the whisper crept
Like growth through childhood. Work and play,
Things common to the course of day,
Awed thee with meanings unfulfill'd;
And all through girlhood, something still'd
Thy senses like the birth of light,
When thou hast trimmed thy lamp at night
Or washed thy garments in the stream;
To whose white bed had come the dream

That He was thine and thou wast His
Who feeds among the field-lilies.
O solemn shadow of the end
In that wise spirit long contain'd!
O awful end! and those unsaid
Long years when It was Finishèd!

    Mind'st thou not (when the twilight gone
Left darkness in the house of John)
Between the naked window-bars
That spacious vigil of the stars?—
For thou, a watcher even as they,
Wouldst rise from where throughout the day
Thou wroughtest raiment for His poor;
And, finding the fixed terms endure
Of day and night which never brought
Sounds of His coming chariot,
Wouldst lift through cloud-waste unexplor'd
Those eyes which said, "How long, O Lord?"
Then that disciple whom He loved,
Well heeding, haply would be moved
To ask thy blessing in His name;
And that one thought in both, the same
Though silent, then would clasp ye round
To weep together,—tears long bound,
Sick tears of patience, dumb and slow.
Yet, "Surely I come quickly,"—so
He said, from life and death gone home.
Amen: even so, Lord Jesus, come!

    But oh! what human tongue can speak
That day when Michael came to break
From the tir'd spirit, like a veil,
Its covenant with Gabriel
Endured at length unto the end?
What human thought can apprehend

405

That mystery of motherhood
When thy Beloved at length renew'd
The sweet communion severèd,—
His left hand underneath thine head
And His right hand embracing thee?—
Lo! He was thine, and this is He!

    Soul, is it Faith, or Love, or Hope,
That lets me see her standing up
Where the light of the Throne is bright?
Unto the left, unto the right,
The cherubim, arrayed, conjoint,
Float inward to a golden point,
And from between the seraphim
The glory issues for a hymn.
O Mary Mother, be not loath
To listen,—thou whom the stars clothe,
Who seëst and mayst not be seen!
Hear us at last, O Mary Queen!
Into our shadow bend thy face,
Bowing thee from the secret place,
O Mary Virgin, full of grace!

Lost Days

DANTE GABRIEL ROSSETTI

The lost days of my life until to-day,
    What were they, could I see them on the street
    Lie as they fell? Would they be ears of wheat
Sown once for food but trodden into clay?
Or golden coins squandered and still to pay?
    Or drops of blood dabbling the guilty feet?
    Or such spilt water as in dreams must cheat
The undying throats of Hell, who thirst alway?

I do not see them here; but after death
    God knows I know the faces I shall see,
  Each one a murdered self, with low last breath.
    'I am thyself,—what hast thou done to me?'
'And I—and I—thyself,' (lo! each one saith)
    'And thou thyself to all eternity!'

The Passover in the Holy Family

[For a Drawing]

DANTE GABRIEL ROSSETTI

> The scene is in the house-porch, where Christ holds a bowl
> of blood from which Zacharias is sprinkling the posts and
> lintel. Joseph has brought the lamb and Elisabeth lights the
> pyre. The shoes which John fastens and the bitter herbs which
> Mary is gathering form part of the ritual.

Here meet together the prefiguring day
    And day prefigured. "Eating, thou shalt stand,
    Feet shod, loins girt, thy road-staff in thine hand,
With blood-stained door and lintel,"—did God say
By Moses' mouth in ages passed away.
    And now, where this poor household doth comprise
    At Paschal-Feast two kindred families,—
Lo! the slain lamb confronts the Lamb to slay.

The pyre is piled. What agony's crown attained,
    What shadow of death the Boy's fair brow subdues
Who holds that blood wherewith the porch is stained
    By Zachary the priest? John binds the shoes
    He deemed himself not worthy to unloose;
And Mary culls the bitter herbs ordained.

Mary Magdalene at the Door of Simon the Pharisee

[For a Drawing]

DANTE GABRIEL ROSSETTI

In the drawing Mary has left a festal procession, and is
ascending by a sudden impulse the steps of the house where
she sees Christ. Her lover has followed her and is trying to
turn her back.

"Why wilt thou cast the roses from thine hair?
    Nay, be thou all a rose,—wreath, lips, and cheek.
    Nay, not his house,—that banquet-house we seek,
See how they kiss and enter; come thou there.
This delicate day of love we two will share
    Till at our ear love's whispering night shall speak.
    What, sweet one,—hold'st thou still the foolish freak?
Nay, when I kiss thy feet they'll leave the stair."

"Oh loose me! See'st thou not my Bridegroom's face
    That draws me to Him? For His feet my kiss,
        My hair, my tears He craves to-day:—and oh!
What words can tell what other day and place
    Shall see me clasp those blood-stained feet of His?
        He needs me, calls me, loves me: let me go!"

Saint Luke the Painter

[For a Drawing]

DANTE GABRIEL ROSSETTI

Give honour unto Luke Evangelist:
    For he it was (the agèd legends say)
    Who first taught Art to fold her hands and pray.
Scarcely at once she dared to rend the mist

Of devious symbols; but soon having wist
>How sky-breadth and field-silence and this day
>Are symbols also in some deeper way,
She looked through these to God and was God's priest.

And if, past noon, her toil began to irk,
And she sought talismans, and turned in vain
>To soulless self-reflections of man's skill,—
>Yet now, in this the twilight, she might still
Kneel in the latter grass to pray again,
Ere the night cometh and she may not work.

World's Worth

DANTE GABRIEL ROSSETTI

'Tis of the Father Hilary.
>He strove, but could not pray; so took
>The steep-coiled stair, where his feet shook
A sad blind echo. Ever up
>He toiled. 'Twas a sick sway of air
>That autumn noon within the stair,
As dizzy as a turning cup.
>His brain benumbed him, void and thin;
>He shut his eyes and felt it spin;
>The obscure deafness hemmed him in.
He said: "O world, what world for me?"

He leaned unto the balcony
>Where the chime keeps the night and day;
>It hurt his brain, he could not pray.
He had his face upon the stone:
>Deep 'twixt the narrow shafts, his eye
>Passed all the roofs to the stark sky,
Swept with no wing, with wind alone.

Close to his feet the sky did shake
With wind in pools that the rains make:
The ripple set his eyes to ache.
He said: "O world, what world for me?"

He stood within the mystery
Girding God's blessed Eucharist:
The organ and the chant had ceas'd.
The last words paused against his ear
Said from the altar: drawn round him
The gathering rest was dumb and dim.
And now the sacring-bell rang clear
And ceased; and all was awe,—the breath
Of God in man that warranteth
The inmost utmost things of faith.
He said: "O God, my world in Thee!"

For the Holy Family by Michelangelo

[In the National Gallery]

DANTE GABRIEL ROSSETTI

In this picture the Virgin Mother is seen withholding from
the Child Saviour the prophetic writings in which his sufferings
are foretold. Angelic figures beside them examine a scroll.

Turn not to the prophet's page, O Son! He knew
All that Thou hast to suffer, and hath writ.
Not yet Thine hour of knowledge. Infinite
The sorrows that Thy manhood's lot must rue
And dire acquaintance of Thy grief. That clue
The spirits of Thy mournful ministerings
Seek through yon scroll in silence. For these things
The angels have desired to look into.

Still before Eden waves the fiery sword,—
    Her Tree of Life unransomed: whose sad Tree
    Of Knowledge yet to growth of Calvary
        Must yield its Tempter,—Hell the earliest dead
Of Earth resign,—and yet, O Son and Lord,
        The Seed o' the woman bruise the serpent's head.

A Ballad of Trees and the Master

SIDNEY LANIER
(1 8 4 2 - 1 8 8 1)

Into the woods my Master went,
Clean forspent, forspent.
Into the woods my Master came,
Forspent with love and shame.
But the olives they were not blind to Him;
The little gray leaves were kind to Him;
The thorn-tree had a mind to Him
When into the woods He came.

Out of the woods my Master went,
And He was well content.
Out of the woods my Master came,
Content with death and shame.
When Death and Shame would woo Him last
From under the trees they drew Him last;
'Twas on a tree they slew Him—last
When out of the woods He came.

Prayer to the Virgin of Chartres

HENRY ADAMS

(1 8 3 8 – 1 9 1 8)

Gracious Lady:—

Simple as when I asked your aid before;
　　Humble as when I prayed for grace in vain
Seven hundred years ago; weak, weary, sore
　　In heart and hope, I ask your help again.

You, who remember all, remember me;
　　An English scholar of a Norman name,
I was a thousand who then crossed the sea
　　To wrangle in the Paris schools for fame.

When your Byzantine portal was still young
　　I prayed there with my master Abailard;
When Ave Maris Stella was first sung,
　　I helped to sing it here with Saint Bernard.

When Blanche set up your gorgeous Rose of France
　　I stood among the servants of the Queen;
And when Saint Louis made his penitence,
　　I followed barefoot where the King had been.

For centuries I brought you all my cares,
　　And vexed you with the murmurs of a child;
You heard the tedious burden of my prayers;
　　You could not grant them, but at least you smiled.

If then I left you, it was not my crime,
　　Or if a crime, it was not mine alone.
All children wander with the truant Time.
　　Pardon me too! You pardoned once your Son!

For He said to you:—"Wist ye not that I
    Must be about my Father's business?" So,
Seeking His Father he pursued his way
    Straight to the Cross toward which we all must go.

So I too wandered off among the host
    That racked the earth to find the Father's clue.
I did not find the Father, but I lost
    What now I value more, the Mother,—You!

I thought the fault was yours that foiled my search;
    I turned and broke your image on its throne,
Cast down my idol, and resumed my march
    To claim the Father's empire for my own.

Crossing the hostile sea, our greedy band
    Saw rising hills and forests in the blue;
Our Father's kingdom in the promised land!
    We seized it, and dethroned the Father too.

And now we are the Father, with our brood,
    Ruling the Infinite, not Three but One;
We made our world and saw that it was good;
    Ourselves we worship, and we have no Son.

Yet we have gods, for even our strong nerve
    Falters before the energy we own.
Which shall be master? Which of us shall serve?
    Which wears the fetters? Which shall bear the crown?

Brave though we be, we dread to face the Sphinx,
    Or answer the old riddle she still asks.
Strong as we are, our reckless courage shrinks
    To look beyond the piece-work of our tasks.

But when we must, we pray, as in the past
    Before the Cross on which your Son was nailed.
Listen, dear lady! You shall hear the last
    Of the strange prayers Humanity has wailed:

Prayer to the Dynamo

Mysterious Power! Gentle Friend!
    Despotic Master! Tireless Force!
You and We are near the End,
    Either You or We must bend
    To bear the martyrs' Cross.

We know ourselves, what we can bear
    As men; our strength and weakness too;
Down to the fraction of a hair;
And know that we, with all our care
    And knowledge, know not you.

You come in silence, Primal Force,
    We know not whence, or when, or why;
You stay a moment in your course
To play; and, lo! you leap across
    To Alpha Centauri!

We know not whether you are kind,
    Or cruel in your fiercer mood;
But be you Matter, be you Mind,
We think we know that you are blind,
    And we alone are good.

We know that prayer is thrown away,
    For you are only force and light:
A shifting current; night and day;
We know this well, and yet we pray,
    For prayer is infinite,

Like you! Within the finite sphere
   That bounds the impotence of thought,
We search an outlet everywhere
But only find that we are here
   And that you are—are not!

What are we then? the lords of space?
   The master-mind whose tasks you do?
Jockey who rides you in the race?
Or are we atoms whirled apace,
   Shaped and controlled by you?

Still silence! Still no end in sight!
   No sound in answer to our cry!
Then, by the God we now hold tight,
Though we destroy soul, life and light,
   Answer you shall—or die!

We are no beggars! What care we
   For hopes or terrors, love or hate?
What for the universe? We see
Only our certain destiny
   And the last word of Fate.

Seize, then, the Atom! rack his joints!
   Tear out of him his secret spring!
Grind him to nothing!—though he points
To us, and his life-blood anoints
   Me—the dead Atom-King!

*   *   *   *   *

A curious prayer, dear lady! is it not?
   Strangely unlike the prayers I prayed to you!
Stranger because you find me at this spot,
   Here, at your feet, asking your help anew.

415

Strangest of all, that I have ceased to strive,
    Ceased even to care what new coin fate shall strike.
In truth it does not matter. Fate will give
    Some answer; and all answers are alike.

So, while we slowly rack and torture death
    And wait for what the final void will show,
Waiting I feel the energy of faith
    Not in the future science, but in you!

The man who solves the Infinite, and needs
    The force of solar systems for his play,
Will not need me, nor greatly care what deeds
    Made me illustrious in the dawn of day.

He will send me, dethroned, to claim my rights,
    Fossil survival of an age of stone,
Among the cave-men and the troglodytes
    Who carved the mammoth on the mammoth's bone.

He will forget my thought, my acts, my fame,
    As we forget the shadows of the dusk,
Or catalogue the echo of a name
    As we the scratches on the mammoth's tusk.

But when, like me, he too has trod the track
    Which leads him up to power above control,
He too will have no choice but wander back
    And sink in helpless hopelessness of soul,

Before your majesty of grace and love,
    The purity, the beauty and the faith;
The depth of tenderness beneath; above,
    The glory of the life and of the death.

When your Byzantine portal still was young,
    I came here with my master Abailard;
When Ave Maris Stella was first sung,
    I joined to sing it here with Saint Bernard.

When Blanche set up your glorious Rose of France,
    In scholar's robes I waited on the Queen;
When good Saint Louis did his penitence,
    My prayer was deep like his: my faith as keen.

What loftier prize seven hundred years shall bring,
    What deadlier struggles for a larger air,
What immortality our strength shall wring
    From Time and Space, we may—or may not—care;

But years, or ages, or eternity,
    Will find me still in thought before your throne,
Pondering the mystery of Maternity,
    Soul within Soul—Mother and Child in One!

Help me to see! not with my mimic sight—
    With yours! which carried radiance, like the sun,
Giving the rays you saw with—light in light—
    Tying all suns and stars and worlds in one.

Help me to know! not with my mocking art—
    With you, who knew yourself unbound by laws;
Gave God your strength, your life, your sight, your heart,
    And took from him the Thought that Is—the Cause.

Help me to feel! not with my insect sense—
    With yours that felt all life alive in you;
Infinite heart beating at your expense;
    Infinite passion breathing the breath you drew!

Help me to bear! not my own baby load,
 But yours; who bore the failure of the light,
The strength, the knowledge and the thought of God,—
 The futile folly of the Infinite!

Compline

DUNCAN CAMPBELL SCOTT
(1 8 6 2 –   )

We are resting here in the twilight,
Watching the progress of a cloudless sunset,
The colour moving away from yellow to a deeper gold.
High on the hillside
Across the sunset the telegraph wires are drawn,
Black on the yellow.
Upward we look through the strands
To the delicate colour infinitely beyond
At the world's end.

The swallows flash in the air
And light on the wires,
They range themselves there
Side by side in lines,
Forming impromptu designs,
Black on the yellow.
An odour rises out of the earth
From dead grass cooling in the dew,
From the fragrance of pine needles
That smouldered all day in the heat.

Love in our hearts is quiet,
Tranquil as light reflected in water
That trembles only when the water trembles.

As gold ages to ivory,
As up from a hidden source there wells
The fragile colour of deep-sea shells,
Ivory is flushed with rose
At the day's close.
And as the present sometimes calls up the past
I see the wires as the old music-staff,
Four lines and three spaces,
The swallows clinging there,
The notes of an ancient air,
The sunset glow—a vellum page
In an old Mass book:—
A vellum page yellow as old ivory,
The fading gems of a rose-window,
The odour of incense—
And a voice out of the past
Imploring in a vault of shadow—

Sancta Maria—Mater Dei
Ora pro nobis peccatoribus
Nunc et in hora
Mortis nostrae.
The golden melody of an old faith
Lingering ethereal in the shadow,
The prayer of the past—
Ora pro nobis.

Pray for us, you swallows,
Now and in the hour of our death;
Now when we are fulfilled in the promise of life
When love is quiet in the heart;
And when we fall like autumn leaves and their shadows;
The colour of the leaves,—the garnered beauty of life,—
With their shadows on the future,
Falling together to the unknown—
Ora pro nobis.

419

May we remember then of all life's loveliest things,
This evening and the swallows' wings,
When infinite love was reflected in the heart
And trembled only when the heart trembled.

We will pray for you, bright swallows,
Now and in the hour of your death;
Now when you fly aloft in the dry air
Rushing together in a storm of wings,
Grasping the wires;
And when you fall secretly in the wilderness,
Where,—none knoweth—
Ora pro nobis.
May you remember then this northern beauty,
The pure lake surface,
And after a long light-day,
Wing-weary, the rest
Of a night by the nestlings and the nest.

The sunset failed in ivory and rose,
All that is left of light is the early moonlight
That trembles in the lake-water
Only when the water trembles;
And the lustre of life alone is left at the long day's close,—
The radiance of love in the heart
That trembles only when the heart trembles.

Solomon

HERMANN HAGEDORN
(1 8 8 2 –   )

Under the sun, groaned Solomon,
There is no new thing, no, not one.
Nothing by man or God devised
Holds any wonder, unsurmised;
And in no throat of woman or bird
Sleeps any note man hath not heard.
New things are but old things reborn;
There is one wisdom, which is scorn.

Solomon, you had too many wives,
Whose little hands held little knives
That softly on your splendor crept
And stabbed your vision while you slept.
Solomon, in too many eyes
You sought the elusive heavenly prize.
Only the steadfast and the true
Find that which is forever new.

Evening Prayer

HERMANN HAGEDORN

She sang her little bedtime air
And drowsy-wise she spoke her prayer.

And as she spoke I saw the room
Open and stretch and glow and bloom;

And in her eyes I saw a ring
Of heaven's angels, listening.

Exile from God

JOHN HALL WHEELOCK
(1 8 8 6 -   )

I do not fear to lay my body down
  In death, to share
The life of the dark earth, and lose my own,
  If God is there.

I have so loved all sense of Him, sweet might
  Of color and of sound,—
His tangible loveliness and living light
  That robes me 'round.

If to His heart in the hushed grave and dim
  We sink more near,
It shall be well—living we rest in Him.
  Only I fear

Lest from my God in lonely death I lapse,
  And the dumb clod,
Lose Him; for God is life, and death perhaps
  Exile from God.

In Shadow

[From a garden overlooking the old Mission, Santa Barbara]

CAROLINE HAZARD
(1 8 5 6 - 1 9 4 4)

Hast thou a heritage,
  Grave olive tree?
The Dove flew back
  With a branch from me.

Dost remember a garden
Fairer than this?
In Eden I sheltered
The first pair in bliss.

Thou knowest, then, Life;
What of Death, gentle tree?
I was awake
In Gethsemane.

"That Which Hath Wings Shall Tell"
—Eccles. x, 20

LINDA LYON VAN VOORHIS
(1 9 0 2 –   )

Think on St. Francis' feathered friends, dear heart,
Nor deem unbroken vigil you must keep.
Stronger their clasp upon the wind-swept bough
When the birds sleep.[1]

Ad Matrem in Cœlis

LINDA LYON VAN VOORHIS

The subtle tracery of the leafless bough
The reminiscent nest of wings grown strong,
The vibrant silence of completed things
Must ultimately bind us as a thong.
We shall be gathered as the herbs to earth,
We shall fly freer than the birds in flight,
When I shall walk in other worlds with her
Who, knowing stars, was fearless of the night.

[1] The claws of birds lock on the branch in sleep and it requires waking consciousness to release the hold.

Dedication

VICTORIA SAFELLE JOHNSON
(*American Contemporary*)

Holy Jesus, Thou art born
For my sake on Christmas morn.
Lord, as Thou art born for me,
I am born again to Thee.

Through the city and abroad,
Thou dost lead me unto God.
Wheresoe'er Thou leadest me,
Master, I will follow Thee.

To Thy love my love I give,
Thou dost die that I may live.
As Thou giv'st Thy life for me.
Lord, I give my life to Thee.

From the tomb I see Thee rise,
When the morning fills the skies.
Lord, as Thou art risen for me,
I will rise from death to Thee.

The Vintage

BELLE COOPER
(*1873 -*)

In Tuscany, the vintage season reigns.
From trailing vines festooning maple trees
The grapes are cut; and everywhere one sees
The great white oxen draw the loaded wains

Up to the vats where, splashed with crimson stains,
    The peasants—men and maids—bare to the knees,
    Treading the clusters, sing and sway at ease,
Till nought but blood-red must and pulp remains.

Rich-colored parable of the plan divine!
    Throughout all Nature life and death are fused.
The grape must needs be crushed before new wine
    Gives forth its life. So man's dark heart is bruised,
Before the true immortal wine wells up,
A fount of strength to brim earth's loving-cup.

A Street Melody

BELLE COOPER

A song soars from a sordid city street,
    A boyish treble, wistful, sweet and clear.
    Why should I hush a burdened heart to hear?—
Wild poppies flame and flaunt in golden wheat;
Brown Tuscan hills lie quivering in the heat;
    Far Apennines their snow-lashed summits rear;
    In Venice trolls a red-sashed gondolier.
A song?—Italia blossoms at my feet!

Clinging Sorrento shines across the blue;
    The Piedmont heights are wrapt in purple haze;
        White oxen plough the wounded Umbrian plain;
Virgilian pastures glint with diamond dew;
    And, far above, fired with the sunset rays,
        Assisi lifts her towers to heaven again.

San Juan Capistrano

ALICE CECILIA COOPER

(1 8 7 6 –   )

Through broken arches moonbeams softly shine.
Long trellised rose-sprays, trained by padres' hands,
Entwine with slender olive leaves in bands
Of wind-stirred tracery. Gray walls combine
With red-tiled roof to guard this lonely shrine,
Upraised by saintly souls at Love's commands.
Despite Time's ravages, this altar stands
In beauty breathless as the night divine.

Oh, shadow-haunted cloister where brown bird
Oft joined the brown Franciscan choir in praise,
Your sanctity the fleeting years increase.
Nought but the leaves down-fluttering now is heard,
Yet your loved bells, in these our earth-bound days,
Awake in us dear memories of God's peace.

In Memory of G. K. Chesterton

WALTER DE LA MARE

(1 8 7 3 –   )

Knight of the Holy Ghost, he goes his way,
Wisdom his motley, Truth his loving jest;
The mills of Satan keep his lance in play,
Pity and innocence his heart at rest.

EPILOGUE:
SIX POEMS
BY
CATHOLICS

Turris Eburnea

ANONYMOUS

What palace-temple of the mystic East
Bequeathed this title to thy Litany?
What wide courts jubilant with minstrelsy,
What tower-chambers whence the weary priest
Might watch the still sky when the psalms had ceased—
Watch the still spires of fretted ivory,
And pass to God in lonely ecstasy,
And with the Angels hold sublimer feast?
Mary, within thy courts all nations meet
To praise the King whose citadel thou art
And temple, and the altar is thy heart,
And thy white soul his chosen mercy-seat;
And by thy stair we shall find strength to part
With earth for heaven, and climb, and reach God's feet.

Regina Confessorum

ANONYMOUS

Thy Knights, O Queen, ride forth by East and West,
By South and North through all the world they ride;
By town and hamlet, coast and countryside,
They bear thy token proudly on their crest,
And in thy name are all men's wrongs redressed,
And for thy love are all men's wants supplied;
Seeing the honour of the Crucified
Is ever in all love of thee confessed.
Such knights are Basil, Benedict, and he,
The Poor Man of Assisi's sainted shrine,
And Dominic, and that dear lord of mine,
Dauntless Loyola. Queen, we too would be
Thy knights made strong with one grave smile of thine
To wear thy favour, and break lance for thee.

The Heart Has Its Reasons

ANONYMOUS

Sing low, my heart, lest we be overheard,
　　This world is not the Paradise we knew.
Let not its mockery trap us in a word
　　Or catch one troubled cry from me or you.

Let the deep song be hidden in the deep
Pulse with our life-blood, waking or asleep,
Yours is the knowledge earth can never know.
Let not its mockery hurt you. Ah, sing low.

Candles

ANONYMOUS

Drop your offering in the box.
　　Light a candle at the shrine.
Join it to those wasting flames
　　Ere the last forget to shine.

Endless darkness gathers round
　　Drowning every star to-night!
Here at least your soul has found
　　One small ring of candle-light.

Grief unuttered, love unbreathed,
　　Burning upward, each alone;
Memories with each flame enwreathed—
　　Add one more, then, of your own.

Some are spent and guttering low,
　　Speechless little hopes and prayers.
You, the wise one, you, who know—
　　Add your midget flame to theirs.

Ask not by that misty gleam
    What your sightless eyes can trace.
Ask not if Murillo's dream
    Hides the beauty of Her face.

Drop your offering in the box.
    Light your candle at the shrine.
Some one, entering in the dark,
    Later on, may see it shine.

Lux in Tenebris

ANONYMOUS

Once, in my darkest hour, in some dim place
Of tears, I saw the light upon Her face.
    Picture or painted glass, I cannot tell.
    I only know it saved my soul from hell.

Oh, not the painter's hand! It was his mind
That through his darkness on my darkness shined;
    But, through his mind, the love I could not see,
    The face he saw in heaven, looked down on me.

There Was No Room on the Cross

ANONYMOUS

I thought that I could follow Him;
    But, when my feet drew near
To Calvary, at dead of night,
    I quailed in utter fear.

Whereat a voice came whispering,
    Through darkness, like a sea:
"Child, child, be not afraid. Your Cross
    Is occupied by Me."

Epilogue

Love Is Life

RICHARD ROLLE

(1 2 9 0 ? - 1 3 4 9)

Love is a light burden that gladdeneth young and old;
Love is that blood-red winter's rose which blossometh in the cold;
He that giveth all to Love hath all that heart can hold.

Fond desire shall fade and fail as doth the flower in May;
Lust is but a fire of straw that smouldereth for a day;
Love that liveth in thy heart shall live and love for aye.

Thou that, on the Cross of Love, wast crowned of lovers King,
Melt this iron Winter, Lord, to Love's eternal Spring;
Hold and fold us all beneath the shadow of Thy wing.

Version by Alfred Noyes

INDICES

Index of Titles

435

Index of Poets

439

May Day

Awake, oh awake! the village bells ringing
Proclaim that all nature is gay;
Sweet odors around us the breezing are flinging
Awake to the merry May Day!

The sun, as he rises o'er yonder hill beaming
Is running his ever bright way —
The green-wood is merry, and nature is seeming
To rejoice in the coming of May!

And see, on the meadow sweet flowers, up-springing
Are budding in fragrant array.
White far o'er the lawn, her airy flight winging
The Lark greets the coming of May!

The violet-bank, its beauty revealing
Is blooming in azure so gay:
Then wake ye! awake! while the merry bells pealing
Shall welcome the lovely May day!

Father Opdenaker

Hymn to Mary

Yes, as a sunburst flushing mountain' snow
Fell the celestial touch of fire ere long
On the pale stillness of thy thoughtful brow
And thy calm spirit lightened into song
Unconsciously, perchance, yet free and strong
Flowed the majestic joy of tuneful words
Which living harps the choirs of heaven among
Might well have linked with their divinest chords
Full many a strain, born far on glory's blast
Shall leave, where once its haughty music
                                    passed.
No more to memory than a reed's faint sigh
While thine, O childlike Virgin! through all time
Shall send its fervent breath o'er every clime
Being of God, and therefore not to die.

Father Opdenaker